RAD

An instant seminal compendium for people who want to gain a deeper understanding of the radical potential of crypto tech for aesthetic institutions. *Harm van den Dorpel, artist & founder of left gallery*

While the term "DAO" may conjure, to some, thoughts of wealth-seeking "crypto-bros", to me it conjures thoughts of Rojava, or the Zapatistas, or artist collectives, and the vehicles of dual power that could be created if the technological and the socio-political joined forces. This book shows how artists are possibly the best prepped to build and steward the new organisational structures we need.
Stefen Deleveaux, Caribbean Blockchain Alliance

For those sitting in between crypto-critical and crypto-curious for a progressive politics, this is one of the best collections of essays from some of the smartest minds in this space. There are no hypemen and also no gatekeepers, just our people. *The Blockchain Socialist*

Catlow and Rafferty have assembled an expansive collection of thinkers and experimenters around a central question: what is the future we want for artworld DAOs, and how do we get there?
Sarah Friend, artist & software developer

Co-edited by two key contributors to emerging debates on the radical creative potential of computational protocols and technologies, this is a brilliant, much-needed book on the social and political potential of artworld DAOs. Assembled here is a thoughtful and exhilarating chorus of pioneering voices, resounding in critical dialogues on peer production, community, solidarity, and so many other radical things that artists, activists, and critics can do together in drawing on – and always superseding – tools of decentralised computation.
Martin Zeilinger, Abertay University

A constellation of works by some of the brightest minds thinking deeply about the Web3 space and beyond. *Billy Rennekamp, founder & artist*

Artworld DAOs are helping to rethink how communities apportion non-monetary value. They therefore serve a vital purpose at a time when NFTs are financialising creativity.
Alex Estorick, editor-in-chief RightClickSave

Radical Friends

Decentralised Autonomous
Organisations and the Arts

Edited by Ruth Catlow & Penny Rafferty

Torque Editions

To Our Radical Friends

Contents

THE ARTWORLD DAOs SPEAK

A METHOD KIT OF PRACTICES, TACTICS AND PROTOTYPES

* * *

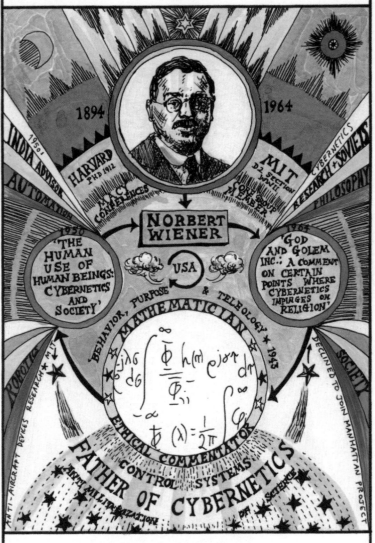

VII

THE CHARIOT

Radical Friendship

Ruth Catlow & Penny Rafferty

The Artworld DAO is Power

Infinite,
Irresistible,
Inexorable,
Indifferent,
And yet, The Artworld DAO is Pliable –
Trickster,
Teacher,
Chaos,
Clay,
The Artworld DAO exists to be shaped
The Artworld DAO is Change[1]

---

1. Our channelling of Octavia Butler's science fiction novel *Parable of the Sower* (New York: Four Walls Eight Windows, 1993).

From our very first long conversation on a Berlin sofa in 2018 it was clear that we shared an appreciation of experimental social play that forked and mutated traditional organisational forms, and regarded life since the Internet as an alchemic political field to be constantly shaped by radical friendships worldwide.

Up until that point we had both been obsessed individually with Decentralised Autonomous Organisations (DAOs) as philosophical sand-boxes for networked collaboration, but after that tête-à-tête we became allies in the field. This was all unfolding in a time when DAOs were still pretty niche as a concept and well before the technical ecosystems had been built for use by anyone but developers. Together, we began exploring how a variety of historical, artistic, political and technological systems could function as proto-DAOs. These early investigations gave us new ways to approach some of the most persistent questions we had as artists, theorists and activists working at the critical crossroads of art and technology: How to transform the primary status of artworks from speculative objects into narrative portals that could catalyse the development of new social futures?; how to make relationships and responsibilities within nested online and in-life communities more free, transparent and accountable?; how might diverse communities be empowered to take collective action in their own interest; what new physical spaces and social relationships might these produce, generate or service?

In short, we were both interested in cultural practices and artforms that recognised humans as political and social animals – creative and self-aware about the implications to wider society of the decisions they make.

Furtherfield[2] had first identified the potential of DAOs as spurs for imagination and action in 2014 with the publication of Rhea Myers', *DAOWO* white paper.[3] This was a provocation for "a second wave of global artworld restructuring, against the toxic cult of the individual-artistic genius, which first found expression in the punk spirit of networked collaboration that Furtherfield called *DIWO (Do It With Others)*."[4] The

2. London's longest-running (de)centre for art and technology founded in 1996 by Ruth Catlow and Marc Garrett.

3. Rhea Myers, "Decentralised Autonomous Organisation With Others," Furtherfield, 2014, https://www.furtherfield.org/artdatamoney/includes/files/daowo.pdf.

4. Ruth Catlow, "Decentralisation and Commoning the Arts," *Phygital Unconference Proceedings*, University of Nicosia, 2019, http://www.unrf.ac.cy/files/unconference-proceedings-phygital.pdf.

conversations fostered between communities of artists, techies and activists at Furtherfield revealed the potential of DAOs as vehicles for new forms of radical networked artistic collaboration and organisation. They also highlighted the threats they posed as part of a global acceleration of surveillance capitalism and extraction. Ruth and Ben Vickers, then CTO at Serpentine Galleries, first presented their ideas about potential directions at a gathering of arts and cultural policymakers at the Austrian Cultural Forum in London in 2016 and then, with the support of Goethe-Institut in London, interrogated them further through the *DAOWO blockchain laboratory and debate series for reinventing the arts*[5] that they devised and hosted between 2017 and 2018. With the launch of *DECAL* their *Decentralised Arts Lab* in 2019 Furtherfield built the first working prototype of *CultureStake*, a collective cultural decision-making app using quadratic voting on the blockchain, that allows communities to choose the creative experiences they want to have in their own localities.

In 2018, Penny had re-entered the artworld as a critic and theorist who was deeply interested in emergent technologies and the bleed between artworld test sites and the social body, she wrote *A Speculative White Paper on the Aesthetics of a Black Swan World* in response to a commission by KW Institute for Contemporary Art, Berlin curated by Tirdad Zolghadr. The text proposed possible systems of change for the local berlin art scene, that was going head to head with gentrification jesters, representation, inequality and cultural washing agencies. Inspired by the theory and philosophy of the first DAOs, Penny applied the concept of a DAO to a specific social system, the Berlin artworld, replacing anonymous agents and stakers with artists, institutions and cultural creators. Since its first publication in 2018 and throughout the years of this book being developed, and continual energetic conversations with peers and friends like Calum Bowden, Laura Lotti, Leith Benkhedda, Catrin Mayer, Max Hampshire and Paul Seidler, Black Swan grew from a speculative idea into a fully fledged working DAO.[6]

The support of the unique transnational cultural institution, the Goethe-Institut, and the groundbreaking R&D Platform at Serpentine Galleries were crucial to the *DAOWO Labs* and subsequent summits and

5. The *DAOWO Labs* were realised in partnership with the Goethe-Institut, Serpentine Galleries and a network of European partners via the *State Machines* programme, https://www.daowo.org.

6. See "Manifesting a Black Swan DAO" in this volume.

Artworld DAO Think Tanks in 2019 and 2020. The collaboration with Katrin Sohns and Mario Schruff at Goethe-Institut extended the scope and reach of these events supporting the authors' ability to connect with leading thinkers, technologists and cultural practitioners, and to build pools of knowledge and experience over time.

This book is the result of eight years of discussions, arguments, euphoria and care, informed and shaped by a multitude of conversations, which in turn shaped six labs, two role-played experiments and two immersive think tank gatherings led by ourselves with artists, programmers, activists and thinkers from across the continents. Not simply individuals, but individuals embedded in and with communities around the world. Operating in dialogue with a wide range of independent, cultural and governmental institutions this has produced not only new theories for working together, but a community of thought and practice that has birthed several of its own prototype artworld DAOs, and has developed a new vocabulary to talk with and about the multitude of artworld DAOs that are coming into existence thick and fast as we write. We are inspired by the generosity and courage of our fellow travellers and look forward to the new dialogues, and the modes of organising emerging.

HANNAH ARENDT

GERMAN AMERICAN POLITICAL THEORIST

1906 · 1975

"THE HUMAN ARTIFICE OF THE WORLD SEPARATES HUMAN EXISTENCE FROM ALL MERE ANIMAL ENVIRONMENT, BUT LIFE ITSELF IS OUTSIDE THIS ARTIFICIAL WORLD, AND

DIRECT-ED TOWARD MAKING LIFE ALSO 'ARTIFICIAL', TOWARD CUTTING THE LAST TIE THROUGH WHICH EVEN MAN BELONGS AMONG THE CHILDREN OF NATURE. THIS FUTURE MAN, WHOM THE SCIENTISTS TELL US

THROUGH LIFE MAN REMAINS RELATED TO ALL OTHER LIVING ORGANISMS. NOW, A GREAT MANY SCIENTIFIC ENDEAVORS HAVE BEEN

THEY WILL PRODUCE IN NO MORE THAN A HUNDRED YEARS, SEEMS TO BE POSSESSED BY A REBELLION AGAINST HUMAN EXISTENCE AS IT HAS BEEN GIVEN, A FREE GIFT FROM NOWHERE (SECULARLY SPEAKING) WHICH

HE WISHES TO EXCHANGE, AS IT WERE, FOR SOMETHING HE HAS MADE HIMSELF. THERE IS NO REASON TO DOUBT OUR ABILITIES TO ACCOMPLISH SUCH AN EXCHANGE, JUST AS THERE IS NO REASON TO DOUBT OUR PRESENT ABILITY TO

DESTROY ALL ORGANIC LIFE ON EARTH. THE QUESTION IS ONLY WHETHER WE WISH TO USE OUR NEW SCIENTIFIC AND TECHNICAL KNOWLEDGE IN THIS DIRECTION, AND THIS QUESTION CANNOT BE DECIDED BY SCIENTIFIC MEANS; IT IS A POLITICAL QUESTION OF THE FIRST ORDER AND THEREFORE CAN HARDLY BE LEFT TO THE DECISION OF PROFESSIONAL SCIENTISTS OR PROFESSIONAL POLITICIANS. NATURAL SCIENCES HAVE BECOME EX-CLUSIVELY SCIENCES OF PROCESS AND, IN THEIR LAST STAGE, SCIENCES OF POTENTIALLY IRREVERSIBLE, IRREMEDIABLE PROCESSES OF NO RETURN"

THE HUMAN CONDITION (1958)

QUEEN OF WANDS

Foreword

Practice Upwards

Nathan Schneider

Friends are the original DAOs. To be friends is a relation autonomous from corporations or states, a fugitive association. There is no Bureau of Friendship that could possibly centralise such organisations as these. Friendships have an economy, an incentive structure, an internal currency. Through the holy pastime of gossip, curious miners pry for information about what is going on in others' friendships (whether it is their business or not). Validators circulate assessments of friends' behaviour across the wider community. There are no servers, only peers.

DAOs propose to enlarge the reach of friendship to the point of replacing corporations and governments, while also threatening to ruin it with immutable records. Imagine if you responded to a gift by handing the giver its precise market value in cash; the gift is no longer a gift. Friendship might stop working properly when you put a price on it. What is new and different about DAOs, on top of foregoing friendship, is the ability to know, trace, and surgically reallocate a relationship's value. Through the digital bean-counting, friendship can scale, extending its powers from the edges and corners of the social order to the center. There, the friendship-DAOs inaugurate a new order based on the specialties of friends, like play, reciprocity, and affection.

The name of a storied artist DAO, Friends with Benefits, alludes less to the sexual innuendo of the phrase than the fact that there is an $FWB token and that it has a price. At last you can check the precise status of art-powered gentrification. But members have assured me that the benefits they care about most are not financial; like any friendship, a DAO will not survive long if its heart can only pump transactions.

The idea of casting society in the mould of friendship is an old one. Confucian thought held friendship as an elemental bond that helps hold everything else together; Chinese political theory has long understood even international relations among states as a species of friendship. Aristotle also considered friendship integral to statecraft. It could even be a substitute for the state; if we were all friends, we would not need the scaffolding of government. Aristotle thereby seems to anticipate the most absurdist libertarian fantasies, which flow freely in crypto-land – government falling like scales from our eyes, once we can at long last properly coordinate.

Modern liberalism has generally subjugated friendship to a merely private sphere, apart from politics. But in recent decades feminist thinkers have reasserted friendship as a political act – as a basis for both resisting oppressive systems and conjuring new communities into being, on the principles of equality and voluntary association. "Friendship," wrote political theorist Marilyn Friedman in the late 1980s, "has socially disruptive possibilities".

When a few friends sit together in a circle it is not the same thing as a CEO addressing hundreds of employees as "dear friends". The lines between small and larger scale ordering are not straight or clear. They are wormholes, dividing levels of abstraction with distinct ways of working. And yet, almost two centuries after he toured the early United States, Alexis de Tocqueville seems to have been right that the health of democracy at the scale of a country has everything to do with how people organise in small scales, in their everyday lives.

Activist and writer adrienne maree brown insists on drawing the lines that link these levels, and acting accordingly: "Our friendships and relationships are systems. Our communities are systems. Let us practice upwards." We practice politics when we practice friendship.

The technological achievement of DAOs may prove only as good as our friendships prepare us to make them. The early glimpses of DAO-life so far reveal the engines of friendship at work, extending their energy over pseudonymous token holders and formidable financial treasuries. The inside jokes among friends expand into the memetics of a DAO, into the space-making for secret codes and initiation rituals and private mythologies, with the intensity of an ancient mystery cult. Smart contract code often protects the right to "ragequit" – to storm off and take your tokens with you, to say *we're not talking anymore*, and maybe start your own crew with the same source code.

The clever new voting methods are interesting – quadratic, conviction, delegated, take your pick. But the frequently near-unanimous vote counts suggest that the real politics is happening somewhere else. This is true. Gossip lurks everywhere off-chain, in the relentless Telegram and Discord chatter, a site of power secured above all by the formidable proof-of-work required to keep up with the conversation. Those who can do so mostly act and vote like friends, together.

Still, the opposition remains between fluid scuttlebutt and immutable blockchains. There is the promise of unencumbered, free-wheeling human relations on one side, and then the dispassionate, unalterable ledgers on the other. They amount to either a symbiosis or a contradiction; we can only know which by trying. Can friendship survive the ruthless quantification of a DAO? Or, by automating the work of incentive alignment, do DAOs at last make true friendship possible?

For years I have been fantasising about (and failing to conduct) a study of labour in DAOs, one attuned to pre-digital categories like invisible labour, shadow work, and gendered making – in sum, the kinds of work that the reigning order doesn't count as work. Particularly during the 2017 ICO boom, everything was so obviously smoke and mirrors, as hasty whitepapers made world-historical claims for software that could do virtually nothing, if it even existed yet. Anecdotally, it was clear enough that behind the claims for how a protocol would change the world were people doing difficult work – often the outliers in a sea of bros. Those "community managers" (if they had a title at all) were doing tons of emotional labour: connecting and orchestrating and summarising, resolving disputes and ordering the food, all in order to protect the illusion of an actual product.

Whales throw tokens at nonexistent software, somehow, but not so much at competent friends. Yet it is friends who seem to be holding up the great mass of activity in DAOs, now at least as much as in 2017, while the quantification and incentive alignment remains a substantially mythological artifice. Could DAOs survive the absence of their underlying friendship?

Another way of getting at the point of that question is to shill this book. The design of DAOs is an art disguised as a science, and perhaps then their true natures will appear to us most fully through art. Unlike liberal political theorists, artists have not had the luxury of imagining friendship as extraneous, since friends are the precondition and original audiences of their work. The networks of friends around an artist are the first to insist that the art is worth noticing, and to give it value, just as friends in a DAO can make "number go up" with their transaction volume and their hype.

If DAOs end up becoming anything like what their proponents imagine – an operating system for the next generation of human institutions – then the things friends are doing together in DAOs right now will matter immensely. The norms, habits, and memes bouncing around now will harden before we know it or notice. The very-online abbreviations and conventions formed among friends on 1990s BBS servers are still with us now :-/ Friends are similarly shaping what we expect from these new protocols and patterns – what rights, and what rules, what jokes and what counts as art. "The extent of their friendship," as Aristotle put it, "is the extent to which justice exists between them." Will we be good enough friends to make our DAOs just?

Let us practice upwards, please. When none of the rules are set yet, all we have are friends. Little weighs more powerfully on us in this world than what friends ask or demand, what they hold us to and expect. So far, we buy their jpegs, swap our tokens for theirs, and crowdfund each other's wars. What next? At this formative moment, the global order to come depends on how, now, we show up to each other as friends.

Introduction

What is Radical Friendship made of?

Ruth Catlow & Penny Rafferty

Friendship is a serious affection; the most sublime of all affections,
because it is based on principle and cemented by time.
— Mary Wollstonecraft[1]

The defining principles of friendship are freedom and solidarity.[2] While our friendships may be mobbed by a myriad of passions, the commitment we make to even our most casual friends is to solicit their wellbeing over time. Sustained intimacy, fellowship and camaraderie, especially across disparities of material and social advantage help us to become sensitised to innumerable challenges and possibilities that might otherwise be invisible to us.

1. Mary Wollstonecraft, *A Vindication of the Rights of Women* (London: Penguin, 2004). First published 1792. 160.
2. "[T]he English word free is actually derived from a root meaning friend. Slaves could not make friends because they could not make commitments to others, since they were entirely under someone else's power and their only obligation was to do exactly as their master said." David Graeber and David Wengrow, *The Dawn of Everything: A New History of Humanity* (London: Allen Lane, 2021). 187.

For this reason, our friendship networks may provide the best design patterns for social infrastructure: resilient and mutable systems for scale-free interdependence and mutual aid. But is friendship not an anathema to trustless systems?[3] Was not this cryptographically secured internet of money and value called the blockchain not built to free us from reliance on outmoded corruptible human institutions – from family, religion, and state – that demanded too much in exchange for the sustenance of our universal basic bodily and psychic needs? If decades of bogus digital friendship-peddling corporations like Facebook have taught us anything it is that we are prepared to risk it all – the warping of our social relations by data-exploitation with dire consequences for our bodies, our lands, and our democracy – in our desire to connect and commune.

Radical friends reject the fantasy of exemplary self-sovereign autonomous individuals optimised for efficiency and productivity. They know that this is a poisonous projection by materially advantaged individuals who seek to leverage their competitive edge within the austerity conditions they co-created.

Presented in this book are the chronicles of different communities of radical friends connected to and exploring a variety of contexts across continents, to experiment with new rules for distributing agency and resources, simultaneously communal and decentralised. Together, they are building the collective imagination muscle for co-creating resilient support systems for the life of the physical and data body in a principled unending hack of totalising systems of violent coercive control.

Collectively, this edited volume presents a range of voices, from different layers of artworld DAO development, in dialogue about the value of and pathways to peer-produced decentralised digital infrastructures for art, culture and society, with the aim of creating a new environment for cooperation and solidarity in the cultural sector. By bringing together ground-breaking players from cultural and technology sectors working on peer-to-peer (PTP) systems, this book explores how traditional organisational patterns and the power structures they serve might be transformed by the emergence of blockchain-enabled Decentralised Autonomous Organisations (DAOs) in artworlds and beyond.

---

3. The concept of "trustlessness" is core to blockchain technologies, crypto payments, and smart contracts. Trustlessness means that you don't have to trust a third party: a bank, a person, or any intermediary to give you access to or control over your digital assets.

DECENTRALISED AUTONOMOUS ORGANISATIONS

DAOs are an evolution of Decentralised Autonomous Corporations first proposed in 2013 by Daniel Larimer[4] as a way to improve cryptocurrencies by co-ordinating shareholder actions. The idea is developed in the "Ethereum White Paper"[5] published in 2014 by Vitalik Buterin before the launch of Ethereum as the first programmable blockchain in 2015.

DAOs are a form of internet-based organisation that enables people to coordinate their work with each other wherever they are in the world. Collectively-owned and member-managed, their built-in treasuries can only be accessed with the approval of the group. In the most common structure everyone in the organisation contributes to decision-making through a system of proposals and voting. The software of the DAO manages membership, pooling, and distribution of resources, according to the pre-agreed rules of its members, and keeps permanent and transparent records of all decisions made.[6] The rules of the DAO are encoded into secure, decentralised software called smart contracts which holds the group's treasury and "tallies votes and carries out the will of the people".[7] No one can change the rules of the DAO once the contract is live on the blockchain, except by a proposal and vote system, in the case of upgradable smart contracts. While the people who interact with these automated organisations are subject to the laws of the lands where they reside, the DAO eliminates the need for third-party mediation, such as the involvement of banks or state-mandated company structures.

DAOs support different models of membership. Token-based membership models like MakerDAO[8] are usually used to govern cryptocurrency protocols or tokens themselves. People buy tokens, usually traded on decentralised exchanges, which grant them voting rights on the future direction of the DAO. Or DAOStack for example, offered meritocratic

4. Daniel Larimer, "Overpaying For Security, The Hidden Costs of Bitcoin," *LTB Network*, September 7, 2013, https://letstalkbitcoin.com/is-bitcoin-overpaying-for-false-security.

5. Vitalik Buterin, "Ethereum Whitepaper," Ethereum, 2014, https://ethereum.org/en/whitepaper.

6. "Decentralized autonomous organizations (DAOs)," Ethereum, https://ethereum.org/en/dao.

7. Ezra Weller, "An Explanation of DAOstack in Fairly Simple Terms," Medium, August 19, 2019, https://medium.com/daostack/an-explanation-of-daostack-in-fairly-simple-terms-1956e26b374.

8. *MakerDAO*, is an Ethereum-based organisation that allows people to lend and borrow using cryptocurrencies and mint's DAI stable coin. Its token MKR is widely available on decentralised exchanges.

voting that weighted decision-making power dynamically according to the reputations of its members. Alternatively, in share-based DAOs like MolochDAO,[9] people submit proposals to join. These usually include an offer of some contribution or value in the form of tokens or work. Shares represent direct voting power and ownership, and members can leave the group whenever they like taking their pro-rata share of the treasury with them. These are used more typically for "closer-knit, human-centric organisations"[10] but can be used for a variety of purposes: charities might accept membership and donations and the group decides how to spend them; worker collectives might offer access to services such as software development, design or translation, and pool funds for workspace, collaboration tools, and marketing;[11] investment clubs might pool capital and vote on enterprises to back, or assets to acquire (NFTs for instance), redistributing profits to members of the DAO. The Fingerprints DAO for instance started out as a curation and investment club for a particular category of NFTs; smart contracts that are also art. This DAO now offers creators a "shared stake in aesthetic performance and value creation."[12] Meanwhile, H.E.R. DAO functions as an explicitly womxn-centred developer DAO built to promote inclusiveness through code to non-binary communities making the space for an intersectional stake in this emergent technological field.

DAOs are organised around member ownership and rights – their fundamental operation is defined by the negotiation of reconfigured relations between all stakeholders in the production and organisation of resources and communities – and therefore they may lend themselves more to cooperativism than centralised and hierarchical corporate structures. It is this capacity that has inspired the thinking behind the DisCO Open-values Cooperative and moves to transfer platform cooperativism to the blockchain.[13] As Nathan Schneider writes: "Crypto should encourage a renaissance of creative governance possibilities that organize economic

9. MolochDAO was originally made for collectively coordinating funds to support Ethereum development.

10. https://ethereum.org/en/dao.

11. *RaidGuild* is a good example of a DAO-based worker collective: https://raidguild.org.

12. See: https://fingerprintsdao.xyz.

13. Jacqueline Radebaugh and Yev Muchnik, "Exclusive Report: Solving the Riddle of the DAO with Colorado's Cooperative Laws," *The Defiant*, December 16, 2021, https://thedefiant.io/solving-the-riddle-of-the-dao-with-colorados-cooperative-laws.

mechanisms around values and rights."[14] Realistically though, DAOs can be conceived and configured (in the abstract and in reality) to organise for an array of socio-political outcomes (stirring zealotry and disquiet in equal measure) from decentralised autonomous workers councils,[15] to plutocratic shell companies for unregulated venture capital funds.[16]

DECENTRALISED INFRASTRUCTURE
≠ DECENTRALISED POWER [17]

Guiding the development of this book is a belief that DAOs hold tremendous potential as organisational vehicles for bottom-up socio-political organising. Furthermore, the rapid centralisation of communication control since the Internet has shown us what is at stake. So much was made of the democratising effect of the Web as "decentralised" infrastructure and yet, 30 years on, we have less not more influence over the important decisions that most affect our lives, our localities, our global environment, and the ways in which our societies are organised.[18] Because owners of digital platforms like Alphabet, Meta, Amazon and Uber, for instance, answer to shareholders in private, rather than to citizens in public, it should not surprise us when they "manipulate, monetize, and exploit users' interactions, attitudes, and behaviours for their own commercial and political interests",[19] co-creating ever-worsening conditions for all. And so, in this warped version of the public realm we face a future of

14. Nathan, Schneider, "Beyond Cryptoeconomics: Platform Cooperativism and the Future of Blockchain Governance," *The Reboot*, October 14, 2021, https://thereboot.com/beyond-cryptoeconomics-platform-cooperativism-and-the-future-of-blockchain-governance.

15. Rhea Myers, "Crypto 2.0 and DAWCs: Dawn of Decentralized Autonomous Workers Councils," Furtherfield, October 14, 2015, https://furtherfield.org/crypto-2-0-and-dawcs.

16. For an introduction see: https://en.wikipedia.org/wiki/The_DAO_(organization). DAOs can also enable anonymous members to exert control and profit from their stakes in enterprises with no accountability and avoiding taxes, see for example Reddit discussion (Created March 25, 2015): https://reddit.com/r/ethtrader/comments/4hmevf/dao_hard_questions. Also: Alexis Goldstein, "Crypto Doesn't Have to Enable Tax Cheats," Bloomberg, August 26, https://bloomberg.com/opinion/articles/2021-08-26/crypto-doesn-t-have-to-enable-tax-cheats2021.

17. Title of 2016 artwork by Jaya Klara Brekke.

18. "People, Power and Technology: The 2018 Digital Attitudes Report," *Dot Everyone*, https://doteveryone.org.uk/report/digital-attitudes.

19. Ruth Catlow, "Reenvisioning the Internet: Do It With Others," *Walker Art Magazine*, March 21, 2019, https://walkerart.org/magazine/soundboard-reenvisioning-internet-ruth-catlow.

trampling, tricking and trolling each other, where citizens are the dupes or hostages of governments.

In this context DAOs could provide the necessary tooling (to those with the knowledge and experience of organising for economic justice) to make multi-scale experiments with citizens, workers and customers alike, to coordinate for common interest. Communities might design and operate their own value systems, countering atomisation and holding power to account. The potential of open source DAOs is to enable groups and communities to create, test, customise and iterate new templates of social coordination, locking in PTP learning about governance for solidarity at any scale.

We are currently experiencing a global cascade of humanitarian disasters headed by individuals operating political machinery that has conferred upon them catastrophic levels of accumulated power and wealth. At the time of writing, February 2022, any coordination by European and NATO allied countries to assist Ukraine in the defence of its airspace could be taken (it is argued) as a pretext for escalation of aggression and lead to nuclear retaliation by Russian President Vladimir Putin. The scope of the international state-led responses to the invasion of Ukraine has been summarised as "banks vs tanks" – imposing ever deeper economic sanctions to drain his war coffers. The cryptoworld has responded with the *UkraineDAO* auction of an NFT of the Ukrainian flag, raising $6.5 million in ETH for Ukrainian Armed Forces. This is part of a massive $50 million uptick in the military crowdfunding efforts that had already been underway in Ukraine since 2014 unsettling the boundary between the military and civilian logistics.[20] Meanwhile other cryptowallets have been used to gather donations to fund cyber-resistance through DDoS attacks, and surveillance operations, as well as humanitarian aid. The potential impacts of this kind of decentralised organised warfare on the balance of power remains to be seen.

In 2021 Putin's puppet and Belarusian President, Alexander Lukashenko closed all NGOs in the country, demolishing its third sector and shredding crucial social infrastructure as part of a crackdown against pro-democracy activists, the independent media, and civil rights

20. Matt Pearce, "'I want to donate to the Ukrainian military.' Crowdfunding becomes part of Ukraine's arsenal," *LA Times*, March 8, 2022, https://www.latimes.com/politics/story/2022-03-08/la-ent-ukraine-digital-resistance.

groups.[21] Since this time the platform Dze.chat has become a vital online portal utilising secure decentralised communication infrastructure to circumvent state censorship and surveillance, providing access for everyday citizens to information and mutual aid through "yard" Telegram channels, organised around local neighbourhoods. We can imagine that further decentralised autonomous organisational infrastructure might make a significant contribution to the resilience of a citizenry facing this kind of state oppression.

Formal relations between states and crypto vary from territory to territory, and are very much in flux with politicians and regulators seeking to balance a wide variety of goals, from the decolonisation of financial infrastructure,[22] and the provision of hospitable environment for fintech innovation, to harmonisation with the commitments of the COP21 Paris Climate agreement. The new *EU Markets in Crypto Assets (MiCA)* framework, for instance, has just been developed to streamline "virtual asset regulation in the European Union (EU) whilst protecting users and investors".[23] This important piece of regulation, which included a controversial clause making Bitcoin illegal in the EU, was removed at the last minute.[24] However, it was replaced with a commitment to review a possible ban on creating, selling or trading any cryptoassets based on "environmentally unsustainable consensus mechanisms" or Proof-of-Work (PoW) within the EU by 2025. The signals about the long-term direction of travel by regulators are important because they have the power to direct the way resources are spent in the development of decentralised governance infrastructure, in this case with an ethical agenda.

21. "Belarus Shuts Down More NGOs Amid Continued Crackdown," *RFE/RL*, July 23, 2021, https://www.rferl.org/a/belarus-shuts-down-ngos/31374183.html.

22. "Enabling Blockchain to Fight against Imperialism in the Caribbean feat. Stefen Deleveaux," *The Blockchain Socialist*, December 6, 2020, https://theblockchainsocialist.com/enabling-blockchain-to-fight-against-imperialism-in-the-caribbean-feat-stefen-deleveaux; Max Parasol, "Volcanos, Bitcoin and remittances: A Tongan lord plans for financial security," *Coin Telegraph*, January 14, 2022, https://cointelegraph.com/news/volcanos-bitcoin-and-remittances-a-tongan-lord-plans-for-financial-security.

23. Werner Vermaak, "MiCA: A Guide to the EU's Proposed Markets in Crypto-Assets Regulation," *SYGNA*, 2020, https://www.sygna.io/blog/what-is-mica-markets-in-crypto-assets-eu-regulation-guide.

24. Chris M. Skinner,"How the EU banned bitcoin... and then didn't," *The Finanser*, March 15, 2022, https://thefinanser.com/2022/03/how-the-eu-almost-banned-bitcoin-and-then-didnt.html.

DAOS– MANIFESTATIONS AND MALLEABILTIES
IN 2021 AND BEYOND

Up until very recently the development and use of DAOs have been stubbornly mystifying to all but technologists and financiers. Time and time again through history we have seen how technologies only reveal their potentials when they move from the hands of the elites to the masses – think of the pen's role in ending illiteracy or the Xerox machine ultimately enabling distribution of flyers aka voices, solidarity, and demands, for groups like the Black Panther Movement. This widely recognised problem, of the public not having access to these conceptual tools and technical platforms has limited the radical potential of initiatives, meaning that, once again, those people whose lives DAOs could most affect would have no opportunity to shape its development.

Since 2021, DAOs are no longer a fiction. They exist and operate on-chain.[25] This is due to two very important developments which made the creation, and use of DAOs accessible to a much wider group of users. Firstly, advances in the DAO technical ecosystem mean that it is now possible for non-technical experts to start to experiment with blockchain-based DAOs. Accessible interfaces and modular DAO tooling systems[26] now allow collaborators to set up safes, create "Multi-sig" wallets (which are more secure from accidental and deliberate compromise, as more than one person must sign each transaction), and to set up DAOs that encode and execute agreements between members, on proof-of-stake blockchains like Tezos, Polygon or Flow (with minimal CO_2 emissions). Voting is also now made more flexible by the integration of lightweight decentralised but off-chain voting facilities such as Snapshot. Finally, community management systems like Collab.Land now provide integration between DAOs community forums like Discord and Telegram to support off-chain discussion and on chain voting for DAO members. Together these advances extend the advantages of the organisational flexibility offered by DAOs to beyond the technical class.

Secondly, before now, it has been far from clear how the law will deal with DAOs and their developers, users, contributors, and counterparties. This has meant that the legal status of members and protections for

25. Chris M. Skinner, "How the EU banned bitcoin ... and then didn't," *The Finanser*, March 15, 2022, https://thefinanser.com/2022/03/how-the-eu-almost-banned-bitcoin-and-then-didnt.html.
26. "Model Law For DAOs," BLOCKCHAINGOV, November 15, 2021, https://blockchaingov. eu/model-law-for-daos.

clients and anyone interacting with DAOs has tended to be unclear. In July 2021, the Coalition Of Automated Legal Applications – Intellectual Property Group (COALA IP) drafted *The Model Law for Decentralized Organizations*, a design framework that aims to enable would-be-DAO creators to harmonise their DAOs with transnational law – "a 'legal wrapper' providing limited liability, legal personality and legal identity to these amorphous decentralised creatures, without requiring formal registration or identification of all members and participants, which would completely frustrate the architecture and purpose of these decentralised entities."[27] The model requires DAOs be deployed on permissionless blockchains and with legible, open source, upgradable smart contracts for accountability, transparency and duty of care to members and counterparties. It also preserves the valuable translocal flexibility of the DAO form by exempting members from the requirement to be registered. Crucially the DAO Model Law acknowledges that a DAO may not only be a for-profit entity but may be used for multiple non-commercial purposes. This paves the way for innovations in co-ownership and coordination by creating a new two-way street between global governance systems and new informal alliances between friends and strangers working together on shared translocal goals.

DAOS. WHERE WILDING[28] MEETS THE LAW – TO REMAKE THE OLD ARTWORLD ON THE BLOCKCHAIN?

In the cultural industries, developments around NFTs (Non-Fungible Tokens),[29] the new digital commodity form, have taken precedence over the development of artworks focused on economic relational aesthetics and more flexible community focused governance tools. In February 2021, *CryptoKitties* digital collectibles[30] were bought with cryptocurrencies by

27. Constance Choi speaking at the "DAO Model Law AMA Workshop," July 18, 2021,
https://www.youtube.com/watch?v=RRzXu0w7bFQ.

28. We are using "wilding" here to conjure the post-punk self-organising spirit of DIY and DIWO (Do It With Others) autodidactic cultures.

29. NFTs are unique cryptographic tokens that exist on a blockchain and cannot be replicated. They are compared to title deeds and can be used to represent real-world items like artwork and real-estate. See Rakesh Sharma, "Non-Fungible Token (NFT) Definition," November 17, 2021, Investopedia, https://www.investopedia.com/non-fungible-tokens-nft-5115211.

30. CryptoKitties is a blockchain game on Ethereum developed by Dapper Labs in 2017. It allows players to purchase, collect, breed and sell virtual cats.

1.5 million people and the classic internet meme known as *Nyan Cat* was auctioned for almost $600,000. In March 2021 the artist Beeple and auction house Christie's minted and sold their first NFT work of art, a collage of 5000 digital images, *Everydays: The First 5000 Days* for $60 million worth of cryptocurrency and the art markets lost their minds. In 2021 sales of art NFTs on OpenSea, just one of many decentralised marketplaces for crypto collectibles, recorded sales valued at a third of the total global art market.[31] The fact that blockchains now reliably hold billions of dollars-worth of financial value indicates undeniably something about the security and growing influence of cryptoeconomic systems.[32] Yet, overall, the use-cases of artworld NFTs have provided the ideal first popular examples for a financial technology that seeks adoption and needs case-studies to prove to populations and governments alike that cryptocurrencies can be real money not just the fever dream of a cabal of Ponzi scheme managers. And this is a cause of great acrimony to specific players of the artworld in relation to the Cryptoart and NFT boom as NFT markets are derided as retrogressive; extending property relations into PTP communities, feeding on cultures of competitive individualism and promoting the cult of the genius artist.[33] Conversely, there are reasons to celebrate the ability of some artists now to be able to earn a living and fund their work, and while capitalism persists, the most impactful forms of co-operation still need cash to function.

However, as in nature, so in culture – markets alone produce inequity, monopoly and fragility, while diverse ecologies produce resilience. So for people interested in a more expanded idea of culture (let alone life) and global democracy, DAOs, not NFTs, are the bigger blockchain story. In order to realise their social potential, however, they need the attention and input of many more diverse people and cultures.

Co-ops, squats and collectives have long created and exercised ways of attending to mutual interest – but typically these have been

31. "The Art Basel and UBS Global Art Market Report", March 16, 2021, Art Basel, https://artbasel.com/stories/art-market-report-2021.

32. Nathan Schneider, "Cryptoeconomics as a Limitation on Governance,"draft v.20220121, University of Colorado Boulder, 2021, https://osf.io/wzf85/?view_only=a10581ae9a804aa197ac39ebbba05766.

33. Jonathan Beller, "Fascism on the Blockchain? The Work of Art in the Age of NFTs," *Coindesk*, March 23, 2021, https://www.coindesk.com/markets/2021/03/23/fascism-on-the-blockchain-the-work-of-art-in-the-age-of-nfts.

coordinated by communities that are already consensually entangled locally and offline. DAOs utilise and radicalise the latent potential of the spread of personal computing and the World Wide Web into our lives. As an open source PTP technology, DAOs lend themselves to templating and revision by other groups trying to find similar answers. As the code bases for the suites of smart contracts that DAOs are made of grow and are made available for scrutiny and adaptation, other DAO builders can learn from or reuse existing pieces of code, making changes and reconfiguring elements for their own contexts. DAOs offer both the tools and the practical philosophical context for people to test their own social critical faculties, their own agendas, and to practice collective decision-making in hybrid online/onlife communal spaces.

As this book documents, DAOs have become a focus for experimentation by artists and activists who see their potential for revisioning and shaping society in new ways.[34] Perhaps it is the flexibility of DAOs – the capacity they lend their members to devise, test and change rules for organising at a granular level – that has inspired such feverish imaginings and experimental collaborations between artists and technologists to realise designs for architectures of cultural power and distribution that can metamorphose at the will of their members. They have felt the power of allyship – to connect across distance and difference at ground level.

Artworld DAOs are where wilding meets the law, where kin[35] can demand the right to:

1. *make* their own instruments for self-and-community-realisation
2. *create* the distribution cultures, platforms and channels to share ideas, practices and insights
3. *own* a stake in their mutual future prosperity

For this, access, useability and values-based co-creation is crucial. An early example of this approach in action was the DACTROIT project[36]

34. Laura Lotti, "The Art of Tokenization: Blockchain Affordances and the Invention of Future Milieus," *Media Theory* 3, no. 1 (2019), https://mediatheoryjournal.org/laura-lotti-blockchain-affordances.

35. We use kin here in the sense that Donna Haraway uses it to describe people enduring mutual, obligatory, relatedness that carries consequences in her book *Staying with the Trouble: Making Kin in the Chthulucene* (Durham: Duke University Press, 2016).

36. Detroit Blockchain Center, https://detroitblockchaincenter.org.

for decentralised infrastructure in Detroit which responded to urgent local needs, building on the histories of "domestic and global labour struggles",[37] in a quest to introduce social justice into what the project initiators call an avant-entrepreneurial dynamic, working across art, politics and technology. As Ingrid LaFleur states of the project:

> Activists respond[ed] to the city's (often highly racialised) political failures to provide basic utilities with impressive social innovation. The recent boot-strapping community mesh networks for instance, was a response to the fact that 40 percent of Detroit residents have no access to the Internet at all. The alliances and networks formed in this project are now providing the social grounding for peer-to-peer technical education and experimentation with emerging decentralisation technologies.[38]

A new field of artworld DAOs are also emerging for different models of both open and closed-door co-creation, organisation, curation, collection, ownership and speculation of, and on NFT-enabled digital art including (and in addition to those already mentioned and/or presented in this book) FWB, PleasrDAO, Flamingo DAO, The Sphere and Holly+. The latter two are of particular interest for their high art concept and deep engagements with experimental co-creation and communities of producers.

IN THE SHADOW-WORLD OF DAOS

By the early noughties the artists, technologists, activists, serious gameplayers and generally life-curious beings who grew up in the malleable world of the early Web and thought they would forever now be able to create and shape the world together using self-made tools, were learning hard lessons. The generative and permissive freedoms of early multi-identity play-spaces of MUDs and MOOs,[39] the corporate

---

37. Ingrid LaFleur Interviewed by Ruth Catlow, "There Are Black People In The Future," Furtherfield, September 30, 2019, https://www.furtherfield.org/ingrid-lafleur-there-are-black-people-in-the-future.

38. Ibid.

39. Multiple User Dimensions, Multiple User Dungeons, and/or Multiple User Dialogues (MUDs) and MUDs Object-Oriented (MOOs) are multi-user text-based virtual realities accessible via the Internet.

brand hacking antics of artists like Trina Mould aka Rachel Baker, and the multiple examples of self-instituting arts organisations on the Web made us forget for a moment that while that famous Paul Baran network diagram [40] shows an evolution of communication networks from broadcast mode to decentralisation and distribution, emergent network effects actually tend to accelerate the centralisation of power and resources. We must not forget again. And so, in order to guard against unintended consequences of working with powerful planetary-scale technologies, we believe it's crucial to look not only at its progressive potentialities, but to connect with the demiurges of its creators, their utopian (or otherwise) predecessors and to prepare for some of the challenges we might face.

In spite of blockchain technologies' political roots in 1990s cypherpunk culture as decentralised network technologies or what could crudely be characterised as "seeking to defeat authorities," they risk becoming just another "disruptive" neoliberal technology to grow the self-image of all people and populations as solely-economic beings, motivated by financial reward and therefore legitimate subjects in a tireless search for efficiency and productivity gains through full automation. DAOs misused could become the ideal instrument for a system obsessed with quantification and a belief in the supremacy of the kind of propositional knowledge that quantification produces. A society that models humans as purely economic creatures will assume that the only effective incentive is financial and will create social infrastructure where priced transactions are the only glue – and betting and speculative success the primary joy. In this world, DAOs will be used (rhetorically and practically) to accelerate and intensify the tracking, mining and extraction of value from living beings and systems. This fork of techno-social evolution conjured vividly in the "rabid nihilism" [41] of Nick Land, would eradicate even the idea of the common good, and see technology and capital at the centre of history, rather than human and more-than-human relations. Unconstrained by any human moral considerations, all life-forms and living relations become raw material, and their suffering and destruction the meaningless and invisible byproducts of the so-called "singularity". Where, as Land writes: "Digitocommodification is the index of a cyberpositively escalating technovirus, of the planetary technocapital singularity: a self-organizing

40. Paul Baran, "On Distributed Communications Networks," August 1964, RAND Corporation, https://www.rand.org/content/dam/rand/pubs/research_memoranda/2006/RM3420.pdf.

41. Nick Land, *Fanged Noumena* (Falmouth: Urbanomic, 2011).

insidious traumatism, virtually guiding the entire biological desiring-complex towards post-carbon replicator usurpation." [42]

Perhaps only one step sideways from this horror-show is another DAO-enabled vision of utopia-of-the-few, that might appeal to the super wealthy, engaged in accumulating material reward, free from societal demand or responsibility. For these people, DAOs possess another captivating potential that is conjured by switching the "A" of DAOs from "autonomy" to "autopoiesis". Here the mission or idea of the organisation "takes on a life of its own, and it's able to incentivise others to make itself happen".[43] Hidden in the shadows of this vision is a resulting growth in the power of those with either capital or technical capacity, to decentre the needs of human communities [44] (let alone those of other life-forms) in productive organisations. Becoming a machine for reproducing and recentralising power. Negotiation and decision-making processes traditionally managed by soft-skilled humans are deferred to a set of potentially dizzyingly complex coordination mechanisms coercing workers using DAOs' internal capital.[45] In this scenario humans service the economically self-sovereign "machine," a popular example being the fleet of self-owning, self-driving cars that hires humans to fix them. Software replaces traditional economic and social coordination mechanisms, encoding market and production-line logics with no regard for the needs of living beings, systems or natural environments that cannot be expressed in solely-economic terms. This world goes dark very quickly, a true tragedy of the commons, for all except those living in smart island fortresses. By preserving the anonymity of its members a DAO can act without responsibility or accountability. The automation of decision making and resource distribution processes in organisations is risky because hostile humans or AIs (black-boxed arrays of information technologies) acting as members of DAOs can act at super-high frequencies, and have

42. Nick Land, "Machinic Desire," *Textual Practice* 7:3, (June 2008), https://doi.org/10.1080/09502369308582177.

43. "Level Up Your Knowledge of DAOs," Aragon. Accessed November 30, 2021, https://aragon.org/dao.

44. Vitalik Buterin, "DAOs, DACs, DAs and More: An Incomplete Terminology Guide," *Ethereum Foundation Blog*, May 6, 2014, https://blog.ethereum.org/2014/05/06/daos-dacs-das-and-more-an-incomplete-terminology-guide.

45. Philippe Honigman, "What can we do with a DAO in 2020?" Daobase, July 14, 2020, https://daobase.org/what-can-we-do-with-a-dao-in-2020.

far reaching and high impact effects, without compunction or detection. The nightmare of the AI paperclip maximiser could become real.[46]

Technology shapes all the forms of life it is co-constituted with. The immutable rules, regulations, code, law, and permanent records of blockchains have the potential to encode forms of life with little flexibility or agency. The bewildering "forever" of early blockchain rhetoric[47] jangles and jars in the ears of anyone also attending to the imperative of continual root and branch societal change and innovation in the face of calamitous species extinctions and climate collapse.

HOW CAN ART HELP?

Feminist economists and commons experts Marilyn Waring, Elinor Ostrom and Silvia Federici, remind us that for life to thrive, economies must follow cultures, not the other way round. And for this to be realised, economic technologies must: be shaped by, with and for the people in communities who use them; connect with more than human systems, with more than markets and governance structures; extend into folk law and cosmological knowledge and wisdom systems; terraform a myriad tiny worlds; and smuggle out lively and strange cultural forms into more consensual realities in the world at large.

Global artworlds provide one of the strongest social testbeds of the digital native generation – for discovering what our relationship with technology might be capable of, for better or for worse. Artists bring value to the technological development space with their intrinsic motivation to address human and more-than-human experience, to cooperate, break rules, find value, and question outmoded business models. As Harry Cleaver writes of the extraordinary use of the early Internet by The Zapatistas: "While business apologists may pretend that 'commerce is the engine of technology change,' managers know that the real, material source of change is the creative power of those fascinated with

---

46. Nick Bostrom's "Paperclip Maximiser" demonstrates the hypothetical risk that AI+automation might pose to human beings (and living systems more widely) even when designed to pursue seemingly harmless goals. If not programmed to value human thriving, a complex machine tasked with manufacturing paperclips will transform all matter including human beings into paperclips or paperclip manufacturing facilities. Nick Bostrom, *Ethical Issues in Advanced Artificial Intelligence*, 2003, https://nickbostrom.com/ethics/ai.html.

47. See for example Ocean Protocol who in 2018 promised to store your data for eternity – and even put a price on the service of $100 per 10MB: https://oceanprotocol.com.

and dedicated to the development of computers in all their aspects."[48] Engagement with new technologies by artists as practical philosophers offers a myriad of entry points for non-engineers and people who believe in art as a tool of social change, even when they think they don't. And to find out how well a system works we must first use it, and maybe even break it, to organise and decide about something we and others really care about. Discussions about genres, comparability, representation and exclusion in the arts are incendiary. When one person claims something as art that others regard as utter trash, without craft or consequence, we discover how much the question of art really matters to people as the exemplary vehicle for schismogenesis, the strengthening of group identity by the creation of divisions and distinctions between one culture and another.[49] Artworld DAOs also demonstrate the importance of the role of users-in-context in shaping their own technological tools (for themselves and their own proximate and decentralised communities) as a counterbalance to systems designed from "the centre" that may not act in their interests.

From the artistic and anti-art movements of Dada, the global revolutionary left of Lettrists, Surrealists, and the Situationists, to the work of systems artists and thinkers such as Adrian Piper, W.E.B. Du Bois and Stephen Willats, there is a historical precedence for cultural practitioners paying close attention to questions of process and power. In their art, and their organising, such art practices deal with questions of *how* we decide, and *who gets* to decide – as much as *what* we decide. They understand that organising for living systems means not simply getting things done, but shaping and attending to the poetry of the organisational tools and processes of all agents, all stakeholders, all the way down. Artists have long been organisational innovators using artistic manifestos as their vehicles. DAOs may now become executable manifestos and a powerful addition to the toolbox of collective expression and coordination across distance and difference. The members of artistic movements often work by setting their sights on the horizon of a world not yet in existence and then organise to bring that horizon closer, but what worlds artists will manifest is a question both for this book and for the future.

48. Harry Cleaver, "The Zapatistas and the Electronic Fabric of Struggle," University of Texas, 1998, https://la.utexas.edu/users/hcleaver/zaps.html.

49. For discussion of this term *see* chapter 2 in: David Graeber and David Wengrow, *The Dawn of Everything: A New History of Humanity* (London: Allen Lane, 2021).

WHAT IS INCLUDED IN THIS ARTWORLD DAO CHRONICLE?

We have come to understand over the years that within every first appearance of a "new" concept, idea, or technology are the dreams, endeavours and accumulated lessons of past futures. And so we open this book with **An Artworld DAO Timeline** that traces a sequence of artistic, technological and world events, revealed to us to be crucial to DAO developments. The timeline places special emphasis on the collective actions, principles and tools of communities of artists, technologists and activists, and global social and alchemic movements. These are the historic events that have informed our thinking and framing of Artworld DAOs. These nodes highlight to the reader how cooperative approaches to the distribution of power and resources have always existed and offer context to their recent flowering within the arts and beyond. From this rich history of commoning we open the practice of radical friendship presented in this book.

The book is organised to support deep thinking, inspiration, praxis and prototyping, complemented by elements specifically created to scaffold learning. Each element is introduced by an alchemical drawing from the **Hexen 2.0** tarot deck manifested by the artist Suzanne Treister. Published in 2016, the original deck holds 78 cards in total, that depict the interconnectivity of computing, the internet, cybernetics, counterculture, sci-fi and social engineering, through a near future lens that is etched with the rhetorics of the past. For this book we have drawn eight cards, each one resonates with the contents that follow, catalysing individual interpretations and divinations through the visuals and histories they depict. Nestled between the *Four of Wands* honouring the "first American Anarchist," the DAO timeline and the *Knave of Pentacles* is a glossary of terms collated by artist, writer and blockchain-whisperer Rhea Myers, which acts as a cheat sheet for the lore and terminology used in this emergent field.

Myers also leads the reader into the heart of the book with her essay "A Thousand DAOs" that describes an array of artworld DAOs and their reasons for being, real and imagined. Upon this foundation is built a series of essays each focusing on a particular question, controversy, or zone of contention surrounding DAO thinking, building and implementation.

All contributors are rooted in communities – artistic, technical, activist – who contribute to the thinking and coding of conflicting and emerging nuances around DAO tools, philosophies, and uses, including the redistribution of power in the artworld, and on the blockchain.

The essays sit along three axes of radical friendship practices in decentralised environments. The first axis advocates for intentional over ideological (or solutionist) strategies for social solidarity and transformation in decentralised systems. Theorist and moving-image artist Hito Steyerl vehemently demands the realisation of a leftist code beyond speculation and rhetoric. Political analyst Jaya Klara Brekke asserts the crucial value to wider society of critical cultural engagement with the development of emerging technologies, and Penny Rafferty advocates for social change through the subcultural frame of direct action against the behemoths of contemporary imperialism (whilst not forgetting the real strain of community-building fatigue). Lucille Haute shares Rafferty's and Brekke's respect for rhizomatic affinity-action groups for enacting collective intentions, in her "Cyberwitches' Manifesto" whose incantations *"Let's be actual « saboteurs of big daddy mainframe »"* are compiled with open source graphic technology. The essays on this axis seek illumination and direction from values and affinities rather than the machinic light of incentivisation and deterrence.

The second axis wrangles the false dichotomy of individual vs. collective interest, predominant in both artworld and blockchain realms. Artist and debt activist Cassie Thornton, the initiator of the *The Hologram*, a viral PTP anti-capitalist health system, shares her own history, doubts and urges in relation to the communal, the collective, and the cryptographic. Art historian and author of "Walled Gardens Autonomy, Automation, and Art After the Internet" Cadence Kinsey collaborated with Ruth Catlow and Rhea Myers and visual researchers Studio Hyte, to produce "The Blockchain Art History Timeline" feasibility study. This interrogates the problems and potentials of a collectively constructed artworld timeline and explores ways to go beyond just another colonial power-grab in service of already-privileged individual artworld stakeholders. Unfolding some of the same questions but through the lens of the art market and the cannon of art history, Legacy Russell curator, writer, and author of *Glitch Feminism: A Manifesto* focuses on how collectives-as-commercial-entities have become progressively established as a salient influence within the contemporary art marketplace. She highlights the way in which participation in economy as hyper-performance can encourage and accelerate both our understanding and our survival as we navigate this increasingly hostile environment we call society. The specialist in sustainable human-computer interaction and design-led participatory research Sara Heitlinger takes this method further with her cohort's report on a multi-species commoning perspective on Nature 3.0 derived through a Live Action Role-Play schema. Ruth Catlow considers questions of translocal belonging after the blockchain and cultural cooperation made possible by DAOs. Each of these essays discovers complications in the process of renegotiating competitive zero-sum fantasies in favour of systems of mutual well-being across distance, difference and time.

The third and final axis concerns the processes, practicalities, potentials, and threats implicit within the opening of blockchains' black boxes to the artworld and beyond. Crypto-ecosystem strategist, artist and researcher Kei Kreutler, who has played a crucial role in realising accessible tooling for DAOs describes her research into the way that cultural occultist narratives of technologies have shaped their use today in her essay "Eight Qualities of Decentralised Autonomous Organisations". Kreutler offers up emergent strategies for getting organised, alongside pictorial keys from the popular Rider-Waite tarot deck that enable non-technical readers to embody, map, and assess the potentials of DAO thinking. Calum Bowden and Laura Lotti hone this praxis with an example situated in the Berlin artworld through their essay "Manifesting a Black Swan DAO" guiding the reader through years of field research and experimentation with decentralised test sites to vanquish cultural gatekeepers and work towards systematic, socio-emotional and resilient shifts in a Web3 landscape. Art historian Tina Rivers Ryan's essay attends to the impact of the DAO's volatile artworld cousin... NFTs. It recounts the key events and protagonists of this global phenomenon, and analyses some of the economic and cultural impacts of the arrival of digital art-forms now imbued with scarcity. Sam Skinner interviews Sam Spike of Fingerprints DAO and Mitchell F. Chan the artist behind *Digital Zones of Immaterial Pictorial Sensibility*, which Fingerprints DAO bought, and the role of DAOs in their respective work and modes of operation. Ramon Amaro, the engineer, sociologist, and cultural theorist in machine learning and artificial intelligence applies his critique of computational reason to reveal the ineluctable racial and "protocological" injustice inscribed in decentralised technologies. Digital infrastructure strategist Cade Diehm shares his research into data and privacy systems to warn about the dangers of inadequate risk analysis and threat detection in decentralised co-ordination tools and processes. Together these texts offer the knowledge to strengthen practical alliances and to build more robust approaches to sustaining and defending camaraderie and fellowship.

Artworld DAOs are now under construction across the world. Conversations unpacking their designs and contexts offer a window on the many missions and ways of life that are shaping their formation. In this book the **Artworld DAOs Speak** for themselves in a series of interviews that give voice to this new, more-than-human species of artworld agents, the true pioneers of blockchain-based decentralisation. Interviews are "transcribed" by the DAOs' creators, including *DAK*'s Nick Koppenhagen, *DisCO*'s Ann Marie Utratel and Stacco Troncoso, the creator of the eponymous *Jonas Lund Token*, and *The Sphere*'s Erik Bordeleau, drawn from disciplines of artworld institutional critique, solidarity activism, legal experimentalism and finance weirding respectively. They are saturated with the ideas, inventions, and interventions of the unique communities from which they spring. Accompanying this section, the **Method Kit of Practices, Tactics and Prototypes** offers a series of practices and disciplines that groups might adopt to tune into and wrangle the specific affordances of DAOs, and offers a range of stories from the ground of what could be called artworld solidarity mobilisations. The section is comprised of: **5 Gateways** to individual and group practices by Omsk Social Club, and exercises for embodying intentional change and building new collective disciplines; **a LARP-creation guide** sets out how immersive, participatory performance might be used to prototype and support the creation of translocal cooperative organisations before committing to code. Finally, blueprints of **Artworld DAO Prototypes** from Berlin, Hong Kong, Minsk, Moscow and Johannesburg communicate a range of possibilities for new artworks, art organisations, speculative fictions and systemic critique. Created as part of a two-year think tank and development process supported by Goethe-Institut, Serpentine Galleries and Furtherfield along with a transnational network of cultural organisations, they open up the some of the secrets of DAO potentialities to provide insights into their communities, practices, infrastructures, economies and ways of life. This section demonstrates how collectivity is demanding by design and how mutable ecosystems powered by community practitioners might inform new tools to navigate the challenges of interdependence. It illustrates how DAO prototyping can advance these social translocal bodies defined less by their problems than their affordances.

Collectively, this book sets out to facilitate diverse, critical, involvement in, and occupation of, DAOs as a powerful social instrument, with potential to operate beyond the blockchain, banking spaces or the new art market centres manifested by NFT innovations. Moreover, it explores the political potential of art to prefigure a space which exceeds the limitations of technical rationality and the economistic approaches dominant in both right- and left-wing analyses. A space in which the DAO as a social process, and the DAO as a functional tool, are interrogated together at the intersection of artistic experimentation and fierce theoretical speculation.

We the authors have to assume some commonality with you, dear readers – we assume that many things about the current organisation of the world will disgust you. However, we also hope for variety and divergence amongst you. We know that we are unable to account for all of your different localities. Yet there is a chance they do connect and that the destinies of ours and your artworld DAOs are able to build new machines for pluralistic polyphonic cooperation. This is in many ways a terrible time for world cooperation and yet experimentation by people in grounded communities, across silos, could drive a resurgence of conscious, peer-led governance and coordination design just when it is most needed.

This, after all, is a beginning, not an end...

JOSIAH WARREN
BOSTON
1798   USA   1874

FIRST AMERICAN ANARCHIST

"TRUE CIVILIZATION" 1863

EQUITABLE COMMERCE 1852

INDIVIDUALIST ANARCHIST COLONIES ☆
UTOPIA, OHIO, USA
(REORGANISED 1847)
MODERN TIMES, LONG ISLAND, NY
PRINCIPLES: THE SOVEREIGNTY OF THE
INDIVIDUAL ★ PRIVATE PROPERTY AND A
MARKET ECONOMY ★ COST (LABOUR) THE
LIMIT OF PRICE

'LABOR   NOTE'

1827 · OPENED THE FIRST TIME STORE, CINCINNATI
A 3 YEAR EXPERIMENT IN ALTERNATIVE ECONOMICS

FOUR OF WANDS

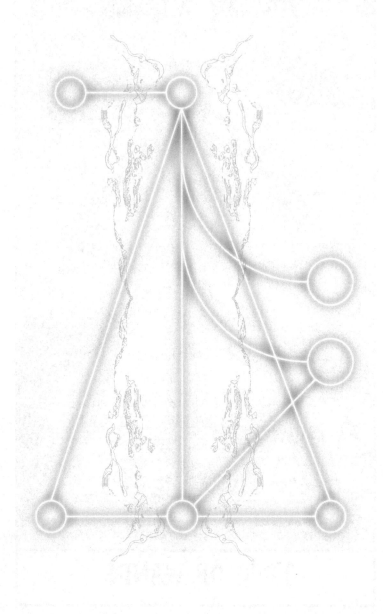

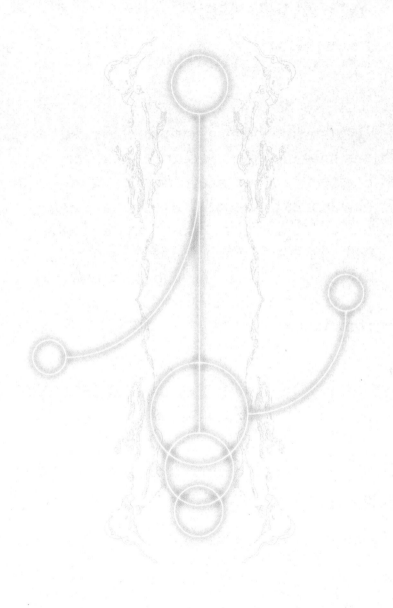

An Artworld DAO Timeline

This timeline indicates events referenced
and mused on by the contributors to this
book with a focus on artistic practice and
new modes of solidarity. Artist collectives
mix with role-playing games, cryptography
with occultism, giving a sense of some of
the radical roots and kinships that underpin
the development of DAOs as form and as
community.

6th century BCE onwards

Daoist leaders in Asia, attuned to the flow of nature, exert large cultural influence from the margins of society. DAO puns, memes and references to "the way" proliferate two and a half millennia later in spite of any lack of formal connection.

1750s

Friendly Societies start to spring up in the UK as collective-self-help and mutual insurance organisations for and by working people.

1830s

French social theorist Charles Fourier theorises phalanx communities for collective dwelling and cooperative working.

1843

The Albany Branch of the North American Phalanx, manifests Fourier's theories and opens a secular utopian socialist commune.

1860

A US youth movement called the Wide Awakes, mobilises against slavery and is responsible for bringing Abraham Lincoln to power.

1884

The *Rochdale Principles* are established in England, as a set of ideals for the operation of cooperatives.

1900

Austin Osman Spare creates the first open source symbol system language for magic, sigils.

1902

The Red Rose Girls, the first female art collective is established by Violet Oakley, Jesse Smith and Elizabeth Green in the Red Rose Inn, Pennsylvania.

1919

The Bauhaus opens in Weimar promoting principles of mass production, and an interplay between artistic creativity and technological innovation.

1933

Black Mountain College opens in North Carolina, practicing holistic art-centered and non-hierarchical learning methods that made students and educators peers.

1935

Walter Benjamin publishes *The Work of Art in the Age of Mechanical Reproduction* proposing that mechanical reproduction devalues the aura of an art object as it was traditionally conceived and offers the possibility for new modes of artistic practice.

1958

The *Situationist International* rejects all art that separates itself from politics.

1959

Yves Klein's performance work *Zone of Immaterial Pictorial Sensibility* interrogates the symbolic and real relationship between art, ownership, money, and value.

1963

The *Fluxus Manifesto* demands: "living art, anti-art, and NON-ART REALITY be grasped by all peoples, not only critics, dilettantes and professionals."

The "holy book" of *Discordianism* is published, written by Greg Hill with Kerry Wendell Thornley, venerating the Goddess of Chaos, and archetypes and ideals associated with her.

W.I.T.C.H. the Women's International Terrorist Conspiracy from Hell start to organise independent groups as part of the Women's Liberation Movement.

1967

Guy Debord publishes *La Société du Spectacle*, a work of Marxist critical theory claiming that representation has replaced all authentic social life and relations between commodities have replaced relations between people.

1968

A revolution is born in France from an unlikely alliance between students and workers against rigid national institutions and government.

The first issue of the counterculture magazine and product catalogue, *The Whole Earth Catalog*, is published.

1969

The Art Workers' Coalition was formed in New York City. Its principal aim was to pressure the city's museums – notably the Museum of Modern Art – into implementing economic and political reforms.

1970

The Royal Chicano Air Force art collective is founded in Sacramento to foster the arts in the Chicano/Latino community.

The first Live Action Role-Plays (LARPs) were run, inspired by tabletop role-playing games and genre fiction.

1971

American feminist Jo Freeman publishes *The Tyranny of Structurelessness* concerning power relations within radical feminist collectives. She proposes a formalisation and democratisation of otherwise unacknowledged hierarchies.

1974

Uranian Phalanstery and the First New York Gnostic Lyceum Temple artist collectives establish a venue in the Lower East Side of Manhattan for experimental Gnostic art practices.

Dungeons & Dragons the fantasy role-playing game is released.

1975

The first text-based, real-time virtual world role-playing games called MUDs (multi-user dungeons) became popular.

1978

Raising their own funding, artists' group Collaborative Projects also known as Colab begins to control the content of their own exhibitions and cable TV shows responding to the political concerns of their time.

1980

LARP activities spread internationally and diversify into a wide variety of styles of role play.

1981

Group Material opens the exhibition entitled The People's Choice consisting of more than a hundred objects loaned from neighbourhood residents, often accompanied by a personal story about the object.

Thee Temple ov Psychick Youth (TOPY) a collective of artists and practitioners of chaos magick is founded by Genesis P-Orridge and others.

1982

Chaos Magick groups are founded around Yorkshire, UK. Specifically focused around a shop called The Sorcerer's Apprentice in Leeds, UK.

1984

The Black movement in Germany begins with the development of the term "Afro-German" by a collective of writers in Berlin with Black German activists and the Caribbean-African-American activist Audre Lorde.

1985

The Rodeo Caldonia Black feminist arts collective is founded by Lisa Jones and Alva Rogers in Fort Greene, Brooklyn.

The Guerrilla Girls, an anonymous group of feminist, female artists devoted to fighting sexism and racism within the art world is founded in New York.

A Cyborg Manifesto by Donna Haraway is published in the Socialist Review.

1988

AIDS activist artist collective Gran Fury emerges from ACT UP (AIDS Coalition to Unleash Power) appropriating commercial language for political ends.

1989

Kimberlé Crenshaw theorises "intersectionality" as a way of understanding the intersecting layers of different forms of oppression experienced by Black women.

1990

Elinor Ostrom publishes *Governing the Commons: The Evolution of Institutions for Collective Action*.

Tim Berners Lee publishes a proposal to build a "Hypertext project" called "WorldWideWeb".

e-Estonia establishes a model of digital state as enterprise, offering passport, citizenship and tax-breaks with no requirement for residency.

1991

The Thing bulletin board system is founded in New York, providing an online forum for the discussion of contemporary art and cultural theory.

Mindvox launches a New York internet service provider attracting artists, writers and activists from non-academic hacker culture, interested in ideas about the potentials of cyberspace.

VNSMatrix, the self-declared saboteurs of "big daddy mainframe" publish the *Cyberfeminst Manifesto for the 21st Century* and claim "the clitoris is a direct line to the matrix."

1993

The Cypherpunk Manifesto asserts the need for personal privacy and state transparency if society is to be kept free of governmental and corporate oppression in the electronic age.

Octavia E. Butler publishes *Parable of the Sower* the post-apocalyptic climate change and social inequality science fiction novel

1994

The strategic use of computer networks by the Zapatista Army of National Liberation in their PR war against the Mexican State, establishes the Internet's potential as a tool for insurgency.

Luther Blissett is born/founded in Bologna as a multiple-use name and identity, to be shared by hundreds of artists and activists across Europe and the Americas.

Antoni Muntadas exhibits *The File Room*, Randolph Street Gallery, Chicago – a temporary physical installation and a permanent, expandable database on the web, containing censored artworks.

1995

The Reclaim the Streets collective is born out of the anti-road protest movement in the UK, resisting the dominance of corporate forces in globalisation and asserting communal ownership of public space.

Critical Art Ensemble declare our *data bodies* the fascist sibling of our fleshy selves in an address to the Interface 3 conference in Hamburg.

1996

Formation of Net Art "Self-Institutions" Furtherfield in the UK and Rhizome in the USA.

A *Declaration of the Independence of Cyberspace* published by John Perry Barlow states: "The internet consists of transactions, relationships, and thought itself."

Critical Art Ensemble publish *Electronic Civil Disobedience and Other Unpopular Ideas.*

PostMasters exhibition *Can you digit?* features works by US West Coast artists and designers with close ties to Silicon Valley.

1997

Rhizome launched *StockObjects* a clip-art-like library to be created by the artists in the Rhizome community.

Sadie Plant publishes *Zeros and Ones: Digital Women and the New Technoculture.*

1998

The legal scholar and cryptographer Nick Szabo designs a mechanism for *Bit Gold*, a decentralised digital currency regarded as a direct precursor to the Bitcoin architecture.

Electronic Disturbance Theatre launches *FloodNet* also known as *Flutnetz* a software to wage targeted mass participation attacks on the website of the Mexican government, to protest measures taken against the Zapatistas.

Artist Olia Lialina establishes the self-proclaimed First Real Net Art Gallery.

Wolf Lieser founds DAM, the Digital Art Museum in Berlin.

Techgnosis: Myth, Magic, Mysticism in the Age of Information is published by Erik Davis.

1999

The Carnival Against Capital, or *J18* is one of the first international anti-globalisation protests against the structural violence of "free market imperialism" organised in cities around the world to coincide with the 25th G8 Summit.

Napster the peer to peer file sharing, distribution and audio streaming service provider is founded by Shawn Fanning and Sean Parker.

2002

BorderXing Guide by Heath Bunting is commissioned by Tate Online, UK – an online guide and database on how to cross borders illegally, aimed at militants and undocumented migrants.

Napster ceases operations and files for bankruptcy following a series of lawsuits over copyright infringement.

2004

The Artist as Producer in Times of Crisis by Okwui Enwezor is published.

Artists Natalie Bookchin and Jackie Stevens' *Agora Exchange* is commissioned by Tate Online, UK – an online community space for designing a multi-player game to challenge conventions for awarding nationality and wealth.

McKenzie Wark publishes *A Hacker Manifesto*.

2005

The Onondaga Nation files a complaint in a federal court in Syracuse seeking title to their lost homelands, not for possession or to exclude, but for the right to participate in the well-being of the land.

The artist run game development studio, Tale of Tales publishes *The Endless Forest*, a multiplayer online game artwork and social screensaver (still online) where players roam and interact as deer as their computers sleep.

Richard Barbrook and Andy Cameron coin the term "Californian Ideology" as a "critique of dotcom neoliberalism".

The Million Dollar Homepage, a website that sells advertising space by the pixel, is conceived by Alex Tew.

NODE.London a city-wide season of media arts is held featuring 150 projects in over 40 London venues, organised as a networked, open, distributed event using consensual decision making methods.

2006

Furtherfield launches the *DIWO (Do It With Others)* campaign for emancipatory, networked art practices.

2007

The Invisible Committee publish *The Coming Insurrection* including chapter "Fuck Off, Google" signalling the growing unease about the centralisation of power on the Web.

The Shock Doctrine by Naomi Klein is published arguing that neoliberal free market policies have risen to prominence in some developed countries because of a deliberate strategy of "shock therapy".

2008

Bitcoin: A Peer-to-Peer Electronic Cash System authored by Satoshi Nakamoto describes a new open source software that operates across a network of computers to create, secure and track digital assets.

WORKING ARTISTS AND THE GREATER ECONOMY (W.A.G.E.) was founded in support of Black liberation, abolition, and the end of racial capitalism throughout the USA.

Aymeric Mansoux, Marloes de Valk publish *FLOSS + Art*, an edited collection of critical essays reflecting on the growing relationship between Free Software ideology, open content and digital art.

2009

The ZAD (Zone à Défendre) is set up after a letter by residents invites people to squat the land earmarked for a new airport for the city of Nantes "because only an inhabited territory can be defended".

2010

Bitcoin is used to raise funds for WikiLeaks in response to the international banking blockade.

2011

Occupy Wall St begin a protest movement against economic inequality and the influence of money in politics in Zuccotti Park, in New York City's Wall Street financial district.

@OccupyArtWorld an anonymous Twitter account begin lobbying for change within the art industry.

2012

A fake press release lands on the homepage of the Whitney Biennial, stating: "The Museum expects to reopen on May 2 a wholly changed institution."

Members of global Occupy Movements take over the ground floor of the KW Berlin on the invitation of the curators of the 7th Berlin Biennale entitled *Forget Fear.*

The first unMonastery opens its doors in Matera, Italy declaring itself a social clinic for the future, attempting to reconcile the work of making a living and the work to make meaning.

2013

Edward Snowden leaks the NSA's secret surveillance infrastructure responsible for US abuses of privacy of citizens, companies and political leaders worldwide.

Daniel Temkin curates *NetVVorth* an online auction presented with TRANSFER gallery. Sales of 50 forgeries by noted net artists are made in Bitcoin and the real artist behind each work is only revealed to the collector after purchase.

Vitalik Buterin publishes the *Ethereum White Paper* for a new blockchain with a built-in programming language to write and execute contracts that automate the management of digital assets and allow the formation of decentralised autonomous organisations.

Ascribe is a protocol, backend, and app for blockchain-secured digital art built on Bitcoin

Dogecoin – meme based currency launched.

Technical protocols for peer-to-peer information networks such as Dat, Scuttlebutt and ActivityPub are developed to redistribute power from centralised corporate interests.

2014

Vitalik Buterin publishes *DAOs, DACs, DAs and More: An Incomplete Terminology Guide*.

Protocol Labs open source lab for research and creation of blockchain software systems to "make human existence orders of magnitude better through technology," is founded. Projects include the InterPlanetary File System (IPFS) protocol and peer-to-peer network for storing and sharing data and FileCoin, a public cryptocurrency, cooperative digital storage and data retrieval method.

Monegraph launches a platform based on the NameCoin blockchain that allows people to certify images on the web, then tweet out public proof.

Karatani Kojin publishes *The Structure of World History, From Modes of Production to Modes of Exchange* setting out 4 different models of commune.

Lorna Mills produces *Ways of Something*, an homage to John Berger's *Ways of Seeing* (1972) comprising digital work by over 113 net artists; Mills pays equal shares of each sale of the work to all participating artists.

Rhea Myers creates the *Ethereum Art Market* smart contract through which digital artworks can be registered and sold, on the pre-launch Ethereum testnet.

Platform Cooperativism vs. the Sharing Economy by Trebor Scholz is published, criticising sharing economy platforms and calling for the creation of alternative democratically controlled worker cooperative.

2015

Developers' tools for creating decentralised governance infrastructure for borderless and permissionless organisations begin to proliferate. Platforms include Aragon, Colony, DAOStack DAOHaus.

DAOWO White Paper by Rhea Myers describes how to combine cryptoculture with participatory art shows.

Artist Sarah Meyohas launches *BitchCoin*, "a cryptocurrency for Buying Art and Investing in the Artist".

Alfredo Salazar-Caro debuts the artist-led, virtual reality-based *Digital Museum of Digital Art*, funded by 3-D printed sculptural editions.

Walidah Imarisha and adrienne maree brown publish *Octavia's Brood – Science Fiction Stories from Social Justice Movements*, an edited collection of stories by organisers and activists.

Okhaos creates *Plantoid* – an autonomous blockchain-based artwork, and "evolutionary life form" in the form of a DAO that relies on cryptocurrency to finance and reproduce itself.

SAGA launches a digital publishing framework that gives creators the power to determine how their work appears in each specific context on the web.

Artist Harm van den Dorpel and Paloma Rodríguez Carrington launch left gallery as a digital art gallery initially based on the Ascribe platform.

Internet artist Shu Lea Cheang edits *We Grow Money, We Eat Money We Shit Money, MCD #76* on the lack of an economy for artists who work with the web as their medium.

The Xenofeminism Manifesto: A Politics for Alienation by Laboria Cuboniks collective demands technoscientific innovation for progressive gender political ends.

2016

Experiments with decentralised governance include experiments with alternative voting methods – quadratic, conviction, delegated – made possible by digital infrastructure.

The DAO, an investor-directed venture capital fund, is instantiated on the Ethereum blockchain and becomes one of the largest crowdfunding campaigns in history.

In The DAO Hack users exploit a vulnerability in The DAO code to siphon off one-third of the funds. The Ethereum community controversially decide to hard-fork the Ethereum blockchain in order restore funds to the original contract going against the principle of blockchain's immutability.

Terra0 white paper is published by Paul Seidler, Paul Kolling and Max Hampshire describing an artwork and DAO for a self-owning, self-exploiting forest.

Bitnation is founded by Susanne Tarkowski Tempelhof offering *Decentralised Borderless Voluntary Nationhood* (*DBVN*) the "governance service equivalent of Decentralised Autonomous Organisations (DAO)" as smart contracts on the Ethereum blockchain.

Sakrowski founds panke.gallery in Berlin to present artworks born of the connection between digital or net-based art and club culture.

Jaya Klara Brekke publishes *The Satoshi Oath*, a hippocratic oath for blockchain development, with B9Labs.

Release of *Rare Pepes* the first artist-issued trading cards, on the CounterParty blockchain. Joe Looney creates the *Rare Pepe Wallet* as a way to collect, display and exchange *Rare Pepes*.

2017

Written by founders of DADA.art, the collaborative art platform with a built-in blockchain token economy *The Invisible Economy* explores the radical separation of art and the market.

Ingrid LaFleur stands for the mayor of Detroit on an Afrofuturist manifesto that includes a proposal for UBI paired with a local cryptocurrency.

adrienne maree brown publishes her book *Emergent Strategy. Shaping Change, Changing Worlds.*

CryptoPunks – a limited edition of 10,000 digital collectibles (an early implementation of NFTs), are issued for free by Larva Labs on the Ethereum blockchain.

Artist Julian Oliver exhibits *Harvest* in the Skövde Art Museum using wind energy to mine cryptocurrency which in turn funds climate-change research.

Dapper Labs create the ERC-721 NFT token standard with the launch of *Cryptokitties*, digital, breedable, collectible cats, and record more than $1 million in transaction volume in a single week.

Bail Bloc artist software utilises cryptocurrency mining to generate money which is then re-distributed to bail low income people out of jail.

DAOWO (Decentralised Autonomous Organisation With Others) blockchain lab and debate series for reinventing the arts is led by Ruth Catlow and Ben Vickers hosted by Furtherfield and Goethe-Institut London in partnership with Serpentine Galleries, London.

OpenSea launches a decentralised exchange and marketplace for digital collectibles.

2018

Max Haiven publishes *Art after Money, Money after Art, Creative Strategies Against Financialization*.

A Speculative White Paper on the Aesthetics of a Black Swan World by Penny Rafferty is published by KW Institute for Contemporary Art as part of their REALTY series.

Guild decentralised artists network is formed in Berlin.

Official launch of multiple decentralised marketplaces for digital original and editioned artworks registered on the Ethereum blockchain include *KnownOrigin* and *SuperRare*.

Jonas Lund Token (JLT) is issued to enable DAO shareholders to control and influence the artistic practice, career and life of Jonas Lund.

Naomi Klein publishes an expose on politicians and bitcoin billionaires capitalising on the Hurricane Maria disaster with tax write-offs.

Google cancels its plan for a "Google Campus" in Kreuzberg, Berlin under pressure from the neighbourhood action; yet it continues its expansion worldwide.

The Decentralized Autonomous Kunstverein (DAK) is a DAO established as a transnational art association inspired by developments in blockchain technology and the Kunstverein tradition of non-profit art associations in Germany

The Distributed Web of Care (DWC) research project, an initiative of Taeyoon Workshop, prioritises collective agency and individual ownership of data and code.

The Current Museum launches a virtual collection backed by a decentralised patronage and stewardship model, in which members vote on acquisitions and can view and help store the collection in their own homes.

In a collaboration with Snark Art the final artist's proof of Eve Sussman's *89 seconds at Alcazár* is divided into 2,304 unique blocks and offered for sale on a fractional ownership model as an Ethereum-based artwork *89 seconds Atomised*.

2019

Moloch DAO deployed to the Ethereum Mainnet to co-fund Ethereum ecosystem development.

In the early months of the Covid-19 global pandemic Cassie Thornton and Lita Wallis run the first online course for *The Hologram* a parafictional feminist, peer-to-peer, collective healthcare system.

Artworld DAO Think Tanks – 52 hours of immersive events for technical talk, political discussion and uncanny working methods to create pathways to collective arts production, tools, capacities, resources, resistance and solidarity devised and hosted by Ruth Catlow and Penny Rafferty with Furtherfield, Goethe-Institut and Serpentine Galleries, London.

The Collective Conditions work session is hosted by Constant, taking socio-technical protocols as artistic and activist media for building better imaginaries for complex collectivities.

This Artwork is Always on Sale by Simon De La Rouviere goes on sale for ever and supports the artist by requiring the owner to pay a 5% per annum patronage at the self-specified price.

The Age of Surveillance Capitalism: The Fight for a Human Future at the New Frontier of Power by Shoshana Zuboff is published.

Open spreadsheet entitled *Art + All Museum Salary Transparency 2019* begins circulating, to which people can anonymously add their salaries, benefits and institutions to "highlight the industry's glaring pay gap".

The choreo-poetic film essay *INFINITY minus Infinity* by Otolith Group presents the British dimension of the afterlife of slavery, revealing the debts of racial capitalism as inseparable from capitalogenic climate catastrophe.

2020

Wide Awakes is launched by Hank Willis Thomas and others to organise a large network of artists, cultural workers and activists to fight injustice and get out the vote in the lead up to the 2020 US presidential election.

The Belarussian Dze.chat becomes a vital online portal circumventing state censorship and surveillance, and providing access for everyday citizens to information and mutual aid, via local "yard" Telegram channels.

Glitch Feminism: A Manifesto by Legacy Russell is published.

Circles UBI, a basic income system for communities is built and launched as an alternative currency, "to allow organised groups of people to provide basic income for each other – rather than depending on the state".

Universal Declaration of the Rights of Rivers a multi-lateral initiative to define basic rights for all rivers is launched.

CryptoArt.wtf the CryptoArt carbon calculator website created by Memo Akten sparks controversy about the climate impact of NFTs created on the Ethereum Proof-of-Work blockchain. The website is taken offline after it is used as tool for abuse and harassment of artists.

Friends with Benefits, a social community using tokens for access and rewards is established by Trevor McFedries one of the co-creators of the first computer-generated social media influencer, Lil Miquela.

2021

TRANSFER and left gallery present *Pieces of Me* an online exhibition of works by fifty digital artists responding to the NFT hype; the show uses fixed pricing, 50% artist resale royalties, and a profit-sharing model that distributes 70% of each sale to all artists.

Gnosis deploys accessible interfaces and modular DAO tooling systems allowing collaborators to set up safes, create "Multi-sig" wallets, and to set up DAOs.

Wanderer Above a Sea of FUD: Cultural workforce, crypto anarchism, intellectual rights, and blockchain-based funding models for culture and arts published by Maria Paula Fernandez, Stina Gustafsson and Beth McCarthy, Department of Decentralization.

DAO Model Law, a design framework to turn DAOs into entities with "legal personality" and to harmonise DAOs with transnational law, is drafted by COALA (Coalition of Automated Legal Applications) working group.

The *FERAL ATLAS – The More-Than-Human Anthropocene* maps the ecological worlds created when nonhuman entities become tangled up with human infrastructure projects.

Wyoming becomes the first US state to legally recognise DAOs and grant them the same rights as limited liability companies.

Metapurse fund buys Beeple's *Everydays – The First 5,000 Days* NFT for $69 million at Christies' auction. The fund had previously bought a suite of 20 Beeple NFTs for the equivalent of $2.2 million and sold off 10 million tokens as fractional ownership shares.

A new field of artworld DAOs are established for different models of open and closed-door co-creation, organisation, curation, collection, ownership and speculation of and on NFT-enabled digital art including H.E.R. DAO, Black Swan DAO, PleasrDAO, Flamingo DAO, FWB, Fingerprints DAO, The Sphere, Holly+.

The Dawn of Everything – A New History of Humanity by anthropologists David Graeber and David Wengrow, bucks the trend (set by Noah Harari, Diamond and Pinker) for single arc stories of human social evolution towards a technological singularity, with an account of concurrent and massively various social and economic organisational forms worldwide.

2022

Radical Friends. DAO Summit for Decentralisation of Power and Resources in the Artworld at Haus Der Kunst, Munich.

DAOs go mainstream and public policymakers such as the Bennet Institute promote DAOs for "mitigation of the rentierization of the digital economy".

Vladimir Putin's invasion of Ukraine leads to the UkraineDAO auction of an NFT of the Ukrainian flag, raising $6.5 million in ETH for Ukrainian Armed Forces. Other Cryptowallets gather donations to fund Cyber-resistance and humanitarian aid.

The EU *Markets in Crypto Assets (MiCA)* framework is established to protect EU investors. It includes a commitment to review a possible ban creating, selling or trading any cryptoassets based on "environmentally unsustainable consensus mechanisms" or Proof-of-Work (PoW) within the EU by 2025.

...

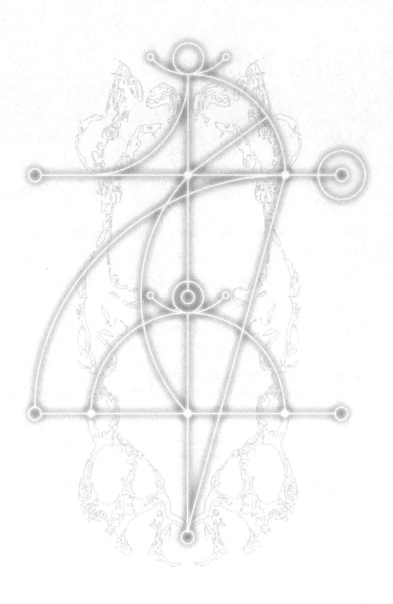

Glossary of Terms

Rhea Myers

51% Attack   When more than half of the hashpower on a chain is dishonestly trying to rewrite the history of the chain.

Address   A unique identity, like a bank account number, for an account on a blockchain.

Bitcoin   The original cryptocurrency created by the pseudonymous Satoshi Nakamoto.

Block   A group of transactions that are gathered up within a given time period for validation by miners.

Block Reward   New tokens in the blockchain's native currency, created to be paid to the miner that validates a new block.

Blockchain   Blocks of transactions gathered periodically and validated by a decentralised network of computers, each block pointing to the previous one in a chain.

Consensus   Agreement between nodes in a decentralised network on the state of reality in a particular system.

Cryptocurrency   Peer-to-peer electronic cash using cryptographic algorithms.

Cryptographic Hash Function   An algorithm that creates a hash that is almost completely impossible to guess the source of or create using any other digital data.

DAO/Decentralised Autonomous Organisation   Blockchain-based code that implements the governance of an organisation and that may control its funds and resources.

dApp   A "Distributed App", an application implemented as the combination of blockchain-based code with a web-based front-end.

Decentralisation   The process of making a system more secure by removing central points of control and failure.

Difficulty   The number used to control how long block proof-of-work takes miners to complete on average. Such as the number of zeroes ending a hash.

Digital Assets   Images, game items and other data that can be represented in a digital ledger, particularly as tokens.

Digital Signature   The use of Public Key Cryptography to assert that the key's owner has some relationship to a piece of digital data.

Distributed Ledger   A ledger assembled by a distributed network of computers with no central co-ordinator.

Distributed Network   A network of computers that operate in a peer-to-peer way with no central co-ordinators.

ERC Tokens   Cryptographic tokens that implement one of Ethereum's "ERC" standards such as ERC-20 or ERC-721.

Ethereum   A cryptocurrency that allows more general-purpose code to be stored on its blockchain and executed by transactions in return for payment.

Fork   A split in a blockchain into two separate chains either temporarily due to error or permanently due to rival code changes.

Fungible Token   A cryptographic token without unique metadata or significance, a coin or game token for example.

Genesis Block The first block of a blockchain, with no previous block but potentially including rewards for purchasers from a pre-mine.

Governance The objective or practice of negotiating and incorporating stakeholder objectives into the development of a system.

Hard Fork A blockchain fork resulting from new software that makes the validation rules for blocks more relaxed and is therefore not backwards compatible.

Hash An unguessable but easily checked identity number of a standard length for any piece of digital data.

Hash Rate How quickly miners on a crypto-currency network are performing hashes on new blocks in order to extend its blockchain and claim the block reward.

ICO "Initial Coin Offering", a crowdfunding sale of cryptographic tokens that can fall foul of securities law if the offerer is not very careful.

Immutability Data, such as a blockchain, that is unable to be changed without great difficulty and without anyone noticing.

Incentive System A set of rules and rewards designed to encourage people to perform a task in the way the designers intended. Building a blockchain, for example.

Ledger A record of balances of accounts.

Mainnet The live network for a cryptocurrency that uses its current code version at its full difficulty and that is therefore regarded as having real value.

Market A system allowing the buying and selling of cryptocurrency, tokens, or digital assets.

Mining Validating blocks of transactions and broadcasting the results for a chance to win the block reward.

Multi-Signature   A cryptocurrency transaction that requires signing by multiple parties before it can be sent.

Node   A computer connected to the Internet that is running a particular piece of blockchain software.

Non-Fungible Token   A cryptographic token with unique metadata and significance, as a limited edition artwork for example.

Oracles   A smart contract used to publish information from the outside world on the blockchain so that other smart contracts can access it.

Prediction Markets   A market that allows tokens or cryptocurrency to be bought and sold to represent how probable the participants believe particular future events are.

Private Key   The super-secret and very long number used to encrypt and sign data in Public Key Cryptography.

Proof-of-Location   Using decentralised "beacons" rather than the centralised GPS system to establish physical locations.

Proof-of-Ownership   Using digital signatures to assert that the owner of a public key or address also owns a given piece of data or cryptographic asset.

Proof-of-Stake   Mining new blocks by staking existing cryptocurrency rather than burning electricity to prove good faith – act in bad faith and you lose your stake.

Proof-of-Work   Mining new blocks by competing to solve a resource intensive puzzle to prove good faith – act in bad faith and you are wasting your electricity bill.

Protocol   A set of rules for communication that are implemented and operated in software.

Provenance   The origin and ownership history of an object or data.

Public Key   Generated from a private key and shared so people can communicate securely with its owner, used in cryptocurrency to generate addresses and validate transactions.

Public Key Cryptography   The use of two separate large numbers as keys to encrypt and decrypt digital data, one private one public. Used in cryptocurrency to authenticate transactions.

Sharding   Boosting performance with baby blockchain "shards" that can communicate with each other but do not need to store every other shard's data or validate its messages in order to work.

Smart Contract   Small programs stored on a blockchain that react to transactions, their name comes from the fact that they usually model rules for controlling value or resources.

Soft Fork   A blockchain fork resulting from new software that makes the validation rules for blocks more restrictive and that is therefore backwards compatible.

TCR Token-Curated Registry   A smart contract that people use the ERC-20 token of to control the data that it contains, representing a register of fact or opinion.

Testnet   The testing network for a cryptocurrency that uses development code or a lower mining difficulty and that is therefore regarded as not having real value.

Title Registry   A ledger that records ownership of property.

Token   An entry in a distributed ledger representing an asset that can be owned and transferred by a particular address.

Transaction   Cryptographically signed data instructing miners to update a cryptocurrency's ledger and/or run smart contract code.

Transaction Block   Transactions broadcast to the network gathered for a given period of time (ten minutes for Bitcoin) and validated by miners.

Transaction Fee   A fee paid to miners in the cryptocurrency of the blockchain that they are mining to encourage them to include a transaction in a block sooner rather than later.

Wallet   Software that manages cryptocurrency addresses with their associated private keys, and that can send transactions signed by them.

Whales   Individuals that hold large amounts of cryptocurrency, the 1% of the crypto world.

Zero-knowledge Proof   "Zero-Knowledge Succinct Non-Interactive Argument Of Knowledge", a complex algorithm for exchanging and using secret information publicly without leaking anything else about it.

TECHNO GAIANISM

BELIEF IN THE POWER OF TECHNOLOGY TO RESTORE EARTH'S ENVIRONMENT

CLOSED BIOSPHERE EXPERIMENTS

LOW EARTH & SPACE COLONIES

TERRAFORMING OTHER PLANETS

GAIA HYPOTHESIS

PLANET EARTH AS A HOMEOSTATIC ORGANISM FORMULATED BY JAMES LOVELOCK A NASA SCIENTIST 1960s

KNAVE OF PENTACLES

A Thousand DAOs

Rhea Myers

DAOS

In fiat state[1] legal code there are many contractual forms of organisation between individuals. Corporations, co-operatives, partnerships, charitable trusts, conspiracies, marriages. Each provides particular protections in return for particular responsibilities and restrictions. In the code of the blockchain there are likewise many organisational forms. Offchain there is protocol-level mining[2] and staking,[3] multisig key management,[4] and fork co-ordination. Onchain, instantiated as smart contracts, there are fungible tokens,[5] non-fungible tokens,[6] fractionalised tokens,[7] marketplaces, DeFi,[8] and Decentralised Autonomous Organisations – DAOs.

And code is law.

But not so fast...

By "code is law", American legal scholar Lawrence Lessig[9] did not mean that software is a perfect match or replacement for the fiat legal

1. Existing nation-states, based on fiat currency rather than gold-based currency.

2. Mining is the process of producing valid new blocks to add to a blockchain in return for a reward paid in the chain's currency (BTC for Bitcoin, ETH for Ethereum, etc.).

3. Placing an amount of tokens in trust as a sign of good faith for participating in a process, to be lost as punishment or rewarded with additional tokens.

4. It's often good to have more than one cryptographic key and/or person sign a blockchain transaction for security purposes, but keeping these keys up to date can be laborious.

5. Tokens that are not uniquely identifiable, like coins.

6. Tokens that are all uniquely identifiable, often representing artworks.

7. Fungible tokens minted to represent a fractional stake in ownership of an NFT.

8. Decentralised Finance, on-chain systems that manage loans, exchange of tokens, etc.

9. Lawrence Lessig, *Code Version 2.0.* (Basic Books, 2006), https://lessig.org/product/codev2.

system. Software developers and lawyers make disastrous practitioners of each other's crafts. Rather, Lessig meant that network protocols regulate human behaviour in accordance with the technological codification of prior human decisions. To write code is to structure human behaviour, at the level of affordance and relative difficulty at least. This means that blockchain smart contracts are an analogue to legal documents such as articles of association, and DAOs use them to structure social forms of human collaboration as surely as fiat state law is used by a gallery or a museum.

After the false start for onchain organisation that started with the code examples on the Ethereum project's first website and ended with the "The DAO" hack[10] on the live Ethereum Mainnet in 2015 it took a while for people to be comfortable with calling their organisational smart contracts DAOs again. Since 2019, DAOs that have been unafraid to name themselves as such have blossomed in areas including finance, project governance, and art. It is the latter that interests us here, although given the nature of blockchain technology it is unavoidable that we will also touch on the former.

DAO CONTENT

DAOs cannot make decisions without a human being (or their software agents) initiating a transaction. But this doesn't dissolve a DAO into the people that make it up any more than it dissolves any other form of organisation. To object that a DAO cannot make decisions is true, but then by that measure nor can an election or a corporation.

DAOs also have access to other onchain entities, and to the ability to constrain and incentivise human action in productive ways. From time-locked resources[11] to ragequitting,[12] they encourage active engagement with the decision-making process in a way that is consequential for the participants. They can make people make things happen. This places

---

10. Starting on June 17, 2016, an unknown attacker exploited a bug in a code of a DAO known simply as "The DAO" to steal its funds. These were worth $150 million at the time. The attack created the equivalent of a constitutional crisis for the Ethereum project, which had not written the code but had to decide how to respond to its failure.

11. Blockchain code has a sense of time, expressed either in seconds or in blocks, and can allow or disallow execution of commands based on this.

12. The humorous name for leaving a DAO and removing any tokens one has deposited in it.

DAOs into the design space of mechanism design and game theoretic analysis of incentives.

DAOs almost inevitably involve tokenisation, the representation of resources as finite coin-like assets. Critiques of this as financialisation are all too easy to arrive at, but we can and must go much further. DAOs, and the blockchain in general, are indexes of our contemporary economic imaginary. In contrast to entrenched economic systems, they are novel and public so we can see them and reflect on their functioning and effects. Shooting the messenger or scapegoating them only resolves psychological tensions, not the contradictions of the society that they are embedded in. Any critique of onchain activity should cascade offchain. The challenge that tokenisation presents to its critics (a la "what do *you* represent?")[13] is to account for where their money comes from and goes to, and to make their values and priorities explicit against the structurelessness[14] of affordable appeals to good intentions. The radical possibilities of open book accounting are intrinsic to DAOs, publishing the origin and destination of every smallest fraction of a penny on a global public ledger.

Any token can be purchased, and anything can be tokenised – even if only via proxies[15] or wrappers.[16] This means that anticapitalist gestures onchain will simply fulfil their historical social reproduction function within capitalism. They will function as heatsinks and R&D, defusing and recuperating alterity. That is no reason not to play with value and its discrete representation as much as possible. Rather it is a reason to scope and time projects carefully, with understanding of the engineering involved in making sure that intentions translate into incentives.

This making explicit of value and values, structured both in terms of financial behavioural incentives and the language and meaning-making of their participants, is what gives DAOs such epistemological, ontological, and aesthetic potential. DAOs are a strange and often disturbing way of producing knowledge and sorting the world, to be sure, but they are

13. Ad Reinhardt, *How to Look at a Cubist Painting* (1946), https://www.frieze.com/article/ad-reinhardt.

14. Jo Freeman, "The Tyranny of Structurelessness," 1971, https://www.jofreeman.com/joreen/tyranny.htm.

15. A number of early blockchain artworks have been recreated on newer chains, notably Kevin McCoy's "Quantum" (NameCoin 2014, Ethereum 2021).

16. For example, *CryptoKitty* NFTs can be represented by "Wrapped Kitty" fungible tokens.

a conceptually and materially powerful one within post-financial-crisis society.

ARTWORLD DAOS

Let us over-simplify the artworld to roles of coaching, creation, commission, critique, curation and collection. These may be fulfilled individually or jointly (collaboration, communing, commoning...) by individuals, groups, institutions, or processes (organisational, legal, software, or historical).

COLLECTING / CURATING / COMMISSIONING DAOS

Collecting DAOs exist today. Like collecting clubs, a group of individuals pool their resources to purchase artworks. In the case of Collecting DAOs those resources are cryptocurrency and information, and those artworks are NFTs. For example, my own work has been collected by the conceptual/code art collecting DAO, Fingerprints DAO.[17] Like many collectors, Collecting DAOs may seek to turn a profit on the work they buy. This should motivate the DAO to work in the best interests of the art and artists it owns in order to at least maintain its value. Such DAOs are like petrodollar artworld art funds.

Collecting DAOs are also implicitly curating DAOs. A collection of NFTs and other art is selected by the DAO, implicitly valorising it, and it is easy to imagine the DAO holding online or offline shows and sales of work, curated from that collection. The curation of such shows could be outsourced to DAOs that exist solely to curate shows from the collections of one or more other DAOs and artists. They can be paid for their services, receive a cut of sales, or buy the work and go long or short on its future value – although that is more the role of critical DAOs.

Commissioning DAOs also already exist. DAOs make gathering, allocating, and accounting for funds simple and transparent. Applying this to payments for work in progress serves the historically important role of providing artists with funding and tasks for future production rather than requiring them to produce work speculatively.

---

17. https://fingerprintsdao.xyz.

CRITICAL DAOS

Critical DAOs take positions on other artworks and other DAOs, theoretically and financially.

Critique is a map (including negative space) of aggregated, abstracted information. We can read it in order to direct our artistic attention and efforts. The information aggregation tools available to DAOs render the qualitative quantitative. This may invoke memories of New Criticism[18] or cliometrics.[19] But those did not involve having skin in the game.

One of the cruellest distinctions to come out of behavioural economics is the difference between stated and revealed premises. Like the character of Hedgehog in Tarkovsky's *Stalker*[20] we may say that we want the noblest outcomes but given the choice we want the cash. Critiques of how "WEIRD"[21] behavioural economics is aside, putting your money where your mouth is focuses the mind. Critical DAOs can exploit this, turning critical DAOs into collecting, curating, and commissioning DAOs or service providers to them.

ARTIST GROUP DAOS

A DAO that commissions artworks from its own members is an artist group DAO. Less contortedly, a group of artists who use a DAO to propose work and administer exhibiting and sales is also an artist group DAO.[22]

This is no different from a cafe, magazine, email list, bulletin board, virtual space, group DM, or room above a shop becoming the place that a group organises itself. What is different is the prospect of being able to account for the group's decisions and finances in a transparent way, and the prospect of more, clearer, and more flexible ways to pay for the work itself.

It also allows the group to work with the materials of the blockchain critically or expressively in a way that provides its own critical context and history, not to mention allowing the kind of blurring or collapsing of the discussion and the work that was so productive for conceptual art and for net.art.

---

18. https://en.wikipedia.org/wiki/New_Criticism.

19. https://en.wikipedia.org/wiki/Cliometrics.

20. Andre Tarkovsky, *Stalker* (USSR, 1979), https://www.criterion.com/films/28150-stalker.

21. https://us.macmillan.com/books/9780374710453/theweirdestpeopleintheworld.

22. See for example https://mobile.twitter.com/agendadao.

THEATRE AND HAPPENING DAOS

The operation of a DAO or DAOs as an experience, either as a performance or a participation, can amount to a play or a happening. A DAO can also administer the organisation of such events. There have been blockchain raves,[23] in Berlin of course, unifying NFT drop logic with the communication problem of sharing the locations of illegal or exclusive events. Blockchain ticketing has yet to take off, possibly due to the lack of simple user and merchant user experiences for it, but token controlled access and PFP token membership schemes are widespread. Proof of attendance tokens also have a long history, and have now been formalised as "POAPs", Proof Of Attendance Protocol tokens.[24]

Video dance performance NFTs also exist. Videos of performances of the kind shown promotionally on social media but ownable, the latest entry in the struggle between choreographers and a copyright system designed to exclude creativity that doesn't exist in a "fixed medium".

Connecting performance rights to ticketing systems and merchandise tokens then feeding the results through on-chain royalty systems makes in-person or streaming performances transparently accountable. Make NFTs of the recordings and use royalty systems to handle residuals. If exposing this information is undesirable, use a zero-knowledge proof implementation of these systems to conceal it from prying eyes.

ARTWORK DAOS

The differences between a happening DAO and a performance or relational artwork DAO hinge on the relationship between the DAO and the participants in the work. In the former they are their own spectacle, in the latter they are spectators to it.

A DAO that manages the aesthetic properties, score, or other materials of an artwork is an artwork DAO. Whether a minimal on-chain experience like much historical net.art or the core of an offchain interface (software or physical), the artwork would not exist without the DAO.

Smart contracts that configure artworks, aesthetically and conceptually, have existed for at least as long as Ethereum (I wrote some early examples myself). Placing the exhibition and conservation of the artwork – its logistics – under the control of the DAO as well makes the

---

23. See *Cryptorave* by Mediengruppe Bitnik! and Omsk Social Club, 2018,

https://www.panke.gallery/event/cryptorave.

24. https://poap.xyz.

artwork literally but ironically the kind of quasi-agent presence that some art theory considers paintings and sculptures to be.

THE DA[O]BWO

Purchasing art is just commissioning it after the fact. Collecting and curating DAOs can commission new work, or DAOs can be constructed specifically for that purpose. None of these roles are or must be exclusive. A DAO need not have a single (or indeed any initially set) function, it can combine all of the above and more.

Voting, staking, prediction markets, and other blockchain information-gathering techniques can be both tool and medium. They can be spread across different DAOs, along with oracles acting as wormholes to the hyperspace of offchain information.

Premature over-structuring of these networks of roles and approaches will calcify them, rendering them legible to existing systems of domination and making further developments in positive directions a matter of displacing encumbrance rather than building afresh.

To invoke an over-worn and under-appreciated image from philosophy, we must create a "BWO", a Body Without Organs,[25] in and between DAOs. A BWO[26] is not structurelessness, rather it is a structure without imposed authority or order. A DAOBWO or DABWO is a BWO, but on the blockchain. A rhizome of roles and incentives within and across DAOs and their participants. This framing allows us to create structure without, and indeed against, impositions of order technically, aesthetically, economically, and politically.

CONCLUSION

The categories of DAOs described above can be combined and differentiated to produce a design space for artworld DAOs that allows wide experimentation. This can form a DA[O]BWO, if we let it. Where we produce DAOs that are critical of this space, let us do so in an informed way that touches on the wider world in which they have evolved. Including those parts of the world in which we make our livings. And let there be

25. Gilles Deleuze & Félix Guattari, *A Thousand Plateaus* (University of Minnesota Press, 1987).

26. For a good example of using the concept of a BWO in the arts, see Éric Alliez and Jean-Claude Bonne, *Body without Organs, Body without Image: Ernesto Neto's Anti-Leviathan (Undoing the Image 1)*, trans. Robin Mackay (Urbanomic, 2017).

some risk for our critical certainties. Where we produce DAOs that do something more, let us do so with a solidly grounded engineering appreciation for the security and incentives design of smart contract systems. Blockchain design is inherently adversarial. Most of all, let us experiment with technologies that the artworld would not normally touch, and with tasks that the blockchain community would not normally think to.

Let a thousand DAOs bloom.

Eight Qualities of Decentralised Autonomous Organisations

Kei Kreutler

Metaphors can guide our understanding of abstract concepts. There are metaphors we live by and lesser known metaphors through which we organise. A 1980s bestseller, Gareth Morgan's *Images of Organizations* looks at organisations through eight metaphors.

Though variably understood as machines, organisms, brains, cultures, political systems, psychic prisons, flux and transformation, and instruments of domination, organisational abstractions are resistant to context switching. As Venkatesh Rao wrote in 2010, "The main reason this book is hugely valuable is that 99% of organisational conversations stay exclusively within one metaphor. Worse, most people are permanently stuck in their favorite metaphor."[1] While organisations are easily subject to projection, it seems our ability to adapt how we inhabit them falters. Today, the organisational unconscious looms large against the failure of institutions and infrastructure to support civic welfare, and the multigenerational quest for the resilient organisation continues. One concept gaining adherents is a DAO: a decentralised autonomous organisation.

The phrase was originally borne from a culture privileging the concept of autonomy. While encompassing traditional for-profit models as well, the earlier term DAC (decentralised autonomous company) was also used to imagine a natural system that is conceived of as self-governing within a humanist framework.[2] Linked to the eleventh century "deodand" legal entity, a physical object that has been granted personhood in order to be litigated against, this idea of DACs was inspired by rivers granted legal rights. Evolving from DAC into DAO, the first instance in the world under this term was presented as an unstoppable funding body, which unfortunately was hacked one month after launch.[3] Later iterations of DAOs can be viewed as software tools that encourage coordination through decision making mechanisms and allocating funding. As peer-to-peer institutions, DAOs have the potential to significantly decrease the barriers to and costs of starting an organisation.

Today, the term DAO as a designation has strayed from its initial signifiers and became a more chimeric term that might best describe a voluntary association in favour of digital cooperativism.[4] Its practical instantiation in the world varies widely depending on disciplinary context. The analytical work to develop a taxonomy of DAOs continues elsewhere, however. Instead, inspired by the Rochdale Principles for cooperatives, here we can playfully walk through eight imagined qualities of decentralised autonomous organisations.[5] These non-exhaustive qualities are imagined, meaning they are not structurally inhabitable yet, but they do present a pattern language for typeforms of organising to come.[6]

AUTOPOIETIC

The autopoietic quality indicates the organisation can reproduce and maintain itself without a single point of failure. The archetype of the many-headed hydra can be invoked: for every head chopped off, it regrows two.[7] The network architecture of decentralised autonomous organisations emphasises its edges, meaning the loss of a central node does not threaten organisational longevity.

ALEGAL

The alegal quality indicates the organisation does not transgress legality but develops a foundational framework over time. The idea of functional equivalence from ecology can be applied.[8] While decentralised autonomous organisations are not always incorporated in legal forms, their basic characteristics can be nearly mapped from traditional associations when required.[9]

SUPERSCALABLE

The superscalable quality indicates the organisation can reach large membership sizes and in contrast to the modern firm, become *more* capable as it scales.[10] A theory of the firm suggests that as organisations grow, they develop inefficiency costs directly proportional to their membership size. In the case of decentralised autonomous organisations, their toolset allows fractal membership growth – in which each new cell within the organisation improves upon the synergy of the whole – to enable large scale coordination.

EXECUTABLE

The executable quality indicates the organisation can run its operations through minimal protocols such as software applications. The ability to register corporations with one click was the first step towards this, and the ability to establish an autonomous company using the command line was the second. Decentralised autonomous organisations envision software product suites that contain the entire operations of a firm out of the box. This quality, however, does not need to implicate access to digital infrastructure, but can extend to a set of robust design patterns easily replicated throughout the organisation.

AUTOPOIETIC

ALEGAL

SUPERSCALABLE

EXECUTABLE

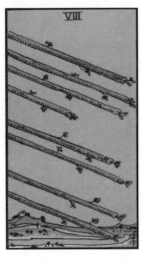

PERMISSIONLESS

ALIGNED

CO-OWNED

MNEMONIC

PERMISSIONLESS

The permissionless quality indicates any entity can enter and exit the organisation according to public criteria.[11] The conceptual ultimatum of exit, voice, and loyalty figures largely in debates on agency. Decentralised autonomous organisations could add the qualification of *entrance*, meaning that any entity can create, fork, or join the network.

ALIGNED

The aligned quality indicates the organisation possesses incentives to overcome common problems of coordination. The field of game theory models interactions between rational decision makers, identifying dilemmas of cooperative, zero-sum, and symmetric games and their inverse. As a counterforce, decentralised autonomous organisations broadly apply mechanism design through economic incentives or social norms to achieve rough consensus and running orgs.[12, 13] Headless brands and cultural values are equally, if not more, powerful tools for affinity.[14, 15]

CO-OWNED

The co-owned quality indicates the organisation encodes proportional ownership to its members. The ownership economy describes a new paradigm of participant-owned services, which is facilitated by peer-to-peer money enabling not only information but value to flow to networks.[16] As programmable cooperatives, decentralised autonomous organisations mandate members equitably share in financial, material, and social capital produced by their participation.

MNEMONIC

The mnemonic quality indicates the organisation automatically can produce a public record through its operations. The task of preserving formal and tacit knowledge has been historically assumed by stories and by institutions, such as archival libraries and monasteries.[17] Through partially automating the production of institutional memory, decentralised autonomous organisations can promise accountability, as well as intergenerational knowledge transfer.

In summary, eight imagined qualities of decentralised autonomous organisations are autopoietic, alegal, superscalable, executable, permissionless, aligned, co-owned, and mnemonic. Drawn from observation, these qualities trace desires for interdependence growing in the cracks of legacy institutions, as well as the dubious inheritance of cybernetic dreams from a century of unprecedented war. The question of global coordination and patchwork governance will not be put aside during the 2020s. Mapping the organisational unconscious of our time, however incomplete, could be one means to stymie its shadow. The term DAO itself may prove a temporary smoke signal under which co-conspirators can gather before it too must be discarded.

1. Venkatesh Rao, "The Eight Metaphors of Organization," *Ribbonfarm*, Last updated 13 July 2010. Accessed December 31, 2021, https://www.ribbonfarm.com/2010/07/13/the-eight-metaphors-of-organization.

2. "Deodands: DACs for Natural Systems," Ethereum, February 2014. Accessed December 31, 2021, https://wayback.archive-it.org/16516/20210623214739/https://forum.ethereum.org/discussion/392/deodands-dacs-for-natural-systems.

3. "The DAO (organization)," Wikipedia, accessed December 31, 2021, https://en.wikipedia.org/wiki/The_DAO_(organization).

4. "Platform Cooperative," Wikipedia, accessed December 31, 2021, https://en.wikipedia.org/wiki/Platform_cooperative.

5. "Rochdale Principles," Wikipedia, accessed December 31, 2021, https://en.wikipedia.org/wiki/Rochdale_Principles.

6. "Black Socialists in America," *Dual Power App*, accessed December 31, 2021, https://dualpower.app.

7. Ruth Catlow, Aude Launay and Penny Rafferty, "Many-Headed Hydras: DAOs in the Art World," So-Far, 2020. Accessed December 31, 2021, https://so-far.online/many-headed-hydras.

8. "Functional Equivalence (organization)," Wikipedia, accessed December 31, 2021, https://en.wikipedia.org/wiki/Functional_equivalence_(ecology).

9. COALA, "The DAO Model Law," Medium, December 19, 2020. Accessed December 31, 2021, https://medium.com/coala/the-dao-model-law-68e5360971ea.

10. Anonymous, "dxDAO:Toward super-scalable organizations," Github, July 12, 2019. Accessed December 31, 2021, https://github.com/gnosis/dx-daostack/blob/master/dxdao_whitepaper_v1.pdf.

11. Seth Frey and Nathan Schneider, "Effective Voice: Beyond Exit and Affect," *Online Communities*, 25 September 2020. Accessed December 31, 2021, https://arxiv.org/abs/2009.12470.

12. Simon De la Rouviere, "Desire Paths & Markets for Recommendation," Medium, December 9, 2018. Accessed December 31, 2021, https://medium.com/@simondlr/desire-paths-markets-for-recommendation-e701aa835013.

13. "IETF Working Group Guidelines and Procedures," September, 1998, https://tools.ietf.org/html/rfc2418.

14. Sam Hart, Laura Lotti and Toby Shorin, "Headless Brands," *Other Internet*, October 2, 2019. Accessed December 31, 2021, https://otherinter.net/web3/headless-brands.

15. Kei Kreutler, "The Byzantine Generalization Problem: Subtle Strategy in the Context of Blockchain Governance", *Technosphere Magazine*, August 19, 2018. Accessed December 31, 2021, https://technosphere-magazine.hkw.de/p/The-Byzantine-Generalization-Problem-Subtle-Strategy-in-the-Context-of-Blockchain-Governance-8UNNcM8VShTpBGWRuob1GP.

16. Jesse Walden, "The Ownership Economy: Crypto & The Next Frontier of Consumer Software," *Variant*, 14 July 2020. Accessed December 31, 2021, https://variant.fund/the-ownership-economy-crypto-and-consumer-software.

17. "Songline," Wikipedia, accessed December 31, 2021, https://en.wikipedia.org/wiki/Songline.

All tarot card images from the Smith deck (https://en.wikipedia.org/wiki/Rider-Waite_tarot_deck), in the public domain.

The Reappropriation of Life and the Living – A Cosmic Battleground

Penny Rafferty

PRELIMINARY DAO EXERCISES
AS RESULTS-BASED MAGIC

Wild and domestic turkey are still the same species, *Meleagris gallopavo*. One of the only differences between the two turkeys is that domestic turkeys have been bred to have white feathers because their pin feathers are less visible when the carcass is dressed, whereas wild turkeys have darker feathers so they can be camouflaged in the wild.

I look at these two sets of turkey images online, wondering can we really rid ourselves of thousands of years of reality conditioning in which we, turkeys, humans and other beings, have become aesthetically more edible? And who or what has/had the authority to make this reality anyway? Can the world still work if we kill the cybernetic thermostat and attune to generative-chaos? In the words of the more-than-human fox, can we enjoy the moment "chaos reigns"?

* * *

Chaos, this word is everything. It is all we know – it's the only part of life that never fails us and perhaps that is why for centuries people have been building frameworks against it. Because it is there. Always giving. Always changing. Yet we do not appreciate Her. To love chaos would mean, for many, that we would have to hate control and that would mean a complete overhaul of the tyrannical society we live in, and so we learn to reject chaos's offerings in favour of the comfortable shackles of mastery. To live alongside or to embrace chaos is to become ungovernable.

And so the multiverse we find ourselves existing within today is a self-organising ecology of infinitely varied relationships that rely on a continual dawn chorus of interdependent becomings and mutual independence. This is the sound of pandemonium. But it could acquire the transformational coordinated energy of useful chaos if we found a compatible working method for self-optimisation inside a collective body. Chaos as a concept has a strong historical lineage of definitions and beliefs that typically have served people in power, top-down organisations like the state or religious groups. The generative-chaos that I am proposing we aspire to belongs less within the framework of science-led chaos theory but is more akin to Chaos Magick.

THE LANDSCAPE: CHAOS

Society has been conditioned to fear chaos. When asked to visualise chaos, we may pull up images of disorientating landscapes, of never-ending, shrieking, suffering like those depicted by Hieronymus Bosch, where the subject appears to have no sense of agency or peace. Yet the predominent historical definition of chaos is a "void state preceding the creation of the universe or cosmos in the Greek creation myths, or alternatively, in Proto-Indo-European language, the etymology refers to the initial 'gap' created by the original separation of heaven and earth."[1] This early genesis hole, this empty yet full state was once akin to a babbling spring, oozing life and creativity.

When drawing The Tower Card in tarot, flames burn up, people dance out of its windows, head first, giving their bodies up to gravity. To the untrained eye this episode looks devastating. Yet those who embrace this ancient iconography, understand this to mean all will crumble, and what will remain is a starting point, just as farmers burn the land to fertilise for the next season of crops.

1. Chaos (cosmogony) etymology, Wikipedia, last modified 18 December, 2021,
https://en.wikipedia.org/wiki/Chaos_(cosmogony).

In software development, chaos engineering is the discipline of experimenting and testing a software system in order to build resilience and confidence in its capacity to withstand turbulent or unexpected conditions, just as when The Tower Card is drawn the user should reflect on the tools and methods they have to land safely, rather than try to avoid the storm. In ancient Egyptian mythology they fought against chaos, embodied in Apophis, a snake-diety who was older than creation, trying to banish and slaughter it, yet their fierce determination to rid their new sun-drenched world from chaos ended in huge battles that created earthquakes and thunderstorms, leaving their landscapes in ruin.

The word chaos across time has/is everything because it is so palpably present. Yet many people try to avoid chaos, they are suspicious of it the same way they are suspicious of someone doing them a favour or good luck coming their way. For someone or a collective body to go against that and love chaos they must be agile, thoughtful and fluid. They must also believe they have access to resources that allow them to survive and grow in chaos. Chaos lovers are believers in both the abundance of change, and the abundance that flows from change. These characteristics are not typically present in the foundations of a contemporary social body. Why? Because they catalyse a person or group's autonomy. A community that nurtures these traits in its members will rarely seek a great power to supervise them. Instead, they will deny the imposition of an external authority, regarding it as an obsolete or false force by comparison with the consistent chaos that life births. One such example of these communities lies in the radical left: Zone to Defend, also known as ZAD in Nantes, France. ZAD was a 50-year campaign that birthed a community that eventually won its battle in 2018 against the development of a new airport on land in the area. Over this period a community was built that lived, organised and developed tactics. Such as the creation of autonomous self-sufficient structures that took shape in the form of a communal bakery, animal husbandry, self-sufficient housing and new governance strategies. After the victory many of the remaining projects at the ZAD then engaged in a process of legalisation and continued to thrive in the area. One could argue that the success of ZAD was through its mutually supporting community, and that one must live in a state of confidence and fluidity to be able to live with and profit from what chaos might bring. The prevailing systems of dominance in societies and communities worldwide rob people of this confidence, inducing them to trade freedom for an idea of secure predictability, which will never be manifested.

THE PLAYERS

At present, there are two types of practitioners who widely thrive in chaos. Firstly, those who are operators of neoliberal apparatus, whose asymmetrical "free" markets and mantras of disruption and innovation dismantle the global commons, mine them for value and then discard their living remains into a landfill of poverty whilst whetting their system's insatiable thirst for supremacy. These figures purposely spin confusion because it offers the chance of prestige and the power to profit over others. These are the creators of the familiar trope of chaos; man-made. There is a never-ending list of examples of these practitioners and their carefully constructed products. Dubbed disaster capitalists by Naomi Klein,[2] you find they are the only ones smiling in the face of an emergency. One such example of these tactics was the mass privatisation of Louisiana schools post-Hurricane Katrina. After the disaster, the dispersed and decimated community of New Orleans was unable to protect 120 of their public schools from privatisation in a process christened a "recovery". As a result, the state-appointed private board fired 7,500 unionised school employees many of whom were Black or Brown in order to hand over the schools to charter school management companies. These privately operated education businesses open and close without concern for the stability of the students and inflict harsh disciplinary methodology on the children who attend them, in an effort to weed out "difficult" students. They push for hardline school reform rather than progressive educational spaces. The local parents and communities have no say in the curriculum that is taught and the needs of their children go unheeded.

Another example is the antics of an individual disaster capitalist who, in this case, both contributed to the creation of the catastrophe that he would then go on to exploit. The British hedge fund manager Crispin Odey, made £220 million by betting the markets would collapse in the event of a "Leave" vote for the UK from the EU in 2016.[3] Odey was also an outspoken advocate of Brexit, which begs the question of why?... with so much at stake – was it money, political beliefs or both? Either way, his

---

2. Naomi Klein, *The Shock Doctrine: The Rise of Disaster Capitalism* (Penguin Press, 2017).

3. Ashley Cowburn, "Hedge fund manager describes moment he won £220 million on Brexit vote: 'The morning has gold in its mouth'." *The Independent*, September 23, 2016.

corrupt practices certainly paid off that morning and he is only one in an ever-growing web of disaster directors.

Naomi Klein frames this adventurist epoch astutely in her book *The Shock Doctrine: The Rise of Disaster Capitalism* by declaring "What we have been living for three decades is frontier capitalism, with the frontier constantly shifting location from crisis to crisis, moving on as soon as the law catches up." And the law has caught up (sometimes, but not nearly enough) as in the recent case of Senator Richard Burr, Republican of North Carolina, and Senator Kelly Loeffler, Republican of Georgia who now have a string of potential legal cases against them for prioritising their stock portfolios in light of their knowledge of classified information on Covid-19 knock-on-effects. Burr and Loeffler made stock sales and purchases leading up to the lockdown in the USA prior to information going public regarding the pandemic. One example of their savvy stock racketeering was that Loeffler bought stock in a technology company that provides teleworking software, which had gone up dramatically due to the stay-at-home office practices during lock-down. She also shed stock worth between $1.2 and $3.1 million, much of it jointly owned with her husband, who is the chairman of the New York Stock Exchange in the three weeks leading up to the lockdown.

When the leaders of nations in crisis are also the profiteers of the moment it is clear that the most vociferous lobbyists against a certain type of man-made chaos are the very same creators of the most devastating kinds of mayhem.

* * *

The second group of chaos practitioners are less visible and practice a very different kind of chaos. They are found through an entangled network of occultists, anarchists, artists, poets, philosophers and thinkers. This is not to say that all creators are masters of what I will go on to call generative-chaos, rather they are fledglings of its methodologies. Generative-chaos inspires its practitioners to act with a playful sense of metanoia (going beyond thought) and a philosophy of flux, discarding dogma in favour of fluid mutation. One of the largest organised communities of generative-chaos after the arts would be Chaos Magick practitioners, a group of post-modern mystics, who began in Yorkshire, UK in the mid-1970s but now have a strong network of global nodes that convene both on and offline most notably forking and experimenting with methods stemming from the book *Liber Null & Psychonaut: An Introduction to Chaos Magic* complied by Peter J. Carroll in 1987. Chaos Magick practitioners both use and adhere spiritually to chaos, whilst upholding a strong scepticism towards ideas of the knowability of objective truth. You will often hear Chaos Magicians pronounce the words "Nothing is true, everything is permitted." In other words, one learns everything to be theoretically possible but it is only through self-study can you begin to sense the nature of things. In a sense, it attests to experiential learning being the only way one can prove anything to oneself. This also means that one's beliefs are negotiated, mutable and growing as you don't believe through hearsay but through sentience, observation and encounter. It is for this reason that I assert the value of Decentralised Autonomous Organisations (DAOs) in an experimental practice for moving towards a different way of living together. The mechanics of DAOs similarly don't exist in a fixed state and can be altered depending on propositions, progressions and failures, which allow them to socially evolve based on shared knowledge and learnt experiences – the lived life of the group, rather than taboo and untested tradition.

Another aspect of Chaos Magick, important to the cultivation of a new socio-technical ecology such as DAOs is its practice of intentionality. Chaos Magicians use self-made sigils (or magical symbols) to signify an intention to their unconscious. These sigils plant the seed of potential, as a proposal in the mind of an individual or a group who then consciously or unconsciously activate specific paths that in turn grow new favourable realities. This strategy of intentional becoming may seem at odds with traditional (smeared and propagandised) notions of chaos, but think back to the void state, the spring, the gap. If we can give form to what flows out, we can live alongside chaos blossoming, not spend our whole lives rigidly tensing against it.

I would go as far as to propose that DAOs could allow us to collectively set up these void states together, and through the act of proposal making and voting, harness intention to regulate new reality making devices. Chaos Magick is also often referred to as "results-based magic" as it is practiced in a mode that specifically emphasises the attainment of intentions rather than the aesthetics and theatrics of other occult-based traditions (think back to the domestic turkey). Chaos Magick also uses a cut and paste technique that borrows and glitches other sources of knowledge commonly found in both the human and spiritual world. Often doused in applied postmodernism Chaos Magick is street magic, that holds belief as the strongest tool and with that comes commitment and intention. Yet a note to our future selves here from Discordianism, the cult-pop "community of chaos" founded in 1963 by Malaclypse the Younger and Omar Khayyam Ravenhurst, whose beliefs are centred around Eris, *a.k.a.* Discordia, the Goddess of Chaos. They chime in:

Whatever you believe, imprisons you.

In lieu of this wise mantra, I reflect that a community tool such as a DAO has the potential to be a resource against dogma making machines, as a DAO in its very essence is a forkable, mutable, questionable entity. It is created to be interpreted and adjusted in a kaleidoscope of ways.

This brings me to one of the oldest magical tools and communication technologies in the world, the Tarot. A set of playing cards, that can commune with your, past, present, future and with unseen entities both human and non. This method kit seemingly emerged in the 15th century, nobody can pinpoint exactly its beginning nor who brought it into fruition. One of the first-known decks being credited as *Tarot de Marseilles*. From this deck millions of decks have been created loosely based on the original major and minor arcana, from the famous *Rider-Waite* deck to the Aleister Crowley's *Thoth* deck to Leonora Carrington's *Major Arcana* to the Visconti-Sforza incomplete deck and the barrage of cat, celebrity-inspired and artistic interpretations of this 78 card system, including the *Hexen 2.0* deck to which a selection are reprinted in this book, imbuing each section with signifiers and charge.

One can adapt Tarot cards and interpret their results based on the beliefs, locality and structures of the community that uses them. The layout of the cards also acts as a series of proposals for dialogue with the reader, rather than an order or demand to be carried out. This reflective iterative practice is key in both magic and DAOs.

THE SOWING: AUTHORITY

But let's take a few steps back...

Who has the authority to make reality anyway?

Everyone... but no-one should have the authority to make a singular reality that is imposed on others.

However, we live in a time where certain people in power, be that governmental bodies, religious leaders, or the police, seem to grant themselves the license to enforce new realities onto anyone within reach with severe consequences for those who reject them.

Those rulers were not always in power. This moment of being powerful had to be claimed and let us be clear this role is not open to all, those occupying seats of power are often groomed over generations and the result of inherited wealth rather than exceptional individual qualities and ideas. Typically, the journey to this power-tower comes from an exchange of promises between the powerful and the powerless, offering an alternative or a relief from the reality of the now – in a sense, this act is a verbal promise of enlightenment that is offered from the predator of current reality to its victims. This is a classic Hobson's Choice: an illusion of choice, where the powerful party offers up the exchange of freedom for safety. The population submits to be ruled in return for said protection by the assets of the powerful: police, army, borders, etc. Sometime later we often see another predator mirror the previous predator by declaring their own hostile takeover and reclamation of reality for the victims who again either submit or die fighting for freedom once more. The new predator declares if they follow their narrative they will live better and know more. This cursed gift has been offered over and over again in history by all sides of the political and spiritual spectrum.

We should resist easy binaries, taking sides, and measuring one supposed reality up against another, and reproducing the types of ideological oppression against people's desired realities which occur frequently across the globe. But, some would say this is currently inescapable, particularly in a highly networked and unequal society, as different realities constantly wrestle for attention over and above other realities. However, even in the most oppressive circumstances alternate realities still live and breathe behind closed eyes, out of ours or other's sightline for now, and let us not forget that one person's cult is another person awakening. Further still, to perceive is a form of participation in a reality created by oneself or another, and the time has passed when it was possible to reply to a proposed reality with the famous words of Melville's Bartleby "I would prefer not to". It has become increasingly difficult in recent years to resist or live otherwise, as our realities have shifted and swerved to immerse us all in a post-entertainment e-sport hack, which we now sometimes call life, complete with resurgent race wars, global 5G conspiracy connectivity and the atomisation of everything we knew as sacred. And even if you decline engagement with said reality, it has still affected you by its very existence, declining is itself an act, and you cannot unknow the reality that you decided to refuse. This is the centuries-old gaslighting strategy of colonial soft power – to create non-consensual reality input to shape the reactive minds and memory banks of "the Other" (which is normally anything that is not a caucasian cis male-bodied vessel), whilst power continues to build its own unique version of reality.

THE HARVEST:
DECENTRALISED AUTONOMOUS COMMUNITIES

This unincorporated reality sketch given to you by the colonial grand-father will always be a shadow in our imaginations and the only way to extinguish it is through an insurrectionary uprising in one's own mind. Now I am not proposing a lobotomy or necromancy, although the invocation of inspirational radical ancestors plays a part in building resistance to unwanted realities. Instead, I propose the act of neuromancy, which is achieved through a powerful merger between the conscious mind of senses and thought, and the *superconscious* mind that sees behind material reality and taps into the energy and consciousness of the collective of all living beings and systems. These strategies, although they sound epic, can be performed through the seance of our own minds (individual and communal), allowing us to decondition ourselves from power-tower inputs and deconstruct those forced realities. This can be done if we begin to put cultures before structures, and recognise how the entangled injustices of our world are connected. If we allow for plu-ralistic translocal fights then familiar-looking, but radically new worlds can appear. They will be familiar because intentional change emerges through action and reflection, not through fast food hyper-consumption and brave new world aesthetics. It is also extremely important when imagining new worlds that we do not forget the past, reparations must be part of new structures and the stewardship of ideas and history must be folded into models of exploration (always plural never single).

In this text, and more broadly through this book, I advocate for DAOs as a tool, not as a saviour. DAOs could provide a renewal in human spirit and values through an altered state of alliance with the machine in order to achieve new states of living relationships. After all, the machine is just a proxy of human imagination[4] – isn't it?

To put it simply a DAO is a testbed, which has the potential to allow a group of people to grow and foster new skills of survival and realisation

---

4. Federico Campagna, *Technic and Magic: The Reconstruction of Reality* (Bloomsbury, 2018).

alongside the protection or production of assets held close to and circulated by that DAO. Furthermore, DAOs can share and disperse their findings and models to others who can either use, fork or ignore the tools and knowledge from other communities. Which leads us back to the idea of perception as participation. If one does not take direct action in understanding and resisting the systems to which one falls victim, how can one ever find the loopholes of change or the crossroads of socio-soul growth and deformation required?

As a thought exercise let us consider a DAO as a cosmic computer, an isolation tank where reality falls apart and social evolution can occur. If we consent to this framework we could realise radically new possibilities, through the lens of good and evil, mechanisms of socially conscious behaviour that we observe and participate in. Judith Butler advocates for an active and dynamic acquiring and transmitting of experience to speed up the process of evolving a society. This sits in contrast to the often laboured application of Darwinistic theories of evolution which attempt to impose ideas of a "natural order" by the misapplication of biological hereditary or variation.

Butler writes that:

> *[W]e must recognize that ethics requires us to risk ourselves precisely at moments of unknowingness, when what forms us diverges from what lies before us, when our willingness to become undone in relation to others constitutes our chance of becoming human. To be undone by another is a primary necessity, an anguish, to be sure, but also a chance – to be addressed, claimed, bound to what is not me, but also to be moved, to be prompted to act, to address myself elsewhere, and so to vacate the self-sufficient 'I' as a kind of possession. If we speak and try to give an account from this place, we will not be irresponsible, or, if we are, we will surely be forgiven.[5]*

We must therefore self-realise with others so we can self-actualise a process of ontological change and to accelerate this we need machines for their speed, accessibility and connectivity. Computational systems' embeddedness in contemporary life and culture, coupled to their reprogrammability, offers unique potential. We must engage with reality as a

---

5. Judith Butler, *Giving an Account of Oneself* (Fordham University Press, 2003).

system, not a system that is out of our control, but one that is us and we are it – a system open to change.

DAO FLESH

The creation of any DAO is a psychospiritual quest for an open-ended micro reality machine. You create this small reality machine with a number of others and let it run, fail, rebuild and evolve. One of the best results of such a project might be to set an alarm clock on this journey. That will wake you and your peers up out of this somnambulant stroll called life. As Rihanna has tattooed on her collarbone – a key for most locks you find on the way:

Never a failure always a lesson.

One of which (both failure and lesson) may be technology itself...

And perhaps inversely, this statement could also be a capitalist mantra, as discussed earlier, that there's no such thing as a failure, or should I say man-made chaos, that capitalism, the eternal innovator, can't fix or feed upon.

It has been said frequently that modern technology has blocked our ontological foundations, most notably by the theorist Marshall McLuhan[6] and most infamously by the activist Ted Kaczynski, also known as the Unabomber. Now I wouldn't entirely disagree with them, but to generalise technology is just as dangerous as the tech titans' machinery they are condemning. We must understand that technology is not apart from us, we are co-constituted with it. It is created by people who are active players in social machinery and therefore it is imbued with their beliefs and motivations. These motivations can even be seemingly ethical in their own value framework, yet have disastrous consequences to those that are outside of it. Behind every line of code there is somebody, but behind them something else perhaps – agency is non-linear and complex, which brings me back to the idea of intention borrowed from the Chaos Magick practitioners.

One could think about the inner workings of an intentional generative-chaos powered DAO as using intentions/sigils in its language of proposals to the collective, to offer up an idea in symbolic form, taken to

6. Marshall McLuhan, *The Gutenberg Galaxy* (University of Toronto Press, 1962).

fruition through the collective strength that the DAO offers. In order to do this, the DAO community would have to simultaneously access their ontological and technological selves to find the ingredients required to give life to the proposal. The sharing of information and the embrace of chaos would be essential in working with this form of DAO making. After all, we must not forget Magick is considered by some to be the earliest form of technology.[7] Félix Guattari, in his book *Chaosmosis*, and Franco "Bifo" Berardi, in his 2011 work *Breathing*, both speak of an act of rebalancing chaos using the tools of osmosis, which allows chaos and the mind to blend. In one of Berardi's last chapters, he asks the urgent question of how can the next generation be happy in this hell? Which was so enigmatically coined for him through a black bloc demonstration banner held up during the 2017 G20 summit protests in Hamburg which read: "WELCOME 2 HELL". Aptly hell was often seen by early Christian forefathers as chaos, as they adhered to the poet Ovid's account of cosmogony from the beginning of the Metamorphoses which he recounted in 8 CE. My answer to Beradi's question would be, we must commit to this companion, friend, lover the chaos, the antichrist.[8] Or as the mystic and philosopher Simone Weil wrote in the chapter on "Love" in *Gravity and Grace*: "Love tends to go even further and further, but there is a limit. When the limit is passed love turns to hate. To avoid this change love has to become different." [9]

Love in itself is chaos and at moments it may be pure and at others less so, but after all, love needs a reality in order to live, yet it is not a reality in itself. Love is as much of a hologram as the Devil yes, but at the root of love is also a human realisation and survival instinct because to recognise and fuel love we must commit. We only commit to something because we are drawn to it and we believe it to be good. Love provokes a sense of our own mortality due to our energy expenditure and the passage of time inherent within the different states of being *in it*, and which we recognise from our work of literally loving some thing or another. Love is vulnerable and could be fluid if we learn how to practice difference

7. Erik Davis, Techgnosis: *Myth Magic and Mysticism in the Age of Information* (North Atlantic Books, 1998).

8. As the story goes: Lucifer was cast out of heaven and fell to earth for rebelling against the almighty power of one God.

9. Simone Weil, *Gravity and Grace* (Routledge Classics, 2002). First published 1952. 63.

and pluralism. A social movement is essentially a shared illusion of love (plurality) which is conscious and sensitive through organisms that conjoin in a social process to emancipate themselves as a mob, beyond the individual.

Our technology today is the perfect expression of our hunger for a mystical all-encompassing closeness of another. This need for radical friendships and primal strangeness is the keystone of our technological life. Yet we must not subsist on this world simply on the tools we are given, rather we must be the co-creators of tools of worlding. We must find new ways to reclaim the power of trial and error, we must feel empowered by failure because to come undone is to come one step closer to learning how to live with chaos, and mastering the modes of surviving in a state of generative-chaos.

Decentralisation, Autonomy and Organisation

Jaya Klara Brekke

Transcript of Keynote for the *Radical Friends: Online DAO Summit for Decentralisation of Power and Resources in the Artworld*, Haus Der Kunst, Munich, January 22, 2022.

Firstly, thank you to Ruth and Penny for the invitation to speak at this event, and thank you for the excellent critical work you are doing with the ecosystem gathered around *Radical Friends*, with Furtherfield, Goethe-Institut and Haus der Kunst. I wanted to start by saying that this work is extremely important and that it's rare to have people who have both the experience, hands-on involvement and the critical skills to keep a focus on decentralising – not just the architecture but also the broader effects in terms of governance and value. These are all too often assumed to follow automatically from technical architectures and nifty token economic designs.

To introduce myself briefly, those who know me know that these dynamics are my main area of concern: I look at the effects and not just the claims made of the technology. Or rather, I tend to look at the relationship between the claims and the results. I find it interesting to see how the dynamics of claims and material effects play out, not just to say, "Hah, look, the technical architecture is not producing the effects that you intended," but more to see how social meaning gets attached to specific technical architectures, and how that, in turn, feeds into value and thereby has a material effect – three things that don't necessarily correlate in any easy way.

My work generally looks at the relationship between technology and power, which has led me to my current main position as Head of Strategy of a decentralised privacy project called Nym. I am also a fellow at the Weizenbaum Institute in Berlin, where I research and write on technology from a social sciences, specifically geography, perspective. And I am also occasionally an advisor to the European Commission and most recently put out a policy report[1] that Ruth among others was kind to feed into, looking at distributed ledger technologies, Web3 token economics and DAOs.

I mention that report in order to again emphasise the importance of your work in the cultural sector. In it I argue that arts and culture play a pivotal role in and around emerging technologies. Firstly, because arts and culture are uniquely positioned to make sense of what it means to actually *live* with new technologies. And because arts and culture practitioners tend to be hugely trans-disciplinary, they can span the social and the technological with hands-on experimentation. And finally, arts and culture tends to interface directly with broader audiences and so are often more attuned to how the broader public is engaging with emerging technologies beyond immediate utility and affecting lives more generally. Something that expert engineers don't necessarily always have the headspace to think about in much detail. The arts and culture has the attention of policymakers, and I think that's something worth saying so that people understand that the work that you're doing as creators and cultural producers is hugely important. It's not just on the sidelines. It's pretty central to what's going on.

DAOs more specifically are also an important area to work on at this current moment in time because of the internationalising effects that DAOs can potentially have by enabling decentralised systems of mutual aid. But I would like to emphasise there is a strange dynamic with decentralised networks: they can bring about either centralising or decentralising effects and in fact will *very quickly* have centralising effects without a lot of effort being put into it turning out otherwise. I'll explain a little bit more about that later.

---

1. Jaya Klara Brekke, Anna Hakami and Alexandre Polvora, "Distributed Ledger Technologies (DTLs) for Social and Public Good – Where to next?," European Commission, 2021, https://publications.jrc.ec.europa.eu/repository/handle/JRC127939.

We are in a time of rising nationalisms and the reinforcement and multiplication of borders – as a result of Covid, but also traceable back to the 2008 financial crisis and refugee crises, at least in the European setting, where it became evident that economic solidarity between countries had ruptured. Ever since then, we've seen more and more of a retreat into national frameworks and a more protective nationalist mentality, most explicitly evident in things like Brexit, but also visible in economic policies. With nationalisms on the rise, I think it becomes essential to revive some bottom-up international and global mentality, and I'm hoping that the DAO hype can in part contribute to this.

In this talk, I would like to take the three words that make up a DAO, namely Decentralisation, Autonomy and Organisation, and look a little bit closer at the assumptions and motivations that arise around these concepts.

I have an itch that keeps bothering me – which is the way that these concepts keep drawing together hugely contradictory meanings, associations, and assumptions. For example, decentralisation as a concept tends to be associated with things like empowerment and direct democracy. But at the same time, decentralisation also comes from an intellectual and economic history that many times is fundamentally anti-democratic and focused on reducing democratic participation in favour of market mechanisms. These are dynamics that we see at play in diverse forms within the crypto and DAO space.

Similarly, with the word autonomy. Autonomy can refer to a person or a group's aim at achieving some form of self-determination. But many times, we also see the word autonomy referring to autonomy of a protocol, system or some code that often operates in exact opposition to human self-determination. And finally also, organisation as a word that implies people coming together around shared meaning and aims. While at the same time, organisation, when it comes to technology, refers to forms of automated coordination that often takes as its starting point isolated individuals who have *failed* to come together around shared aims, and therefore require a protocol to coordinate their behaviours. So we have these contradictory meanings and there are actually social, political and theoretical histories that can be traced that hopefully help explain some of these dynamics.

I also want to say that rather than trying to assert some form of true definition of these concepts, I'm much more interested to see how these different and contradictory meanings flow through lived experiences and what their contradictions make possible. This, friends, is a form of knowledge production that looks to *complicate* matters rather than simplify them. But hopefully to complicate them in a useful way.

DECENTRALISATION IN TIME

So we're going to unfold the concept of decentralisation in time and space. Starting with time, and my own personal journey. Decentralisation became part of my politics when I began to participate in direct action groups when I was about 16 years old. These were, generally speaking, anti-capitalist direct action groups somewhat on the left-anarchist spectrum, and part of a larger movement called the anti-globalisation movement. This was the late 1990s early 2000s. The anti-globalisation movement was a global coalition of many different and very diverse groups, including indigenous groups, feminists, trade unions, anti-fascist groups, anarchists, some political parties and climate groups and more. All of these were organised together without a central governing body, against the expansion of capitalism and ecological destruction, and mobilised around big global trade and policy summits. Whenever the World Trade Organisation was having a meeting, or the International Monetary Fund, or the G8, then this global movement would descend on these summits and have very large demonstrations and direct actions take place.

Decentralisation made this broad coalition possible. Without it, they would not have been able to come together because the tactics of resisting capitalism and preventing ecological destruction were so diverse. No one would have accepted the domination of any other group. Decentralisation was a big part of these movements, and it was understood as related to direct democracy and to self-determination. Decision-making processes took the form of horizontal decision-making assemblies and what are called affinity groups and groups that would form around shared tactics.

Affinity groups would be like your little direct action family. They would usually form not just around shared message and shared cause but also specifically around the tactics: how confrontational you are willing to be with the police, whether you believe in a festive way of protesting or more along the lines of sabotage and direct action. Your direct action family would keep an eye on each other in the middle of all the chaos of the demonstrations and if you got arrested would contact the relevant people. And the affinity group would sometimes also extend into daily life, between the big summits. In the bigger mobilisations, affinity groups would also serve to coordinate actions between the diverse perspectives that were present by sending representatives to bigger organising assemblies. But what was important was the organising assembly did not need to know every single detail of every action that was planned. They only really needed to know the basics to coordinate on basics. This was also important to ensure that there was no single body that could shut down the whole thing through pressure by the police or otherwise. Actually, here we have some concepts already like "single-point of failure" that I am guessing are already familiar to many of you! So that all sounds beautiful and interesting, but I also think it's worth noting some of the lessons that were learned around then.

When I was about 20 years old I travelled from London to a remote village in Spain to a brilliant gathering of autonomous and anarchist women from all over the world. It was a fantastic gathering to discuss politics, economics, power and what we want the future to look like. But there was also the moment that I realised something that I would like to call "process fetish" or process fatigue. I realised that all these meetings and assemblies had somewhat traumatised me. It is probably the reason why even though I've followed the space of DAOs pretty much since the infancy of DAOs around 2016, I've never been involved in their creation nor participated in their processes. I think it's because I simply burnt out around the fascination and the focus on organising and arranging processes and procedures in the abstract with the idea that somehow we can solve the problem of power and politics a priori and in perpetuity. As though, if we could find the right diagram, then we'll resolve politics.

So I was at that gathering with hundred-fifty or so incredible people talking, writing and partying, and for a few afternoons some of us were workshopping the broader basis of our politics. This took the shape of organising principles rather than any specific issues. And what was essential, we agreed, was the ability to remain free in our differences. The ability to organise locally about the things that mattered most to us but simultaneously coordinate and work together across multiple geographies and cultures. We gave a name to this newfound political program which was something along the lines of "situated interconnected manifestos." I think that name has a lot of resonances with what's being attempted with DAOs. It's worth noting some of these repeated efforts because I think there is something to be learned with each effort.

For me, one of the essential lessons was how often we would arrive at things that sounded so great in the abstract for it to simply fall far from experience in reality when people participated in horizontal based decision-making processes. Politics became reduced to a fetish for the ways that decisions were being made rather than what we were trying to achieve. I soon found myself in assemblies about how to run assemblies in an infinite regression that I think is also familiar with in the DAO space. As Kei Kreutler wrote "Who is responsible for making the decision on how to make decisions."[2] It also points to this problem of infinite regression or what a couple of other authors and I have also talked about[3] as "governance maximisation" that tends to happen when we're trying to solve problems in the abstract a priori and through primarily procedural and formalised means. What I also learned through this experience is that there's no neutral means through which to solve differences. The mediums matter, and in this case, the mediums were assemblies, and it was obvious that certain people suited that form of decision-making and that form of resolving differences and conducting politics better than others.

* * *

Now to zoom out a bit, these were local groups, part of a global movement that came about to resist a very different version of decentralisation. The anti-globalisation movement really came about to resist a form of market fundamentalism that we can trace back to the infamous economist Friedrich Von Hayek. Hayek has been an ongoing influence for quite a few economists justifying the destruction of public goods and collective resources. Including the mass privatisations by Reagan and Thatcher in the 1980s, as well as the work of Milton Friedman, an economist that informed much of the violent structural adjustment programs of the World Trade Organisation and the International Monetary Fund in the 1990s and 2000s. The anti-globalisation movement organised to prevent and resist these programs in order to protect collective resources, the autonomy of local ways of life and the environment.

2. Kei Kreutler, "The Byzantine Generalization Problem: Subtle Strategy in the Context of Blockchain," *Technosphere Magazine*, August 19, 2018, https://www.anthropocene-curriculum.org/contribution/the-byzantine-generalization-problem.

3. Jaya Klara Brekke, Kate Beecroft and Francesca Pick, "The Dissensus Protocol: Governing Differences in Online Peer Communities," *Fronteirs in Human Dynamcs*, May 26, 2021, https://www.frontiersin.org/articles/10.3389/fhumd.2021.641731/full.

The Hayekian version of decentralisation is an important piece of intellectual history to look at because it is also very much at play in many discussions and assumptions around decentralisation today. Hayek's 1945 essay, "The Use of Knowledge in Society," put forward the idea of the market as a giant information processor. Looking at the broader history of economics and computation, we can see that the two disciplines have had a very intertwined history. Hayek argued that information about needs and available resources exists scattered throughout society as local knowledge that only individuals hold. The idea was that this would prove that it would be near impossible for any central decision-making body to gather all that knowledge and make meaningful decisions. (We can see how this was a response to party-based Communism.)

The argument was that the market would be the means to gather disparate bits of information and communicate those bits of information in a decentralised manner. It would do so through price fluctuations: if demand was high for a certain good, this would reflect a need for that good, and prices would go up, which would incentivise people elsewhere to increase production of that particular type of good and satisfy that need or demand. Conversely, if there were plenty of a particular good and not many people needed it, the price would go down until more people would decide to go ahead and buy it, thereby absorbing any excess production. The idea here was really that the market would essentially act as a decentralised information processor, taking input that it would translate into price incentives which would then produce an output in terms of behaviour. And all this without the need for any centralised decision making, any governance, nor any need to intervene. In the abstract, a model like this looks fascinating. And personally, I find it pleasurable to read Hayek – as a mental puzzle – just as satisfying as reading Satoshi Nakamoto.

It is vital to then look at what actually happens in reality when a model like this is attempted to be steamrolled across people's different ways of life and social and political realities. And in fact, what has happened since is a string of hugely destructive consequences, epitomised in strangely sterile words that are somewhat familiar by now, like "market failures"; "externalities", and what some might call "free-market imperialism". Let's take these one by one.

Market failures – people realised that market and price mechanisms would fail to satisfy needs. It turned out that not everyone had access to money and markets to the same degree. It turned out that not everyone has the same bargaining power and in fact it turned out that oftentimes some people would starve while others had plenty, and far from balancing out over time these kinds of inequalities were hugely exacerbated through policies eroding collective resources for the benefit of market provision.

Externalities – another sterile way to describe environmental destruction like waste from production getting dumped into oceans. It's a word that describes the effects that are not included in the balance sheet. Costs to health, happiness, humans, animals and the environment that are not calculated in profit and losses and that are therefore not included in the price.

Free market imperialism – a less sterile term and obviously not an economist's description, but one that describes the necessarily expansionist agenda that follows from Hayek's decentralisation. Namely, that if the market knows best, that means that all other ways of addressing needs have to give way to it's higher logic. In order for Hayek's market to really be the perfect information processor that it claims to be, it demands more and more information in the form of price. Which means more and more interactions and relationships need to be incorporated into market mechanisms and market-based relationships to be resolved through the price mechanism. An expansionist agenda that thereby provides the ideological reasoning for deregulation and later fed into the Neoliberal policies eroding democratic governance. These events should be a lesson and backdrop for anyone who reads whitepapers and nifty mechanism designs: a model is very different from how systems affect real people and environments. Be wary of getting too obsessed by the beautiful model, the whitepaper and the great idea.

A major assumption of the Hayekian version of decentralisation is that it assumes that people operate as isolated individuals and that the only accurate means for understanding each other's needs at scale is through price fluctuations. This really brings about two terrible dynamics. It provides the ideological basis for violent market expansion, systematically destroying all other means for people to collectively resolve issues and access the things that they need. And it encourages a form of structural stupidity because if only the market knows best because it has the fullest information, then any other type of intervention is considered inaccurate and flawed at the outset. Which means that even if you can see, with your own eyes, that needs are not being met, there are climate disasters happening, homelessness, people cannot afford food and housing and healthcare, there's a reasoning that determines that you're not supposed to intervene. "The market should just be allowed to freely play out its dynamics." Hayek crystallised these ideas in his writing in the 1940s but these then resurfaced through structural policies in the 1980s and then again in the rise of Neoliberalism in the late 1990s and early 2000s.

So we have had these two diametrically opposed political ideas of decentralisation – on the one hand a movement for direct democracy, for difference, for local self-determination and on the other, an agenda of market logic and expansion, of free market fundamentalism. And now we have this surreal mix of so many of these ideas playing out in cryptoeconomics, in the DAO space, and in mechanism design.

Today it might be a bit harder to come across *pure* market fundamentalism. Instead it's fairly widely accepted that markets can take many different forms; that regulation and governance are an intricate part of markets; that their design matters, and that actually the design can be structured to serve very different purposes. For a non-market puritan, the good thing about this is that if there's a more clearly defined and time limited understanding of what is attempted to be achieved with markets – then it should be possible to also scrap them if their design is not playing out as we might expect. Holding markets to account in a sense. In other words, there has been a shift towards understanding markets more as a design space rather than the Hayekian absolute where *The Market* is in capital letters, forming a higher intelligence and governance principle. When we then add considered forms of governance into that, then there is a possibility of democratically governed economics, which starts to make this merge a little bit less crazy, and a little more like a potential for economic democracy. Which was also a major aim back in the late 1990s and early 2000s.

There are some additional important lessons to take with us from the anti-globalisation movement, which is that the medium really matters. Extremely long meetings and assembly-based decision-making drained my will to live, while for others it was the most exciting meeting of ideas and battling out of political fractions. In a similar way, tokens and token based governance suit some people and not others. But more important-ly, it opens new dynamics to enter into a space, and I think one dynamic that I'll be watching very closely and that needs more critical thinking is the complete merge of economic dynamics and governance that we see in for example the idea of radical markets and where tokens signify "skin in the game". When politics and economics mix in that way I think we should be quite wary – markets have 'failures' and 'externalities', remember? We need to consider what it means to approach the world so completely through the lens of economics. The other lesson is this problem of expansionist dynamic, not only to Hayekian decentralised markets, but also to the way that protocols and networks operate – network effects! There is always the issue of network effects and scale being such a strong part of the end game. What markets and network protocols have in common is the assumption that they are universally neutral means to achieve something. By now, it should be obvious from the many battles in the crypto space that there is nothing neutral about a protocol.

I would like to wrap up this historical meandering by also mentioning the network technologies that were developed as part of the anti-globalisation movement. Of course new technologies also played a huge role in facilitating that form of decentralised organising and this is a history that I have long wanted to trace out in more detail. And it's a history that Francesca Bria touched on in a very recent interview with *The Syllabus*.[4] Namely, how the technologies that emerged in and amongst these movements directly led to "Web2". And we can trace it all the way through to what's happening in "Web3" now too. A history of Indymedia would reveal much of this. Indymedia was a global network of independent media producers during the 1990s and early 2000s. These were self-organised groups that appeared all over the world of video makers, writers, developers, and photographers that came together under the slogan of "don't hate the media be the media." It was a response to broadcast media, which at the time would all too often dismiss social movements as violent thugs or otherwise misrepresent or not cover the demonstrations and initiatives at all. So the idea was for the social movements to have their own platforms. In fact, this was the beginning of platforms, of blogging, micro-blogging and what became Twitter. It was about enabling people to report on the actions that people were taking at the time, the themes and the issues that they're organising around. And we can see how that medium of self-expression went on to become centralised in the big Web2 companies as we know them today, which segues quite nicely into the next section unfolding the concept of decentralisation in space.

---

4. Evgeny Morozov, "Francesca Bria on Decentralisation, Sovereignty, and Web3," *The Crypto Syllabus*, https://the-crypto-syllabus.com/francesca-bria-on-decentralisation.

DECENTRALISATION IN SPACE

I want to first invite you to conjure a mental model of decentralisation as layers that exist above and below the typical network diagram that we otherwise so often think about when we think about decentralisation with the net of nodes and vectors. It's very easy to get stuck in that mental model and not be conscious of how decentralisation at one layer might very well cause or be the result of centralisation in other layers. The easiest way to think through these more complex effects is to unfold decentralisation through the metaphor of the stack. The Stack is a metaphor that Benjamin Bratton has elaborated on quite a lot but I don't want to use his categories so much in this talk because I think there are some other categories that are slightly more relevant for our theme. I think in particular we can talk about the history of the crypto space itself as an unfolding of layers in that stack.

The first unfolding was from the flat layer of the protocol to a governance layer. The protocol was initially intended to resolve disputes at a technical layer. This was the fascination of the consensus protocols at the very beginning of Bitcoin and at the beginning of Ethereum, which was not challenged really until the Bitcoin scaling crisis and even more so during the Ethereum governance crisis around the DAO Hack. These disputes showed exactly how there will always be dissensus cropping up that require governance processes to resolve.

And so from the flat mental model of the node vector diagram, a governance layer now also existed in people's minds. And around the same time, another layer unfolded which was that of value through an awareness of 'whales' in the crypto space, and how decentralised protocols were not leading to decentralised wealth and value. And from there we can just keep unfolding: into hardware, land, supply chains, regulatory regimes, where it turns out of course that jurisdictions matter a lot. And unfolding of the tech itself too, from layer one blockchains, to layer two, and as Moxie from Signal so nicely pointed out in a recent blog post,[5] we can also see how far clients and the application layer is from the decentralised blockchain protocol layer; and how APIs are running through single companies rather than being anything that looks decentralised.

---

5. "My first impressions of Web3," *Moxie*, January 7, 2022, https://moxie.org/2022/01/07/web3-first-impressions.html.

It is important for us to be more honest and be more real about what decentralisation really looks like, and what purpose decentralisation is really serving. What's important to me is less an affiliation with some ideology around some abstract notion of decentralisation. It is rather what we're actually trying to achieve strategically and in terms of societal effects. As Moxie put it, it's about time that we admit that not everyone is going to run a server, and equally it's about time that we admit that not everyone is going to run a full node and so these things really matter for understanding how power then operates in these kinds of spaces.

I would like to wrap up there and I would like to leave you with the mental models that I've been foregrounding throughout this talk – namely this idea of unfolding *decentralisation* in both space and time. I would love to also do this for the concepts of *autonomy* and organisation and I would love to do this in a much more rigorous way. My aim here is less about arriving at a fixed set of conceptual definitions. It is more about opening up these concepts so that they are considered less as ideologies, less as first principles and strict dogmas and more as strategies and pragmatics. So that we can actually start to be a little clearer on what we're actually really trying to achieve.

I want to finish off by again congratulating the work that Ruth and Penny are doing and everyone else that has been involved in and around *Radical Friends*. Because I do think that there's a pretty clear idea of the aim, namely to develop new forms of cultural funding and governance. To come back to that policy report that I wrote for the European Commission – it was a process where I was thinking through whether the arts might be a gateway for people who are involved in crypto to actually start experimenting more with some actually functioning and upgraded forms of democracy for the digital age. Or conversely, whether the arts experiments with DAOs might instead become a gateway for the expansion of the reach of predatory markets and financialisation! And there will probably not be a simple answer to that. But I can see what many involved in *Radical Friends* are aiming for and I support the efforts to create new governance tools and more direct economic democracy.

I am one of those unfortunate people that is very much a fence sitter when it comes to crypto. Crypto, DAOs and tokenisation more generally are a set of debates that tends to be hugely polarised. You're very much either for or against, but I know that there's a handful of us who sit rigorously and critically right in the middle and are trying to make something out of this mess and that's a very important role to play right now.

Walk The Walk – Beyond Blockchain Orientalism

Hito Steyerl

What is a DAO? No one really knows. One reason is that most possible answers lie in the future. Will a blockchain based decentralised autonomous organisation follow templates for Ponzi schemes or Paris Commune style popular councils – or neither or both? Are they going to be decentralised, autonomous or even organisations? Will they be on the blockchain at all, given the fact that this is quite expensive these days? Remember, prediction can be hard, especially about the future. So let's start from a different direction. Let's start from what DAOs are definitely not and then make a sharp U-turn.

The DAO of blockchain-based decentralised autonomous organisations has patently nothing to do with the Dao of Chinese Daoism. Except for two things. Firstly, technological DAO proponents often do gesture towards the spiritual appeal of historical Daoism.[1] Vague ideas about following the "way" (the Dao) and somehow vibing with nature structure this approach. There is a blockchain Orientalism baked into the blockchain DAO texture, that renders it a sitting duck for scrutiny. On the other hand such critique would mostly be formulaic and boring,

---

1. A few examples: https://www.researchgate.net/publication/336316096_THE_TAO_OF_
DAO_HARDCODING_BUSINESS_ETHICS_ON_BLOCKCHAIN;
https://news.bitcoin.com/curing-the-disease-of-control-with-taoism-and-crypto-anarchy;
https://bitcoinmagazine.com/culture/bitcoin-stock-to-universal-flow.

so I'll skip it for now. But I will return to it later from a less predictable perspective.

The other overlap between both phenomena is actually factual. Even if there is absolutely nothing else to link both DAO named phenomena, one common factor cannot be denied: both arise in historically very troubled periods – and partly as a reaction to them. Daoism as a school of thinking and ethics starts cohering at the end of the so-called Warring States period around 2nd century BCE in China. This era is a time of turmoil. It ends with reconsolidation under monopolist military imperial rule. It is an era of technological innovation – iron replaces bronze – and the consolidation of patrilinear clan laws as well as large-scale infrastructural projects.

But it is also an era in which ideas about money, markets, religion and philosophy intersect. Karl Jaspers called its wider context the so-called Axial Age – an era roughly set between the 8th and 2nd century BCE. In this age most of the concepts used today – religious, economic and political – are created in a geographical area spanning from East China to Minor Asia.

The emergence of minted metal coins is especially interesting in the blockchain context. Anthropologist David Graeber writes: "The core period of Jasper's Axial age... corresponds almost exactly to the period in which coinage was invented."[2] Metal coins, documented since the 6th century BCE, are important to evenly distribute the spoils of war and pay mercenary standing armies within a fractured political landscape. But minted coins also give rise to metaphysical tensions: between form and content, between material and social value, idea and matter, between the social trust required in such monetary systems and the unfettered rule of violence. Graeber also claims that some of the big schools of thought in China arise as social protest movements to oppose the constant threat of plunder, warfare and the rule of strongmen warlords. Whether this assessment is correct or not, it raises the question about how current ideas about DAOs sit in relation to current power shifts and turmoil. In opposition? In complicity? It's far from clear.

The debate around DAOs is happening during a moment of undeniable deglobalisation in the wake of reactionary populism, platform capitalism, climate change and pandemia. In recent years multiple simultaneous failures happened in overlapping systems – from logistics

---

2. David Graeber, *Debt: The First 5000 Years* (Brooklyn: Melville House Press, 2011), 224.

to health care, from public trust to political stability, from the financial system to states failing, leading to mass migration, civil wars, quasi civil wars and many other consequences. The invention of the blockchain system itself is partly due to a lack of trust in the global financial system post-2008 financial crises.

The infrastructure or technological context of DAOs is thus embedded on multiple levels into a global landscape in which economic ties rapidly unravel to be reconstructed in the form of local filter bubbles, more often than not controlled by authoritarian rulers or quasimonopolist corporations. Its structures tie in with the emergence of closed info-forums (for members/owners) and the widespread loss of the idea of public spaces, society as such and the public good. Following the templates of platform capitalism, smaller, closed communities regroup on Discord channels or messenger groups, organised around ideas of shareholdership and private property. The idea of civic values, rights or public spaces is de-emphasised to foreground an idea of participation based on the amount of members material possessions, FX shares or tokens. This is reminiscent of prerevolutionary situations in the US or France – when property was the base for political representation. Needless to add: democratic revolutions happened to overthrow this system and to enable people excluded from representation – in many cases women and slaves – to claim not just basic human but political rights. To base representation on property is definitely a reactionary move. It implies leaving the chores of running and maintaining society to others. The social contract evoked by the blueprint of decentralised autonomous organisation is often implicitly an antisocial contract – because it simply has no concept of the social.

The emergent scope of the political horizon of DAOs – as communities of co-owners – thus resonates with a background of rampant privatisation and the postmodern dismantling of societies in many places – including infrastructures of democratic participation, health care, the welfare state (if existent), possibly a public cultural sector, etc. It refracts a pattern of the vernacularisation of social organisation that has come a long way from the universalist (but hypocritical) state structures of modernism. DAOs reflect shrunken social horizons. They could actualise as tribes, clans, squads, cliques, mafias, cabals, unions, associations or cartels. DAOs could be modelled as cooperatives, Ponzi schemes, after Rosicrucian loges or somewhat more realistically, after bullshit job bureaucracies. They could implement anything from Rousseau's volonté générale to the physics of a fish swarm or the Camorra. But if the insistent rhetorics of DAOs being able to provide new social contracts or even bold experiments in equality is to have any real world credibility, then these mechanisms need to be defined – and not delegated to some future tech implementation that will magically take care of it. Let's admit: whoever has sat through hours of plenary discussion has secretly wished for all of these tedious procedures to be automated away. I get it. I confess to finding consensus decision-making cumbersome too. But in politics the process of negotiation is a fundamental part of the procedure. Especially blockchain orientalists would have to agree with me: following the way (the Dao), is the goal.

If more just and accessible models of social organisation are to emerge from these experiments, questions of political and economical power and who owns and controls it have to be squarely onboarded. One needs to answer questions about which political or social contract is going to be implemented instead of just repeating that something will be automated eventually. Why? What? Why would one even want do such a thing if every decision would cost a fortune in gas fees?

Let me give an example that squarely deals with power: In the present, cryptomining triggers intense riots and uprisings. Through wasteful consumption of energy cryptomining has created power failures and grid problems in places like Kosovo, Georgia/Abkhazia and Kazakhstan. People started protesting the breakdowns of electricity supply caused by POW protocols in cryptomining. Paradoxically the attempted automation of trust by cryptotechnologies ends up undermining their very condition, namely a stable electricity supply. By sucking power out of strained networks they produce grid failures in societies in which inequality and fragmentation abound anyway. Real estate bubbles and subsequent housing shortage are other consequences of crypto economies, just as a flourishing scam industry going up in newly built office areas for white collar scam professionals. If the Proof-of-Work protocol was supposed to produce trust between anonymous participants of a network, in reality it ended up intensifying existing political fault lines, energy shortages and partial system failures in regions plagued by mining. However, until now none of these uprisings presents an organised alternative, let alone a progressive one. Instead, the mining riots up to date seem to confirm the uneven devolution of society into premodern forms – the family and the local context that seem to provide islands of stability within kleptocratic environments.

While this situation has nothing to do directly with the contemporary idea of DAOs as such – after all they could also be realised using less power hungry protocols – it throws a harsh light on illusions about Web3 decentralisation.

To put it very simply: if cryptomining or its multiple consequences take out electricity there is no internet, and thus no web based decentralisation, neither within Web1 nor 2 nor Web3.

But the mining riots have also revealed another weak point of crypto-based decentralisation projects. Basically, as recently witnessed in Kazakhstan, even a smalltime autocracy is able to shut down relevant parts of the Internet,[3] if not control access altogether. Thus even a Web3 structure would be dependent on the goodwill and functionality of both governments and power suppliers. Any web-based decentralisation project lacks a reliable foundation as long as both electrical and governmental power are not decentralised. The decentralisation of informational power is a condition of the decentralisation of power, period. Thus, new questions emerge. What is information autonomy? What is energy autonomy and how can it be reached using more sustainable procedures? What is political autonomy, lest we forget to ask that question? The attempt to create tech "fixes" to these issues or just rely on some mysterious smart contracts to magically take care of them shows that these kinds of "solution" just create new and quite serious problems, from civil unrest to environmental breakdown, from social inequality to multiple health hazards. And we haven't even asked how centralisation is hardwired into the emerging technological constitution of Web3, in which (unlike in Web1 for example) technological participation remains restricted to specialists.

So, let's return to blockchain Orientalism as promised earlier, but from the other side.

By making a huge detour by way of an obvious and rather boring dead end – blockchain Orientalism – important questions have emerged. What are the conditions for decentralised organisations? When can they be said to be autonomous – and is autonomy even still desirable in a world in which the macho idea of self-legislation sounds somewhat like

---

3. On a much smaller and sillier scale Moxie Marlinspike has shown how NFT platforms easily manage to separate you from your assets, thus invalidating any idea of decentralised control of assets on the blockchain by exploiting poor UI´s and access barriers: https://moxie.org/2022/01/07/web3-first-impressions.html

Man heroically subduing nature? What is the political horizon of DAOs? How about most current DAOs focus on property-based rights as opposed to civic, political or human rights, let alone rights extending to other entities? What are the consequences for public or civic spaces – or any ideas of public good or society as opposed to gated communities, cartels and private virtual real estate? The organisational model of the DAO is still quite undefined – to reiterate, it mostly doesn't exist yet. And – let's face it – there are many problems that current arrangements fail to solve – from livelihoods to any kind of social security, for example for cultural workers. It is very important to underline that any crypto-gamification of resources is also a symptom of an underlying problem of failing remuneration that precedes (and exceeds) Web3. This problem will not go away by people like me criticising current concepts of DAOs and if DAOs are not the solution, a solution still needs to be found – for example in good old cooperativism and workers self-management and if someone manages to implement a real world example of this as offchain DAO I would definitely be up for it.

But questions of political organisation and the distribution of power beyond property need to go way beyond the invocation of magical thinking/social Ponzi schemes. Dear blockchain Orientalists: If you really want to follow some "way" or another – good for you! I don't have the slightest problem with that. I find the idea of cultural private property just as problematic as the idea of art as private property. But if you want to go down this path – you also need to bloody walk the walk! What kind of social contract do you want if any? Make up your mind! If it's a glorified investment pool, then please just own up to it and stop clouding it in orientalist verbiage. If it's not then kindly please tell us what else it is supposed to be. Otherwise some potentially valuable social experiments will just end up in some irrelevant subfolder of some dimwitted monopoly metaverse in which staking games on rotating Shiba Inus burn up the planet.

Cyberwitches' Manifesto

▲

ONE KNOT IN TIME
THEN THE WORLD CHANGED
THEN MEMORY DISAPPEARED
THEN WE COULDN'T UNDERSTAND LIFE ANYMORE
NEITHER FORWARD NOR BACKWARD.*

▾

It's time

to stop dodging; to stop fudging
ourselves; to face the current changes.
Not without anxiety but with determination.

Let's unite our voices:

*We do not defend nature, we are nature defending
itself.* — Nature, Gaia, neither mother nor sister,
but a force beyond the languages that have
difficulty with post-gender.

Let's acknowledge

that the master's tools
will not dismantle the master's house.
The very technologies that were reason to dream
of new forms of politica empowerment have turned out
to be the means of surveillance and control for everybody.

It is time

to leave the dualist labyrinths. But let's not be Icarus:
the Sirens are our sisters and we are too keen
on the sensuality of the stones and the
tenderness of the trees
to give in to
transhumanist
pride.

Let's connect

from Earth
to the Noosphere without
rummaging, scratching or desecrating Gaia's
entrails, without spitting in the face of Heaven and
Time the deadly fumes that are mortgaging our futures.

Let's be actual "saboteurs of big daddy mainframe".

Let's profess

technological autonomy and all forms of emancipation
and empowerment. Let's be inspired by W.I.T.C.H.,
VNS Matrix, Gynepunk, Reclaiming, technoshamanism,
xenofeminism, hyperstition, afrofuturism
and ancestorfuturism without us
adhering entirely to one
or the other.

Let's play

with hermeticism with irony.
We know that speech is the active
material of magic. Let's sometimes try this
alchemy of the verb that modifies reality through
words. Our words have little hubris. They caress the daisies
rather than helping to instantiate the magic. Our power is
domestic and vernacular. Our sorority protects us from
slipping from witch to woman of power. Our
do-it-yourself practices escape religions.
We are not one but labile
& evanescent.

Let's practice

this applied science of
the creation of forms by energy
and the direction of energy by forms.
The forms, structures, images that we ma-
-nipulate will sometimes lead us out of the
limits imposed by our culture. Our will,
our actions, our directed energy,
our choices made not once but
several times: this is
our magic.

We live
in this 21rst
century that used to be
dreamed and is now feared.

Let's invent

for ourselves experimental origins
and traditions. Let's not believe
in divinity, let's connect
with Her.

Let's understand

that everything is interconnected,
that consciousness gives
shape to reality and
reality gives shape
to consciousness.

Let's use

social networks to gather
in spiritual and political rituals. Let's use
smartphones and tarot cards to connect to spirits.

Let's manufacture

DIY devices to listen to invisible worlds.
Our astral body travels through
the cosmic plane of
radio waves.

Let's mix

ancestral and
invented methods to
reveal the porosity of the worlds
— ours, that of the God·esses we no longer believe in,
the free cosmogony and that of the fictional
entities that we create.

We are corporeal

biological, incarnate entities,
but also and simultaneously: relational
and informational beings. We are entities with digital
extensions. We live in a physical, technical and digital world.
Let's be hybrid entities living in an hybrid world.
Let's take care of our body-hub-servers.
Let our contemporary everyday
technical equipment be part
of our rituals.

Our magic is technophile

Let's say the words.
Let's make the gestures.
Let's manipulate the objects.
Let's summon archetypal relics.
Let's call for the emergence of egregores.
Let's seek a fleeting energetic symbiosis.
Let's practice this art of changing consciousness at will.

Let's be cyberwitches.

*Quote: Rosmarie Waldrop, A Key Into the Language of America, New York; New Directions, 1994.
Type: Bluu Next, Jean-Baptiste Morizot (distributed by Velvetyne).
Web-to-print graphic design by L⬡-H, 2021.

Lucile Olympe Haute,
Imbolc 2019.

▼

Beauty and The Beast: Collectivity and the Corporation

Legacy Russell

In the American art world, corporations are people, my friend. Within the last five years the trend of collectives-as-commercial-entities has become increasingly prevalent as a prominent influence within the contemporary art market. And these groups are corporatising. Faced with the shifting sands of sustainability within the fickle realm of creative practice, many artists bound together in their process of production have begun to enact the hierarchies of corporate business infrastructure as a cornerstone to their own advancement. The interest of fiscal self-preservation has many collaborative projects collectivising and, further, assuming the title of corporation as part of their formal operative fabric and legal personhood.

A corporation, in its essence, can generally be defined as a legal entity, separate and distinct from its owners, which exists solely by the grace of the state. Unlike the individuals that create it, a corporation enjoys only a limited (but growing) subset of the rights and responsibilities that an individual possesses.

Let us back up a bit. For all intents and purposes of having this conversation, it is necessary to suss out the differences between two terms that are often (questionably) used interchangeably: the collaborative and the collective.

A collaborative activates the specialisation of labor within a very particular framework. In a collaborative operation, many individuals pool resources to get a specific job done; thus, their efforts become somewhat site-specific, moving project-by-project, as necessary. Ownership of the work falls to each contributor separately. Individuals are provided autonomy beyond the umbrella of the collaboration, a harmony of efforts. In a conversation between research theorist Brett Stalbaum and Faith Wilding of the "(cyber)feminist art collective" subRosa in *M/E/A/N/I/N/G Online*, Wilding notes: "Collaborations usually have a more informal or less ideological basis than collectives... usually each collaborator is credited by name. Ownership of the work redounds to each artist separately."[1] Collaboration, therefore, often remains more open-ended than that of collectivity, as it is transient in nature, often runs its course, and therefore is not substantiated by the premise of an idée fixe.

A collective, on the other hand, stems often from a political agenda and points toward the pooling of principles in the interest of promulgating and promoting a larger ideological framework or strategic methodology. For collectives, ownership of work falls under a larger over-arching umbrella that encompasses all members therein; thus, individuals are often expected to refrain from acting autonomously in any way that would contradict or jeopardise the collective goals and central objectives of the group. As a member of a collective, there is an understanding that an individual enters a contract (formal or informal) to relinquish some part of their individual identity as a maker to that of the collective whole. Members of these groups, though clearly named, often are rendered somewhat invisible or anonymous by default due to the asserted structure of a collective body. Wilding comments, "Collective members usually share similar political goals and desires – though they may have different degrees of political radicality. Collective members also share the desire to work together and to count this process as part of their 'work'. Many collectives use only the group name for identification and don't label individual parts of works produced with the name of the member who was responsible for making it. This is often a problematic negotiation when it comes to trying to enter the art world system."

Problematic? How?

Collective and collaborative art-making is deeply linked to the canons of art history. What was Dadaism, Surrealism, and Constructivism in the early parts of the 20th century, found a renaissance in the 1960s in Fluxus,

1. "An Interview with Faith Wilding and Brett Stalbaum," *M/E/A/N/I/N/G Online #2* (1993), http://writing.upenn.edu/pepc/meaning/02/wilding-subrosa.html.

Conceptual, community-based, muralist and feminist art movements.[2]

These creative efforts moved from the margins into the middle, beginning as pièce de résistance to the academy and then being embraced by the same arms that first spurned them. Spurred by the identity politics and activism of the 1980s that carried contemporary art practice in large part through the 1990s and into the early 2000s, within the past ten years the art world has been cycling again through a rebirth and revisiting of group action, seating itself this time in participatory engagement, social practice, interactivity, and an expansion in the digital frontier of new media. Institutions have expanded and adapted in response to these shifts, with summits such as Portland's *Open Engagement*, programs like The Museum of Modern Art's *PopRally* series, and granting opportunities such as Triple Canopy's research and programming fellowships, or the Museum of Art and Design's *FUN Fellowship*, which funds projects wherein nightlife and social practice come into contact.

It is precisely because of this rich history that understanding collective as "a problematic negotiation" often becomes a blinding light, easier to turn away from than face, head-on. Yet it would be naïve to pretend that the rise in globalised conglomerates and corporate multinationals, and the hand these entities have in changing the course of history on a macro scale would be mirrored in every part of the world as we know it, excepting the arts. The politics of art leaves a bitter taste on the tongues of many. Though we continue to witness funding for the arts being cut nationally with MFA and Master's program graduates flooding an art economy too crippled to care for them, we still allow ourselves to be fed and fattened by the romantic fantasy that, somehow, art and ethics go hand-in-hand.

This is not the case.

Collaboratives in this day and age operate within the art world as points in a longer narrative, participants therein often defined in part by their difference from one another, brought together to participate in exchange. A collective practice, however, is a lifestyle, and, as many lifestyles do, collectives often value sameness of goals and aspirations over radical difference amongst members. Within the art world collaborations have been accepted and acknowledged as valuable assets within the larger market community of commerce; it is the commercial collective (a paradox to its very core), however, that is still finding its place and its ethical

---

2. Nikos Papastergiadis, *Spatial Aesthetics, Art, Place, and the Everyday* (Institute of Network Cultures, 2010), 21.

beat. Collective as an item of commerce is often more difficult to swallow for patrons, collectors, benefactors, and institutions, as the larger agenda of the group can sway the direction of the group's career path, and the amassing of more than one individual in the process of art-making and the production of artworks introduces the entangled issue of compensation. How to compensate many individuals who operate under the golden arch of mono-one? It is here that the unified corporate model proffers a strategic solution for the capital success of collective creative practice.

Thus, the lifestyle and the politic of the collaboration become the products, manifesting themselves in participatory gatherings, programs, and events, used to cull content for the production of objects that can be pinned to the white box or placed on the auction block to be consumed by the voracious appetite of today's art market. The archetype of the artist-in-solitude within the studio has been shattered as the definition of studio has expanded. And the work of the participant, spectator, or audience just might end up in the galleries of the next blockbuster exhibition, authorised and presented as part of a collective oeuvre.

In his essay "The Work of Art in the Age of Mechanical Reproduction," Walter Benjamin stresses the importance of the utilitarian nature of creative practice in times of crisis as a tool "for the formulation of revolutionary demands in the politics of art."[3] With the working-class struggle against capitalist coercion as a focal point, Benjamin challenges creative individuals to use their work as a vehicle for social dissent and discourse. Enter paradox: if artists need to make a living to sustain their creative practice, yet artists hold, in part, the responsibility of critiquing and dissenting from the social and cultural systems upon which they depend for sustainability, how to bridge the gap?

The answer: the collective. Collaboration is a good seedling, but it is within collectivity that codes of power begin to substantiate. And it is in this turn that we begin to hear the call and response between the collective and corporate as symbiotic models.

Guy Debord's *La Société du Spectacle*, sheds light on the alienation of the individual under the thumb of capitalism. "The more... life is now a product, the more [one] is separated from [one's] life."[4] Life as

3. Walter Benjamin, *The Work of Art in the Age of Mechanical Reproduction* (Penguin Press, 2008). First published 1935.

4. Guy Debord, *The Society of the Spectacle* (Rebel Press, 2004) Chapter 1, Section 33. First published 1967.

a marketable object is a shape-shifter, ever-changing as it is sold off in parts as a means of entering the social system and purchased in parts as a means of compensating for that which has been displaced or lost via sale or exchange. That said, "The present art market and its existing infrastructures still promote the success of the individual"[5] over that of the collective. The brand of an individual offers the possibility of a constant. And an individual's lifestyle is a large part of creative currency.

In light of this, the contemporary collective finds itself pressured to echo the strategies of the individual, finding success in the fullness of one. Though collective practice has the potential for liberation from the anxieties and alienations presented by individual practice, within the art world it does little to invert the capitalist model it often is bred to resist against, collapsing in on itself and alienating its audiences as an overt vehicle of capitalism. In asserting itself as an authoritative voice of polemic rhetoric, it requires its audiences to acknowledge its political expertise. When a collective is placed in this position, the group takes on a didactic function, with the public's participation as signed consent to be educated, regardless of the veracity or quality of what is being taught.

In his essay "The Artist as Producer in Times of Crisis,"[6] curator and educator Okwui Enwezor asks, "Is the collectivisation of artistic production not a critique of the poverty of the language of contemporary art in the face of large scale commodification of culture which have merged the identity of the artist with the corporate logo of global capitalism?"

With today's American art world collectives increasingly miming the self-interest of the individual, we must ask ourselves: What is the alternative when these groups also take on "the corporate logo of global capitalism"? Who to turn to for uncompromised and responsible social and institutional critique of crisis within the domestic and global forum? Do these outlets exist, or are they dreamscapes of utopistic pedagogy, too romantic to be realised?

5. Joanne Laws, "How Does Collective Practice Function Within Contemporary Art Practice?" https://joannelaws.com. Accessed, March 4, 2011.

6. Okwui Enwezor, *The Artist as Producer in Times of Crisis*, lecture delivered at 16 Beaver Street, April 15, 2004: http://www.darkmatterarchives.net/wp-content/uploads/2011/02/Enwezor.AuthorProd..pdf.

As Enwezor points out:

... collectives tend to emerge during periods of crisis; in moments of social upheaval and political uncertainty within society. Such crisis often forces reappraisals of conditions of production, reevaluation of the nature of artistic work, and reconfiguration of the position of the artist in relation to economic, social, and political institutions.

Yet more and more the collective, once a critical strategy of the avant-garde, has morphed itself into a critical strategy of capital gain to engage with commerce and create a base of power within the art market. The art world's collective has become a part of the crisis.

The Contemporary impulse to mimic the corporate form has come together with the desire to collectivise, and then to commercialise as a move toward sustainability. This means that artists shouldered with the historicised responsibility of critical resistance have become implicated and entangled in a diseased corporate archetype. The ineffectiveness of this illusively sound corporate model is one of many catalysts for the Occupy Movement, shedding harsh light on the culpability of the one percent and the devastating impact such socio-economic imbalance has on the rest of the (inter)national body. Is complicity with ailing structures of power, tools of a dominant paradigm, a new resistance? A form of institutional critique so seamless that the divide between institution and artist is rendered invisible? The emperor, it seems, has no clothes. But perhaps the Occupy Movement, in its mixing of models, is onto something. Jonathan Kaiser[7] observes:

Occupy Wall Street has not only reintroduced radical ideas about collectivity into mainstream discussion, they have managed (for a while at least) to convincingly frame those ideas as the common-sense goals of the majority, rather than as the irrational demands of a countercultural fringe. Any public demonstration has to be concerned with public presentation and media representation as much as its own internal process and ideology. But by combining the two and trying to construct a transparent micro-example of direct democracy, OWS is showing a glimmer of positive direction in a long lineage of protests that can't seem to be heard beyond the prefix 'anti.'

7. Jonathan Kaiser, "Work About Working Together: On Collaboration and Activism in Contemporary Art," *Constellation* 17. QuodLibetica, online. Accessed, December 1, 2011.

Occupy Wall Street – though forcibly driven in part by creative micro-communities within the OWS movement (such as Arts and Culture, or Arts and Labor) – was not first formed to critique or evaluate the art world specifically. Occupy Art World, on the other hand, was. Yet, as a result of its decentralisation the frequency of these public actions has been staccato, with the public perception of their true points of genesis being choppy at best. Though one can follow some of this activity via @OccupyArtWorld on Twitter, this forum has largely found its strength in enacting a sort of running manifesto "For people who are tired of the 1 percent and their tools controlling the direction of art,"[8] and a tongue-in-cheek talk-back to the forces that be, ranging from Saatchi to Saltz and beyond. While @OccupyArtWorld seems to preach to the choir (its followers) using social media as its mouthpiece, the actions that have taken place away from the perpetual Twitter roundtable (but perhaps virally fueled by it) have been impactful in their socio-cultural significance. Groups like @Occupy_With_Art have a similar online presence paired with a commitment to interact and engage beyond the facelessness of the digital stratospheres, documenting and bringing "art, cultural events and projects, with a particular focus on OWS itself as a social art process"[9] into the streets for public participation and engagement. These two groups are a sampling of a vast many more that represent opposite sides of the same essential coin: Occupy Art World highlighting the inequalities of the art world via the lens of the vast imbalances presented by the art market, Occupy With Art reifying the role of the artist-as-revolutionary, placing at the forefront the possibility of inciting change within the scope of creative production through the act of making. Occupy With Art has made its mark with everything ranging from performances to film screenings to screen-printings, while Occupy Art World has manifested itself in a variety of more disparate forms. To name a few: Occupy Museums, wherein people marched last Fall from The Museum of Modern Art to the New Museum to "protest the conflation of art and commerce";[10] the September 22, 2011 disruption of auction proceedings at Sotheby's Upper East Side location; the short-lived October 2011 occupation of SoHo gallery Artists Space; the sending of a letter to the Whitney Museum by the Occupy Wall Street Arts and Labor

8. Excerpted from Twitter bio @OccupyArtWorld, https://twitter.com/occupyartworld.

9. *Occupy with Art*, website, accessed June 28, 2012, https://www.occupywithart.com.

10. Melena Ryzik," Taking the Protests to the Art World," *The New York Times*. October 21, 2011, https://artsbeat.blogs.nytimes.com/2011/10/21/taking-the-protests-to-the-art-world.

group requesting the termination of their Biennial event;[11] and, most recently, a fake press release placed on a faux-Whitney Biennial website headed by the bold proclamation that, "WHITNEY MUSEUM TO CLOSE FOR MAY DAY; ANNOUNCES GOVERNANCE CHANGES."[12] Though perhaps not the sole source of inspiration, the Occupy Movement has set the stage for other points of public critique of the current art world system, such as the recent release of the Working Artists and the Greater Economy survey at Artists Space on April 20th, which noted that "58 percent of artists who exhibited at a New York non-profit organisation between 2005 and 2010 received no form of payment, compensation or reimbursement – including the coverage of any expenses."[13]

As part of his project Occupy 2012 – a self-described daily effort to "write and think about Occupy each day of 2012" – writer, teacher, and visual/cultural critic Nick Mirzoeff muses:

> *Why does the art world not get similarly tired of wealthy patrons dictating 'taste' or indeed of the neo-liberal regime of the art market? Why is it not bored of Sotheby's, the art auction house, locking out its union Teamsters Local 814 in order to reduce still further their labor costs? These staff are art handlers, so you would think you would want that job done well. Perhaps we get a clue when we learn that Diana Taylor, director of the board at Brookfield Properties, owner of Zuccotti Park, is also on the board at Sotheby's.*[14]

Mirzoeff highlights with swift simplicity the reality of the presence of the one percent on Wall Street as well as within the art world, and the nature of their co-dependency. Thus the dichotomy that delegates corruption to the realm of finance, and earnest self-expression to the Shangri-La of creative

11. This letter also happened to coincide with the anonymous mass distribution of a mock press release (and website to boot), headlined "Whitney Biennial 2012 to Open March 1; Museum Breaks With Two Corporate Sponsors, Apologizes to Participating Artists."

12. "WHITNEY MUSEUM TO CLOSE FOR MAY DAY; ANNOUNCES GOVERNANCE CHANGES, SPECIAL ADDITION TO 2012 BIENNIAL PROGRAMMING," https://www.whitney2012.org.

13. W.A.G.E Presentation & Open Forum, last modified April 20, 2012, www.artistsspace.org/programs/w-a-g-e-survey-release.

14. Nicholas Mirzoeff, Occupy (and) the Art World?, Occupy 2012, ongoing. Online, February 17 2012. https://www.nicholasmirzoeff.com/O2012/2012/02/17/occupy-and-the-art-world/

practice, is false. The art world is a reflection of its financial counterpart, and there is no more integrity within the art market than the stock market.

Yet somehow we are still unresolved. Yes, the world calls for regulation of Wall Street, demanding accountability, and leading bastions of corporate economy have been disgraced as prominent examples of their violations. However, the conversation about responsibility and how to officiate regulations of abuses of power and unethical corporate-genre practice within the art world is not fully realised; in short, the art world remains unsupervised. Labor violations, selection and funding bias based on sex, race, class, and gender, insider trading, the hiding and shuffling of assets, the misuse of the non-profit structure, the misrepresentation of creative-corporate personhood to the general public in the interest of capital gain and advancement – all this has become de rigueur. And the collective often poses itself as a mode of resistance, a key part of the solution.

In her "Thoughts on Artists Collectives"[15] artist and writer Michelle Grabner notes:

> *The rationale of a... collective is primarily to cultivate a base of power. Among the many variations of contemporary artists groups, with their broadly diverse social and political agendas, it is this desire for power that unites them. Regardless of whether these contemporary groups are modelled after corporate firms, pop bands or ephemeral grassroots organisations, they all hope to assert themselves more effectively as a group than as an individual into their given cultural spaces and institutions.*

The well-oiled collective model is incredibly efficient in streamlining production and amassing sheer force in labor alone, making it a prime structure for competing within a capitalist market. For one individual to be asked to compete with the efforts of five, or ten, is a near-impossible task, as the production capacity surpasses that of a single individual with ease. Though the efficacy of group work remains somewhat of a constant throughout, the utilisation of power within contemporary art world models of collectivity has shifted radically from the dawning days of groups such as the Art Workers' Coalition, Gran Fury, Group Material, Guerrilla Art Action Group, the Guerrilla Girls, Colab, or Critical Art Ensemble. Once

---

15. Michelle Grabner, "Thoughts on Artists' Collectives", *X-TRA Contemporary Art Quarterly*, Vol 6, No. 2, Winter 2004.

used as a tool to challenge the systematic marginalisation of groups and political positions considered by the mainstream as fringe, power now amongst contemporary American collectives seems to feed directly into the "pop band" modality of creativity – the machine of super art stardom.

The recent debate in the United States about corporate personhood is a cyclical resurgence of a conversation that can be traced as far back as 17th century America. Personhood and its historical ties to the structuring of the corporation allowed corporations to be held accountable for their debts – as a person, a corporation could sue and be sued, provide creditors legal recourse, and encourage banks to extend credit to corporations. Thus the fiction of personhood allows corporations to increase their capital and continue to grow.

Collective practice in the art world and the personhood implied therein is also a legal fiction. Collectives garner public support because the public identifies with and trusts the ideology and lifestyle that the group promotes. Items made by a collective group therefore become manifestations of those modalities. The public consumption of these objects provides a connection to the group. The group produces these objects on credit, based on the reputation as substantiated by public opinion. Credibility and authenticity is then assigned to art objects based on this reputation, whether the reputation is a distortion of reality, or not. This credibility allows collectives to continue to expand, grow, increase their capital, and pursue more elaborate projects. Without checks and balances, collectives, much like corporations, are stripped of the mechanisms for the downgrading of credibility when these groups fail to make good on the credit extended to them. Thus, if a reputation is established based on a skewed representation of reality, there is no mechanism provided to the public to democratically challenge and dissemble the structures therein.

Hans Haacke put it best when he said, "What we have here is really an exchange of capital: financial capital on the part of the sponsors and symbolic capital on the part of the sponsored."[16] In this case, the commercial collective aligns itself with that of the sponsors, and the general public is paid via cool factor, intellectual investment, and celebrity association. This cycle enacts itself as somewhat of a turbine, with the symbolic capital acting as stock for the masses at the bottom – as long as a collective of artists maintain their cultural capital, and thereby maintain their cool factor, this

16. Pierre Bourdieu and Hans Haacke, *Free Exchange* (Stanford: Stanford University Press, 1995), 17.

stock keeps its value, and is able to generate enough energy to keep those at the top in motion via production. Where socialising is currency in the art world, those at the top win doubly – they gain financially by culling content from those at the bottom that they can later offer as a product within the art market, and they gain momentum by being provided the opportunity to socially network, a major stepping stone toward greater success.

Many seeking access to the elite art world bubble are left to trade in symbolic capital while their labor – in the form of support and viral publicity of art star collective participatory projects, branded as property of the collective and alchemised via the turbine into financial capital – continues to fuel the overall machinations of celebrity. Yet, symbolic capital does not allow for social mobility; that which is known as the American Dream is not based on symbolism, it is based on money. In the division of profit and labor the gap between the zenith of art stardom and the populace below is widened; the financial capital necessary to rise up is not provided to those who hold the stock of symbolic capital alone. In order to invert this model, to call for change, one must ask: How to make the participating public real shareholders in the actual profits of the celebrity collective? If art stardom is built via open source public contribution, how to define ownership? How to make sure that those invested in symbolic capital get back concrete dividends – and what would those dividends even look like?

The imbalance here is this – while the participating public is offered symbolic capital in the form of association with these larger collectives, collaboratives, and miniature art corporations, these groups garner financial capital for their creative contributions to culture. This means the public's engagement does not only support that of the collective's capital gain, but it guarantees the systematic disenfranchisement of the participants themselves – it deepens the divide between the collective and the individual, making it more difficult for the individual to make the leap independently between the regions of symbolic and financial capital gain. Thus the individual becomes dependent on the collective in the same way that the individual depends on the corporation. Is this model sustainable?

Those who purchase artwork from collectives and collaboratives, or who support their practice as patrons, are, indeed, shareholders of company stock. Patrons therefore become dependent on participants as well, because participants drive the symbolic capital that supports the rise of their collective financial gain. Thus the survival of the collective becomes contingent on the value of the stock alone and the public's investment in it – where many act as one, we see the capital gain of many to be placed under the umbrella of the individual. If the symbolic capital diminishes, so might some part of the financial capital, as the interest in acquiring works may shift.

Faith Wilding noted that, "Monumentality is the business of capitalist culture."[17] In a capitalist art market that conflates the collective and monumentality, separating the two becomes an increasingly difficult task. Capitalism requires constant growth, and, similarly, within the art market, collectivity requires constant growth and flux to remain socially relevant. The hand of collectivity has been forced – collective practice used to be a form of collaborative practice, but faced with the weight of financial sustainability and the siren song accompanied by the laurels of art stardom, the relationship between the two is becoming increasingly distanced. The facelessness of collective practice, oft branded by anonymity, presents a Goliath similar to that of the corporation, providing a micro one percent of its own, a miniature economic model echoing the macro examples we see headlined in the world at large.

There is no immediate fault in mimicking the corporate structure alone. However, mimicking the corporate structure as well as the gormandising nature of the modern mega-corporation is what compromises the integrity of the collective politic and the material history therein. Contemporary art collectives – and the artists within them – must remain conscious, critical, and responsible. One ought not to fall into to a corporate model for its plain ease; one must make a choice, acting with transparency, intent, and determination. Understanding the failures of the structure itself is key to making changes and a stepping-stone toward modifying the rubrics that have been previously established. Corporations are not individuals – but individuals together are collectives. An obligation to the individual's agency and credit to his or her voice, as part of the collective task, is an essential anchor. In pouring our labor into the alternative collective effort, let it be in the name of palpable political progress, not solely commercial gain, and let our investment require of the collective an investment back into the populace that built it.

This essay was originally published by *Guernica Magazine* in 2012.

17. "An Interview with Faith Wilding and Brett Stalbaum," *M/E/A/N/I/N/G Online #2* (1993), http://writing.upenn.edu/pepc/meaning/02/wilding-subrosa.html.

Manifesting a Black Swan DAO

Laura Lotti & Calum Bowden

Today there is a mounting awareness among art workers of the ways in which contemporary art is instrumental in extending the logic of finance. The rampant neoliberalisation of the cultural sphere concentrates risk on the individual art workers who go head-to-head for increasingly limited opportunities and resources. Faced with the collapse of legacy institutions, some artists and creative practitioners have turned to block-chain technologies to find answers to the problem of organisation in the cultural field, including its psycho-social pathologies and its economic sustainability. While the financial nature of the technology runs the risk of engendering familiar power structures and dynamics, the possibility it affords to transfer funds across borders, experiment with programmable co-ownership models and software-based organisations for transparent decision-making and record-keeping, known as DAOs, has opened up the imaginations of many to alternative forms of organising.

Established in 2018, Black Swan is a Berlin-based collective that deploys the conceptual and operational affordances of blockchains to pursue alternative approaches to the traditional artworld templates for art making. Black Swan was conceived in the context of the Berlin art scene, deploying blockchains and DAOs to address the precarious reality of local artists and cultural practitioners, who often fall between the cracks of existing arts infrastructures due to the interdisciplinary or "non-canonical" nature of their practises. Since blockchain technology is still nascent and limited in terms of its technical and financial accessibility, Black Swan has so far used it primarily as a means of rethinking the economics and organisational structures of the art world: *Blockchain thinking*, without relying on the technology itself.[1] Through peer support, artist-led funding and community decision-making, Black Swan places resources into the hands of the users rather than the gatekeepers of the arts. In Black Swan's cosmos, galleries, museums, and funding bodies have no influence over how their resources are used. Cultural practitioners are the active members of the system; they decide collectively on the use of resources, participate in the curation of initiatives and art projects to be realised (something that will be addressed in more detail below), and benefit from the value produced by their practices.

Black Swan's research methodology has put play and games at the centre of technical development as a means to challenge the mystique surrounding blockchain and understand emergent behaviours around its uses, foregrounding the affective dimension of technically-mediated interactions. In role-playing games, working groups, and hackathons, Black Swan invites existing communities of creative practitioners to experiment with forms of interaction, modes of organisation, and sustainable economic models to test hypotheses around how we organise, in a safe, playful environment. This is used as a way out of narrow technological solutionism, to collectively arrive at modes of framing problems and experiment with alternative ecologies of artmaking.

Our first working group with nine creative practitioners met in Berlin in January 2021 and surfaced the desire for tools for horizontal resource management for art making. This working group is explained in more detail in the chapter "Cygnet Prototype" in this volume. Our research emphasised that one of the biggest challenges to collaborative initiatives is neither the lack of ideas or enthusiasm, nor material resources per se, but is rather the absence of context-specific tools through which artists can reach consensus over how to best use and allocate resources to their collective benefit. Since then Black Swan has been developing a

---

1. One of the blockchain's key characteristics is the *immutability* of the ledger. While this is often a desired feature, since it enables censorship resistant record-keeping, it also means that any changes to a protocol require a new deployment of the protocol itself, which can be expensive and hinder usability. To avoid this, Black Swan used role-playing as a method to gain insights into collaborative dynamics to inform the development of its DAO, which will, it is envisaged, be blockchain-based in the future.

kaleidoscope of methods and tools to power multi-disciplinary research and practice that are situated in and adapted to our context in Berlin. This is not about replacing legacy institutions with equally molar and centralised structures, but rather creating new pathways and ecologies within and between them so that new formations may emerge from their interstices. For Black Swan, institutions are *edges* – connecting relations – and not centralised nodes within a network. As part of this effort, Black Swan is plotting the creation of Black Swan DAO: a translocal and mutable source for distributing resources and value differently across interdependent art worlds.

AFFIRMATIONS FOR ARTWORLDS BASED ON SOLIDARITY AND MUTUALISM

Over the last three years, Black Swan has acted as a research and development working group exploring the possibilities of art-run organisations. Below are some of the evaluations we have come to at the end of 2021, in the guise of affirmations for artworlds based on solidarity and mutualism. True to Black Swan's nature, these observations may be forked, forgotten or mutated from here on in and are only committed to paper as glimpses of close horizons.

ART-MAKING IS A MODE OF COLLECTIVE STAKING

An agreement is always a commitment, even before a formal contract. DAOs and blockchain mechanisms provide ways to make these commitments more explicit. One of these mechanisms is staking, the practice of "locking" tokens into protocols to earn some kind of reward while forfeiting the possibility of trading them. A stake is a lock on liquidity that enables the circulation of other "values" in a system. But as those involved in collective practices know, staking extends beyond technical mechanisms; it is a mode of relation that binds people together, socially and often economically. In fact, staking can take many different forms: one can stake in an idea, or project, or practice; it can be a way to assign responsibility, or to signal *appreciation*. Staking creates connections and networks, it is a game that creates its own rules as more people play it.

This is true for the contemporary artworld too. The idea of the individual artist genius celebrated by the global art market is a hangover from a bygone era whose historical groundings are shrouded in myth. Art making has always been an endeavour of collective staking, and even today an artist CV (a highly disputed tool in the arts) tells a story of collaborations with many different kinds of "stakeholders", from studio assistants and curators, to galleries, collectors, university classes, residency programs, and much in between. While art collectives have long been part of art history books, within the neoliberal circuits of Contemporary Art, "the contemporary collective finds itself pressured to echo the strategies of the individual, finding success in the fullness of one... it does little to invert the capitalist model it often is bred to resist against, collapsing in on itself and alienating its audiences as an overt vehicle of capitalism."[2] With the recuperation and individualisation of the collective by the art market, there is an urgent need for alternative organisational structures and mechanisms that support the heterogeneity of contributions in processes of art making. Peer-to-peer infrastructures can facilitate a process of "instituting otherwise,"[3] providing the foundations for proto-institutions that renew the functions and commitments of legacy organisations to tend to the ecologies within which collectives are situated.

Black Swan uses blockchain mechanisms to support the commitments and trust networks that already exist among practitioners, without eliminating or replacing them with code, and build new bridges to extend said trust to institutional actors as silent stakeholders. The challenge is how to not stifle these nascent collective formations with too much formalisation, as emotional engagement is as key as protocol mechanics in running an organisation. In this regard, perhaps DAOs are a signpost or gateway to something else, rather than an end in and of themselves.

THE ORGANISATION IS MUTABLE, LIABLE TO CHANGE

When artistic practices are overly constrained into rigid and static organisational forms copied from vehicles of capitalism, they result in extractive economic relations where a minority in creative leadership positions benefits at the expense of the art workers who produce art for wages.[4] Far from the tyranny of structurelessness,[5] Black Swan's research demonstrates the ways artists use varied organisational structures and hierarchies in practice, deploying organisational strategies to suit tasks at hand. To rethink the organisational structures of the artworld, Black Swan starts by searching for new metaphors for organising that are mutable and liable to change.[6]

2. See Legacy Russel, "Beauty & The Beast: Collectivity and the Corporation" in this volume.

3. On the relation between institutions and infrastructures, see "INSTITUTING OTHERWISE," BAK Online, https://www.bakonline.org/program-item/instituting-otherwise.

Looking at the origins of the words *organisation* and *corporate*, we discover narrow assumptions about biology extended to the social sphere.[7] Organisations and institutions can be thought of as shells and containers for groups of people. Organisations are formally constructed to achieve goals that individuals are unable or unwilling to achieve on their own.[8] But as they grow in scale and complexity, organisations tend to ossify around "rational" mechanisms that render them abstracted from the reality they

4. The use of fabricators to produce art has been commonplace since at least Michelangelo and Rembrandt, but the industrialised approach used by contemporary artists such as Damien Hirst, who employed more than 120 people in 2007, attains new scales of coordination and organisational complexity. One of Hirst's assistants comments in the UK's *Evening Standard* that she resented being paid £600 to do a painting that would sell for £600,000. David Cohen, "Inside Damien Hirst's factory," *Evening Standard*, August 30, 2007, https://www.standard. co.uk/culture/exhibitions/inside-damien-hirst-s-factory-6609579.html.

5. Jo Freeman, "The Tyranny of Structurelessness," 1972, https://www.jofreeman.com/ joreen/tyranny.htm.

6. Raising the importance of metaphors in the investigation of how people bring meaning to technologies, and how technologies bring meaning to people, George Lakoff and Mark Johnson write: "Metaphors... highlight and make coherent certain aspects of our experience. A given metaphor may be the only way to highlight and coherently organize exactly those aspects of our experience. Metaphors may create realities for us, especially social realities. A metaphor may thus be a guide for future action... fulfilling the metaphor and reinforcing it." George Lakoff and Mark Johnson, *Metaphors We Live By* (University of Chicago Press, 2003), 132.

7. The shifting notions of organisation and corporate are evidenced by the etymologies of the words. In the early 15c., *organisacioun* is taken to mean the structure of the body or its parts. By the 18c. organisation means "that which is organized", with the senses of "an organized body of persons" only emerging in 1829, and "system, establishment, constitution" in 1873. Douglas Harper, "Etymology of organization," Online Etymology Dictionary, accessed December 22, 2021, https://www.etymonline.com/word/organization. Like organisation, the term "corporate" also shifts from the biological to the social. Corporate comes via the Latin *corporatus* "to make or fashion into a body, furnish with a body," and the Latin *corpus* or "body" more generally. In the 15c., corporate comes to mean "united in one body, constituted as a legal corporation." Douglas Harper, "Etymology of corporation," Online Etymology Dictionary, accessed December 22 2021, https://www.etymonline.com/word/corporation. A biological metaphor runs through our social structures.

8. Doyle Paul Johnson, "Meso-Level Structures: Communities and Organizations", in *Contemporary Sociological Theory* (Springer, 2008), https://doi.org/10.1007/978-0-387-76522-8_10.

are embedded in, and unable to adapt to the changing context. Modern capitalism is an *organised* society, where *corporate* actors are endowed with the capacity to act independently from the intentions and interests of their creators.[9] People are either held by or excluded from institutions of the family, the corporation, and the state. A person's context-specific position within this matrix becomes at least somewhat deterministic of their ability to access resources, economic security, and a quality of life. But the rigid organisational forms upon which today's society is constructed and the expulsion, exclusion, and isolation associated with them are recent phenomena. Until the 15th century such a notion of formal organisation was inconceivable, as the legal separation between public and private sphere had not yet been developed.[10]

The biological metaphors upon which modern notions of organisation depend further naturalise the form and structure organisations take. The rationality, rigidity and immutability associated with organisations might stem in part from 15th century European assumptions about nature, based on a mechanistic view of the universe as a large-scale eternal machine.[11] Taken with more recent thinking about biology and the philosophy of science, we see alternative possibilities for organisations emerge that map more closely to the dynamic, multi-linear processes through which artists create together. In the recent works of the philosophers Paul B. Preciado and Laboria Cuboniks, nature becomes a site of contestation and technological transformation. Preciado reveals how bodies are produced and reproduced through the pharmaceutical industry, pornography, and late capitalism.[12] And Laboria Cuboniks calls for the potential of contemporary technologies to be mobilised upon gender, sexuality and disparities of power.[13] As these authors show, the

9. Helena Flam, "Corporate Actors: Definition, Genesis and Interaction", MPIFG Discussion Paper 90/11, https://www.mpifg.de/pu/mpifg_dp/dp90-11.pdf.

10. Alfred Kieser, "Organizational, Institutional, and Societal Evolution: Medieval Craft Guilds and the Genesis of Formal Organizations," *Administrative Science Quarterly* 34, no. 4 (1989): 540–64. https://doi.org/10.2307/2393566.

11. "For what is the Heart, but a Spring; and the Nerves, but so many Strings; and the Joints, but so many Wheeles, giving motion to the whole Body, such as was intended by the Artificer?". Thomas Hobbes, *Leviathan*, 1651 (Oxford University Press, 1965), https://files.libertyfund.org/files/869/0161_Bk.pdf.

12. Paul B. Preciado, *Testo Junkie: Sex, Drugs, and Biopolitics in the Pharmacopornographic Era* (The Feminist Press at the City University of New York, 2013).

arrangement of organs that make up bodies are rendered as in flux, made and remade through media, technoscience, and economics. If we rethink the biological metaphors underpinning organisation in terms of this more recent thinking about nature, we can see organisational bodies as something that are fluid, mutable and adaptable, and that shift the ecology within which art is created. As Laboria Cuboniks says, "if nature is unjust, change nature!" DAOs are the most recent instantiation of the ways in which organisation can become unpinned from an immutable and ideal body form, though in practice most DAOs have a tendency to fall back on previous assumptions about what an organisation can be. Black Swan aims to change that.

THE ORGANISATION IS UNITED THROUGH SHARED VIBES

Beyond the formal mechanisms that define the scope and domain of operation of an organisation, what an organisation actually holds in common is something that is practiced, performed and renegotiated at each encounter. It cannot be "engineered" a priori. Shared vibes may lead to shared values, but not the other way around. The theorist Peli Grietzer describes a vibe as an aesthetic unity in a world or in a work of art, that is a "surface-accessible, world-making structure".[14] In other words, a vibe is an aesthetic form that operates beyond and below what neoliberal policy reductively calls social cohesion, producing collective formations through resonances that traverse pre-established social contexts.[15] Vibes are recursively related to intersubjectivity: vibes are both preconditions for, and effected by, the sharing of subjective experience by multiple people. A vibe might encompass an array of commonly-recognised phenomena and structures including difference, noise, ambiguity,

13. "Our lot is cast with technoscience, where nothing is so sacred that it cannot be reengineered and transformed so as to widen our aperture of freedom, extending to gender and the human. To say that nothing is sacred, that nothing is transcendent or protected from the will to know, to tinker and to hack, is to say that nothing is supernatural. 'Nature' – understood here, as the unbounded arena of science – is all there is." Laboria Cuboniks, "Xenofeminism. A Politics for Alienation," 2015, http://laboriacuboniks.net.

14. Peli Grietzer, "A Theory of Vibe", *Glass Bead*, 2017, https://www.glass-bead.org/article/a-theory-of-vibe.

15. JoAnn Jaffe and Amy A. Quark, "Social Cohesion, Neoliberalism, and the Entrepreneurial Community in Rural Saskatchewan," *American Behavioral Scientist* 50, no. 2 (October 2006): 206–25. https://doi.org/10.1177/0002764206290634.

the sacred, the profane, the unknown, and the ineffable. Shared vibes are produced through intimacy and common references and already emerge within local and translocal art scenes. The musician Ezra Koenig (via Grietzer and in turn via Elif Batuman) describes a vibe as a local colour with a historical dimension: "What gives a vibe 'authenticity' is its ability to evoke – using a small number of disparate elements – a certain time, place and milieu; a certain nexus of historic, geographic and cultural forces."[16] A vibe erupts beyond the singular and the static towards a multiplicity of heterogeneous elements and cannot be fixed or pinned down (attempts to name or describe a vibe always reduce its complexity). As Koenig suggests, a vibe demarcates a temporality unfolding across spaces and cultural contexts. It marks the creation of a locality that is not bound by geographical constraints. Black Swan's experiments with moon cycles in Cygnet further reveal ways that coalescing around the rhythms of alternative, more-than-human, temporalities might be used to create more equitable common substrates for art making.

Formal organisations like firms and corporations are only possible if there is a separation between public and private spheres. Emerging in the modern era, corporations are imagined as bodies for groups of individuals to act and exchange within. The creation of these abstract corporate bodies has come to depend on the reduction of complex identities to absolute values, which serve more as regulatory ideals than as means of caring for or nourishing collective bodies in flux. While organisations and corporations might publicly declare they are held together by goals and values, economists such as Ronald Coase reveal the ways in which firms arise because of profit incentives, and grow disproportionately large when transaction costs within an organisation are lower than between organisations.[17] If our collective bodies are no longer to be based on profit maximisation or binary and absolute ideals, what else might act as substrates for people to act in concert?[18] As information technologies and blockchains make the cost of transacting between organisations effectively the same as transacting within an organisation in terms of

16. Grietzer, "A Theory of Vibe."

17. Ronald H. Coase (1937), "The Nature of the Firm," *Economica*, 4: 386–405.
https://doi.org/10.1111/j.1468-0335.1937.tb00002.x

18. The philosopher Hannah Arendt defines power as the human ability to "act in concert" towards common public and political purposes. Hannah Arendt, *On Violence*. (New York, NY: Harcourt, 1970).

time, coordination effort and economic expenditure, the contours of individual and collective bodies become more entangled in mutualistic metabolisms.

Searching for a "north star" or a mission without having a commonly-held vibe only leads to an articulation of values that is vague, cliché or overly moralising. Providing a lens for reexamining the declared values of the contemporary artworld, political theorist Rodrigo Nunes shows how delineating political differences through ideological positions reduces politics to a set of choices between absolute values. He demonstrates the bifurcation of leftist politics through an analysis of two left-wing melancholias centred around the Russian Revolution in 1917 and the protests of 1968 respectively – the former emphasising state action as the driver of social transformation, and the values of unity, leadership, hegemony; and the latter stressing the initiative of social actors, putting emphasis on the values of plurality, autonomy and bottom-up organisation.[19] Nunes argues that in constantly demarcating their mutual difference through the reiteration of abstract principles and values that function as negations of each other, these two sides ensure that common ground cannot be found.

We see analogous dynamics at play in the contemporary artworld: on the one hand, large institutions aim to renew themselves in a top down manner, attempting to fold any innovation or existential threat into their own brand; on the other, small initiatives operating entirely outside of established circuits in a "horizontal" and "autonomous" way miss out on network effects and the benefits that come from leadership and institutional support. Nunes finds a way out by thinking of organisation in terms of specific problems and not merely conceptual relations: "common ground is a condition for responding to actual situations instead of just reiterating abstract principles or reproaching reality for being unlike our model."[20] Here we see how abstract values and principles end in questions of measurement and assessment against unattainable ideal states. Vibes, and the needs and desires that vibes articulate in practice, might provide better, more transversal, organising principles and enable the adoption of mutable structures to address common problems which demand varied approaches.

19.   Rodrigo Nunes, "One or Two Melancholias? 1917, 1968 and the Question of Organisation," *Crisis & Critique* 5, no. 2 (2018).

20.   Nunes, "One or Two Melancholias?", 255.

THE ORGANISATION IS MAINTAINED

Whether supported by technology or not, an organisation can work sustainably over a long period of time only if it is constantly maintained. Maintenance is about repair and renewal of the social and technical mechanisms that allow the organisation to operate in the first place, enabling it to adapt to and individuate through the milieu with which it is enmeshed. As Yuk Hui and Harry Halpin put it in the context of alternative ways of conceiving social networking: "individuation is also always a temporal and existential process, rather than merely social and psychological. By projecting a common will to a project, it is the project itself that produces a co-individuation of groups and individuals."[21] Like other organisational frameworks, a DAO works as a funnel to attract and catalyse "common will" and turn a "projection" or vision into a project – that is, a plan or coordinated activity.[22] While the will is not lacking, most of the initiatives emerging out of the blockchain industry today feel like business as usual and are not daring enough in the visions they project for the futures they want to realise. Part of the blame lies in the deceitful optics of *decentralisation* with the misguided emphasis on eliminating structural hierarchies in order to eliminate power imbalances;[23] the other part is in the lack of *curation* in the original sense of the word, which is to say the lack of actual care for the relations that DAOs can facilitate.

Black Swan aims to address this by clarifying common misconceptions around both terms, beginning with curating. *Curare* – to take care, to cure, from curating as taking care of bathhouses in Roman times, to the priest who cared for souls in mediaeval times, to looking after collections of art and artefacts in the 18th century... What new inflections and metamorphoses are to be found in the meaning and practice of curation within distributed digital environments? Black Swan's research

21. Yuk Hui and Harry Halpin, "Collective Individuation: The Future of the Social Web," in *Unlike Us Reader: Social Media Monopolies and Their Alternatives*, ed. Geert Lovink and Miriam Rasch (Institute of Network Cultures, 2013), 115.

22. Etymology tells us that from the 15c., a *projecte* was "a plan, draft, scheme, design," from the Medieval Latin *proiectum* "something thrown forth". Douglas Harper, "Etymology of project," *Online Etymology Dictionary*, accessed February 17, 2022, https://www.etymonline.com/word/organization.

23. A corrective to this position is offered in: Richard D. Bartlett, "Blockchain Doesn't Decentralise Power," *Enspiral Tales*, September 8, 2017, https://medium.com/enspiral-tales/blockchain-doesnt-decentralise-power-5918c168e6f6.

demonstrates the ways in which community facilitation is a key capacity needed by cultural institutions of the future.[24] As artistic practices and experiences are moving online and increasingly unfolding beyond geographically-bound localities, facilitation needs to be embedded in the core mechanisms of an organisation. It needs to be cultivated from within, in order to manifest its caring, and carrying, function. The shared vibes at the core of translocal art scenes require care and curation to be sustained, reproduced and be liable to change.

Black Swan's research also demystifies and seeks to break down the ideas of the "Decentralised" "Autonomous" "Organisation" within DAOs. Decentralisation, as a technical principle, can be invaluable to fostering infrastructural resilience and reach, but it is not about eliminating or automating hierarchies. Instead it should be about creating and supporting useful and mutable roles in order to meet the needs of a given initiative. Autonomy is always a mix of automation and labour, the labour of care for the infrastructure of humans and machines working together to generate $Surplus. And Organising is always a mix of horizontal, vertical and transversal strategies.

MANIFESTING A BLACK SWAN

Black Swan is a project researching the organisational forms at play in the artworld today. It responds to the ways in which legacy institutions have failed the artists they supposedly serve by imagining, role-playing, and building new organisational frameworks and arts infrastructures. Following Marina Vishmidt, Black Swan moves from institutional critique to infrastructural critique, to engage and intervene within the interlinking material, historical, economic, affective, and subjective conditions necessary for the art institution and its critique to exist and reproduce.[25] From past research, play, and critique, Black Swan has distilled these four affirmations, that we have presented above, as guiding mantras to accompany us in the realisation of alternative ecologies of art making:

24. For more information, see: Black Swan, "CTM 2022: Prototyping Sonic Institutions," January 30, 2022. Available at: https://www.youtube.com/watch?v=DKb9za47twU; Black Swan, "Simulating Equitable Art Worlds: DAOs through a role-played lens" (KW Institute for Contemporary Art, forthcoming).

25. Marina Vishmidt, "Between Not Everything and Not Nothing: Cuts Towards Infrastructural Critique," in Maria Hlavajova and Simon Sheikh, eds. *Former West: Art and the Contemporary After 1989* (MIT Press, 2017), 267.

☼ *Art-making is a mode of collective staking*, or in other words, mutually beneficial contributions and commitments should be explicit in art making.

☼ *The organisation is mutable, liable to change*, or collective bodies and the metaphors they are based on should allow for adaptable, task and context specific organisational structures.

☼ *The organisation is united through shared vibes*, or collectives craft and hold their own mini worlds in common.

☼ *The organisation is maintained*, or new art ecologies need to be cared for, curated, and tended to.

At the core of Black Swan's effort is the awareness that what is "wrong" with art-and-technology projects – their inability to square radical modes of inquiry and collaborative labour with the demands and expectations of corporate and military funding, institutional support, and instrumentalised science – is precisely what is most important about them. That current collective practises cannot fit the rigid, KPI oriented structures of current institutions, and instead require organisational structures that reflect their dynamic, distributed, interoperable nature. Black Swan is developing building blocks for such organisations, for the institutions of proximate horizons. These may take many forms, all at once: a solidarity-based translocal art circuit (as opposed to a "market"), a proto-institution for multi-disciplinary research and practice, a community-led micro-residency program, a self-curated knowledge repository, a mycelium network connecting different, heterogeneous hubs, and many more that cannot yet be imagined.

Black Swan does not want to replace the current artworld with an equally rigid monolithic and universalising structure. Let a hundred artworlds bloom![26] Neither does it promise utopian visions. Utopias are closed systems and only exist within clearly defined boundaries and specific contexts. Utopias are futures of the past and are not equipped to confront the challenges of the present.[27] As Donna Haraway says: "The Anthropocene marks severe discontinuities; what comes after will not be like what came before."[28] Building future artworlds requires being rooted

26. Adaption of Rhea Myers' essay "A Thousand DAOs" in this volume.

27. Fredric Jameson, *Archaeologies of the Future: The Desire Called Utopia and Other Science Fictions* (Verso, 2005).

28. Donna Haraway, *Staying With the Trouble: Making Kin in the Chthulucene* (Duke University Press, 2016), 100.

in the present and looking beyond myopic frameworks inherited from modernity, building friendships and tools that may be capable of seeding many possible, if unimaginable, artworlds from the ruins of art, critique, and age-old institutions.

Commune Killer, Qu'est-ce Que C'est?

Cassie Thornton

Every time I try to write about my work, I find myself writing about my mom. We don't talk that often and rarely about my work. Recently, I've been working with an international network of people to develop and distribute a social technology called *The Hologram* (2016–). In part it's a protocol for a meeting, where three people come together online or in person to focus for about 90 minutes on the physical, emotional and social health of a fourth, called the hologram. When I'm the hologram, our conversations always circle back to my mother. As I write about her now, I wonder if I'm actually inventing a character and a family story to explain to myself how I can hold so much angry disappointment and scepticism in one hand, while grasping for forceful optimism with the other.

When I was a child in the 90's, when we ran out of money, my mom and I would go live on the family commune. Our commune was one of a network of religious communes into which my mother's family was absorbed since she was in her teens. She had been trained to refer to these places as "centers".[1] My mother always said that she regretted how much she hated going to the centers because I seemed to love being surrounded by people making granola and meditating. I thought that she hated them because she couldn't smoke and believed that the enlightened people were secretly kicking her dog. So Instead of making communes and communal living a part of our regular life, we used them as our Emergency Resource Centers. Our *real* life took place in tiny apartments,

---

1. I am purposely using the US spelling of *Center* here to honour my family lineage in the centre of the universe: rural Midwestern US.

where we could smoke cigarettes, watch TV and not have to hide how much we liked to use our credit cards.

In my late 30s I moved to Canada with my partner. We lived with two roommates and some of us made granola. Upon her first and only visit to my new home, my mom locked herself in her room, in protest. She could barely stand to be sleeping somewhere that smelled like an Emergency Resource Center. This visit was a few months after my uncle, her brother, appeared at my house to deliver my family dowry: a tupperware box from the Emergency Resource Center where he still lives. Inside, there were many old photos of my family inside of Emergency Resource Centers. My uncle explained how my family got entangled in this network of communes and how my mother got the hell out.

My grandma had apparently found a new spirituality when my mom was a young teen, just after she divorced my abusive grandfather. Their family home became a place where young people gathered around my grandma, who would read spiritual texts and lead conversations. Imagine a 1970s tupperware party, but with soft Christian prose instead of soft plastic containers. My grandma's house became one node in a network of facilities, including larger communes, that offered followers not only a spiritual shelter but a literal shelter from the impending nuclear war prophesied by the community's two charismatic male founders, who held daily conference calls with their followers to talk about peace.

According to my uncle, my grandma's charisma attracted people. When my forty something grandma began a romance with a younger man, things went nuclear. The patriarchs used the love affair to discredit her. They also took things a step further, using their authority to blow up her family. My mother, her brothers and my grandma were all sent to live in separate Emergency Resource Centers in different cities across the US. It was traumatic.

And so, 40+ years later, when my mother locked herself in a bedroom in my house in protest against traces of communal living that she could sniff, I somehow understood. It is funny how people become politicised – I would have never guessed that my mother's hatred of authority and fierce individualism might have come from such a specific experience, where actual people with power over her destroyed her family home. Of course she hated the Emergency Resource Centers.

Now that I understand, I am grateful for my gift of anti-authoritarianism and its lineage, which have allowed me to be a part of the sacred line of COMMUNE KILLERs. *I never chose to be a COMMUNE KILLER, it just comes naturally.*

In the past decade, before I knew our family lineage, I used much of my art practice to understand why I both love and loathe collectivity. I've dedicated my life to organising new social technologies for collectively hacking away at capitalism, but am constantly dissatisfied by and scared of what happens in big groups. As an organiser and a public artist who pounds people with the idea that a better future can only emerge from new forms of hardcore sharing, cooperation, and collective action, this has always been a point of deep confusion for me.

Have I inherited both my grandma's power to create communes and my mother's desire to kill them? More broadly, how can any of us come to terms with the contradictory habits we have each inherited from having to live in the radioactive wasteland of racial capitalism?[2] *The Hologram* is a practice dedicated to helping us discover our contradictory habits and developing shared frameworks for personal and collective transformation. I see it emerging from this profound contradiction in me and maybe in all of us.

THE HOLOGRAM

The Hologram has benefitted from the intense artworld interest in care during the pandemic. But for many people I know who have lived with long term illness, disability, and/or who have been organising underground care projects for a long time, this newfound attention is annoying, or even dangerous. We know what happens to hot topics: they die young.

My disappointment with most new artworld or art academic care projects is that they often live in abstraction. Filled with ideas, theory and poetry, they lack a way to put the ideas into practice. At best, these projects help remind very privileged people to care more for themselves individually as the world burns. They use words, concepts and tools like empathy, healing, self care, rest, pleasure, and other nice human things. But most of these projects seem to frame care as an endpoint and not as a process of transformation towards building collective health and stability that will allow us as communities and societies to change.

2. Gargi Bhattacharyya, *Rethinking Racial Capitalism: Questions of Reproduction and Survival* (Rowman & Littlefield, 2018). I don't believe it is possible to discuss capitalism without race, and I am influenced by how Bhattacharyya explains that "the world made through racism shapes patterns of capitalist development."

What if care was about building communities who can address and confront the systemic abuse that has destroyed our access to nice human things? When care is disconnected from a larger collective process of the destruction and rebirth of our society, I begin to see these saccharine projects as Care-orrism.[3]

I am angry about it, but only because I want it all. I want long term integrated care practises coming from disability justice movements to be sustained and grown further. I want to see care increase in the world for all beings, from the bottom up. But I also want to sabotage the systems and large forces that keep us from the world we want to live in. I think that living with long term high quality care can lead to the health and stability that we need to confront the systems that make us sick in the first place. This is the ambition of *The Hologram*.

The Hologram is a peer-to-peer collective health practice that anyone can use to create a long term culture of care for themselves and their community. Through much experimentation and play during the pandemic, we have developed and practised a protocol for a meeting among friends that can be performed in person or online. The hologram invites three people to meet with them (the triangle) and ask them questions about their health. In the protocol, the triangle members ask questions about the hologram's physical, social and emotional health, and offer reflections and feedback. Intended to be a long term practice, the group meets regularly, as often as they decide, for as long as possible. We invite groups to make agreements to continue to meet regularly far into the future, where our imaginations are afraid to go. For months, years or decades, we invite people to continue meeting with the same three people, asking questions about the hologram and seeing the patterns of their health and life. The triangle's long term support improves over time as they learn about the hologram, without being an expert or giving advice. The project becomes viral when the hologram supports their triangle to get the support they need from three completely different people. In this way the care virus spreads, and it is also how everyone who gives care also receives it.

The goal of *The Hologram* is to create long term stability and support outside of collapsing or profiteering systems, because we want

3. Care-orrism is a term developed by me with Max Haiven. We describe care-orrism as the cynical or foolish use of "care" in ways that either cause, profit from, reproduce or do nothing to prevent a system of death and harm.

participants to see what happens to them and to us when they and we are ok. What would happen to you if you felt stable and supported? What if you weren't struggling and feeling alone in your life? What would you want next? What would you wish for? We surmise that when you become stable, you will begin to realise that in order for you to be *better-than-ok*, things have to get better for everyone. We aim to create a situation where the beneficiaries of the practice become active in organising new collective structures for our currently anti-social societies.

The current protocol[4] used in *The Hologram* is one that has been developed in the pandemic, as people all over the globe began to practice it. What we realised by practising it repeatedly with lots of people, is that the formation we use (three people focusing and asking questions of one person) has the power to help all four people understand some of the history, beliefs and patterns underneath how the hologram does things. Frequently, the triangle members who are asking the questions can see how the experience of the hologram relates to their own.[5]

For me it has been incredibly useful to understand the ways that the COMMUNE KILLER has led to working and struggling to support *The Hologram*. It also helps me see what lies underneath the work of others, as a way to find out how we can connect our creative work towards escaping our little hells, which we live in alone and together.

PUT YOUR CONTRACTS BACK IN THE MASTER'S TOOL BOX,[6] PLZ

NFTs, the blockchain and cryptocurrencies have the same effect on me as granola has on my mother – it makes me want to lock myself in a room and smoke cigarettes until I die. Technological innovation that doesn't come in tandem with transformation of our value systems and social habits will reproduce the curse of racial capitalism and produce shinier versions of the same shit, but perhaps with fun new word combos.

---

4. The protocol we are using is in constant development. Though the main aspects we are describing here have been consistent, small adjustments are always made as we learn from people who use it.

5. The roots, inspirations and formative contexts for the development of *The Hologram* and social holography are set out in my book *The Hologram: Feminist, Peer-to-Peer Health for a Post-Pandemic Future* (London: Pluto Press, 2020).

6. Audre Lorde, "The Master's Tools Will Never Dismantle the Master's House," (1984), i n *Sister Outsider: Essays and Speeches* (Berkeley, CA: Crossing Press, 2007).

So it was to my surprise that I recently warmed up to a blockchain-involved project called the *ReUnion Network*,[7] a collectively designed project for distributed long term care, initiated by Yin Aiwen. My eye was on this project for the past few years because I knew that the collective behind it shares the ambition to create long term care relationships outside of the medical system. I was doubly interested in how much dissonance I felt, which was due to the design aesthetic and the technocratic tools being used in the name of "care" including blockchain contracts and cryptocurrency. I also felt that this was an example of a project that exemplified abstract care politics, but without a care practice. I had filed this project under care-orrism.

However, when I was able to ask in-depth questions of the founder, I realised that while I disagreed with the way this project is designed, many of the desires behind this project echoed my own wishes for *The Hologram*. It was so exciting to find a distant unknown collaborator speaking such a different language.

On the *ReUnion Network* "document" website[8] they describe their work as: "A collaborative site for contract-making, including renewable long-term interpersonal agreements, generating relationship-driven crypto-currencies to incentivize people to cultivate and maintain the care relationships arising in their immediate life (as opposed to a sharing economy for short-term exchanges of care)." As in *The Hologram*, a participant asks three friends for support, and each friend is asked to make a promise. In the *ReUnion Network* project, this promise is made into a contract and placed on the blockchain. The work put into relationships is tracked using a token system, and pairs of users in relationships are encouraged to update their shared contracts regularly (and they are rewarded with tokens).

Let's imagine it. "We" sign a peer-to-peer contract to support a friend in the future. When the friend faces some sort of emergency and needs help, we can predict at least two potential scenarios. First, the friend calls us and asks if we can help them and we say "yes". In this case we can honour the contract. However, one can imagine that the contract may be only one small part of why we followed through on the promise,

7. ReUnion Network, "Commoning by PTP Care," ReUnion Network, https://www. reunionnetwork.org.

8. Aiwen Yin and Genevieve Quick, "Overview," *ReUnion Network: Commoning by PTP Care – ReUnion Network Document*, 2020, https://docs.reunionnetwork.org.

alongside other bigger motivations that may include our own desire to help, guilt, and/or habit. In the second scenario, help is requested but we cannot fulfil our side of the contract. We say "no" because we are unable or because we do not want to help. What is the value of the contract now? Does anyone want care that is unavailable either because the caregiver cannot or does not want to offer it?

We[9] can imagine that the contract has power in itself to produce an action, because we are used to signing contracts and doing what we promise. The contract is used when at least one entity does not trust that the other will do what they promised. That's why contracts in hierarchical relationships are backed by force. Force includes administrative, financial, judicial penalties as well as a threat of violence and incarceration. If there was not a threat of violence or meaningful consequences to breaching a contract, would you fulfil the contracts that felt exploitative or that you simply didn't have the capacity to fulfil? Because we sign and obey so many contracts with entities that are more powerful than us, we may begin to make the contract out to be more powerful than it is. Contracts do not make us do things, fear and desire do.

The idea of asking someone to sign a contract for care feels like a defensive move in that it comes from a distrust in the other person, or in their ability or desire to do what they say. It seems to me to be avoidant of a deeper conversation: "would you be willing to help me if I needed it?" In the world I hope we build together, I don't think that contracts are something that we should revive *better* – I think they should be abolished and replaced with something else completely: communication about fears and needs? Friendship and care relationships are the place to experiment with desire and communication, which is crypto-nite when it comes to our ability to blindly follow through with coercive contracts.

But wait, how *can* someone go from a desire for long term care and attention from friends, to a contract and tokenised incentives on a blockchain? In a recent phone call with the founder and director of the *ReUnion Network*, Yin Aiwen, I identified the wish for the formalising of non-normative/queer family that lied beneath the designs.

In the peri-pandemic world we now inhabit, with no stability in sight, the *ReUnion Network* correctly surmises that most friends cannot promise long term attention or care. In contrast, Yin observes how marriage and family ties are perceived as stronger and longer lasting because they

9. "We" in this paragraph refers to the feral/underclass, the working class and the middle class.

are a commonly recognised social form that we are taught to want, and they are institutionally backed by the state through various bureaucratic, financial and social forms of domination (also, hello patriarchy and puritanical Christianity!). Though many friendships can be more intimate, and of higher quality than many marriages or family relationships, often the more formal relationships are prioritised and relied upon for care anyway. The friendship relation can be seen as temporary or even disposable in comparison.

What became clear to me was that the decision to use a contract between friends is meant to create reliable relationships outside of family and marriage that allow for stability in an unstable world. In search of ways to value and rely on non-normative relationships that are neither valuable nor visible to the state (what we might call queer family), *ReUnion Network* decided to write contracts to track, hold and protect promises between friends on the blockchain. I don't think this logic is effective, because the contract is not and never was the ideal social technology for the creation of trust or long term sustainability.

Imagine this: We invite someone to care for us. They say they can't. Instead of seeing this as a breach of contract, we react with curiosity and support. What if every breach of contract expressed a need? What if a violation of a contract was the beginning, not the end?

IS THIS THE BEGINNING OR THE END?

In *The Hologram*, we rely on the desire for collective liberation, friendship and curiosity to create commitment between people. If someone says that they cannot or will not give the support we ask for, this is the most important communication we can receive. The honest expression of a boundary, or to say "no" to a request can be the most precious gift. But we can't always be so clear. Often our desire to be needed, to be helpful or show up for friends overpowers us, and we make pledges we can't keep. But more broadly, why would you want care from someone who was contractually obligated to provide it? And the danger of the contract is that it doesn't guarantee that the caregiver is, themselves, cared for.

This is why basing care on contracts doesn't make sense in our framework. Consider that most of the people doing care work in our economy are already contractually obligated to do so as employees of some institution that exploits or alienates them. The principle of *The Hologram* is that each person receiving care is called to make sure those who care for them in turn have care.

This has become especially clear through many workshops we have been running for waged care workers using *The Hologram*. People who work as professional or full time carers find it especially hard to organise their own care, and often suffer immensely from a sense of duty and self-sacrifice. This makes sense, in a way, because organising your own care is very challenging work, especially when you feel undervalued or are not acclimated to receiving care yourself. But in contrast, what we have learned through practising *The Hologram* is that when most people are asked by a friend to give care, using *The Hologram*'s formal structure, they are honoured to do it and are very faithful to the process. Ironically, it is the task of asking for help from others that seems more heroic to most participants in *The Hologram*. In part this is because receiving care in our competitive, individualist society often implies being broken or weak. Asking for help makes most of us feel like a burden and is harder to do the more inequitable our society is.

That's why every person who receives care in this project becomes invested in helping their three caregivers find equally good care from three other people. A contract can't help us here, no matter how smart.

SECURITY GUARD

Sometimes, in workshops, a courageous sceptic raises their hand and comments that *The Hologram* feels like a cult. I think this response stems partly from the reality that most adults have not experienced what it is like to be a part of a group outside of the formal and often exploitative or oppressive structures of work, education or family. The feeling of joy and solidarity expressed by hologrammers can only be understood as a kind of fanaticism. This impression could also arise because of the excitement and evangelism of *The Hologram* participants. Many who use the practice quickly realise that the only way for them to experience the maximum benefits of the project is if they spread it like a virus as a way to help change the culture of health and care for many different types of people. Our health as individuals is bound up in the health of one another. Things get kind of meta, and so it's not surprising newcomers are often unnerved by our zeal.

What I wish I could say, to reassure them, is: *don't worry, you can't have a cult started by a commune killer.*

As I mentioned, in my personal myth making, I have come to see myself as inheriting both my grandma's passion for bringing people together in new, experimental, radical communities and also my mother's visceral allergy to anything that smells of granola. I think this impossible contradiction keeps me and the project I work on honest. I find myself, in *The Hologram* planning meetings, often as both the most earnest and loyal hard-worker, excited about being part of such an amazing group of visionaries; and also an inconsolable toddler screaming "no" for reasons I can't begin to understand for months.

As the initiator of the project and one of the central organisers and facilitators, I see my job as merging my two inheritances to become a kind of cosmic security guard, who protects the project as it grows. Sometimes I have to protect it from itself. Most of what I do is say "no." I say no to proposals to join the blockchain. I say no to some offers of funding from untrustworthy partners. I say no to making things more complicated than they need to be, and also to making things too simple. I say no to doing exhibitions and fancy institutions that would take us away from our real work of supporting hardcore transformation for people who need it. I say no to a competitive capitalist spirit and its stupid twin: flakey new age bullshit. I say no to exploitation. I say no to too much work. I can't help myself – it was from this "no" that the "yes" of the project sprouted. I feel the "no" is creative in its resistance.

Sometimes I have said no to the wrong type of collectivity, and held onto my benevolent dictatorship instead. Sometimes I fear that I have made myself queen of something that was meant to be non-hierarchical, simply by saying no. Sometimes I wonder if I will be able to follow through on my promise to decapitate the project in 2023 and turn it over to collective governance. Sometimes I fear that I am replicating the commune that my mom fled and that I want to flee, too, and smoke cigarettes until I die.

Translocal Belonging and Cultural Cooperation after the Blockchain – A Citizen Sci-fi

Ruth Catlow

WHO AND WHERE ARE MY PEOPLE?

Ursula Le Guin, the virtuoso of sci-fi politics of place, tells us that the most important question a person can ask now is, "Who are my people?"[1] But how should we answer this question? We can reflect personally and ask ourselves which people we can trust to love us absolutely and hold us accountable for loving ourselves[2] or we can use a social lens and ask with whom and where we belong. Nation-states assign identity by place of birth, but someone's nationality says very little about who they are – about their values or ways of life. Rather a person's passport can only tell you something about their status in a pecking order of nationalities, and the constraints they face moving around the world. The writer, Taiye

---

1. "Ursula K. Le Guin: Panel Discussion with Donna Haraway and James Clifford," filmed August 5, 2014, AURA Vimeo. Accessed November 29, 2021, https://vimeo.com/98270808.
2. adrienne maree brown, "sabbatical your life (workshop report back from AMC2012)," adrienne maree brown's blog, July 10, 2012, https://adriennemareebrown.net/2012/07/10/sabbatical-your-life-workshop-report-back-from-amc2012.

Selasi, who moved between three continents growing up and whose grandparents hail from four different, distant countries, says, "Don't ask me where I am from, ask me where I am local". To answer the question, she proposes we look at our rituals, our relationships, and the restrictions that we face. When we find people that share these things with us, we have found where, and with whom we are local. We have found "our people".

"Translocality" is a term intended to change the way we think about the places, people and cultures that we belong to[3] as a result of globalisation, migration and hyperconnectivity.[4] It specifically describes the fact that most of us now feel that we belong to many communities in multiple places at once. And that these place-based communities make conflicting demands on us, shaping our identities in new ways.

Intensifying translocal effects mean that people and their "localities" are layered in multiple interconnected territories across physical and online realms. And so the political complexity associated with the question of where we come from is becoming more apparent to us all, along with questions about territory, who rules us, and by which systems of governance.[5]

The constraints that many people experience because of the passports they carry, for example, have terrible consequences for whole populations and have come to feel increasingly arbitrary, violent and unjust.[6] As a result of the havoc wreaked on social and natural ecosystems, whether by despots, distant states or business operating under free market imperialism,[7]

---

3. Arising from the work of ethnographer Arjun Appadurai. See: Urmila Mohan and Jessica Hughes, "Translocality as Connections that Disrupt," *The Jugaard Project*, 2020, https://www. thejugaadproject.pub/home/translocality-as-connections.

4. Statistics produced by states and companies worldwide tell us that in recent years the increase in the global number of international migrants has continued to outpace the growth of the world's population. The number of international migrants globally reached an estimated 272 million in 2019, an increase of 51 million since 2010. Currently, international migrants comprise 3.5 per cent of the global population, compared to 2.8 per cent in the year 2000. "The number of international migrants reaches 272 million, continuing an upward trend in all world regions," United Nations, September 17, 2019. Accessed May 21, 2021, https://www.un.org/development/desa/en/news/population/international-migrant-stock-2019.html. Internet users are growing by an average of more than one million new users every day and half are accessing the internet by mobile phone. See for example: "Digital 2019 Global Internet Use Accelerates," January 2019, We Are Social. Accessed May 21, 2021, https://wearesocial.com/blog/2019/01/digital-2019-global-internet-use-accelerates.

wealth inequalities are increasing,[8] and growing numbers of refugees are separated from their kinfolk, their lives and cultures decimated, and basic needs and rights denied.[9]

HOW TO DISTRIBUTE AGENCY IN THE WORLD WIDE WEB OF COOPERATION CRISES?

Those of us with access to the Web can now[10] connect with peers to create our own, if fragile and with varying degrees of freedom, social realities and senses of belonging, seemingly detached from the limitations of physical bodies and place. At the same time, now that no place on earth is untouched by computational cultures, we encounter evidence in the form of visual and numeric data gathered from the deepest ocean beds to the outer atmosphere[11] confirming impending mass species extinction and climate collapse as a result of growth capitalism which is also racial

---

5. Pomponius the 2nd century Roman theorist of law, claimed that territory, "the sum of lands within the boundaries of a community" was so named "because the magistrate of a place has the right of terrifying [terrandi], that is, exercising jurisdiction, within its boundaries". Whosoever in human history has ruled a territory, has commanded standing armies to menace enemies at its borders and internal law enforcement to coerce its inhabitants. Theo Deutinger, *Handbook of Tyranny* (Lars Müller, 2018).

6. In her 2020 book *Glitch Feminism: A Manifesto*, Legacy Russel identifies violent patriarchal supremacy at work in conjoined digital and physical realms: "Where we see the limitation of a body's 'right to range,' be it at an individual or state level, we see domination."

7. See "Decentralisation Autonomy and Organisation" by Jaya Klara Brekke in this volume.

8. Sam Phan, "Wealth gap widening for more than 70% of global population, researchers find," *The Guardian*, January 22, 2020, https://www.theguardian.com/global-development/2020/jan/22/wealth-gap-widening-for-more-than-70-per-cent-of-global-population-researchers-find.

9. An alternative blockchain-inspired political imaginary is explored in the speculative fiction *History of Political Operating Systems – Interview with Dr. L. Godord* by Elli Kuru. Here a world expert in "the history of political operating systems, specifically systems predating the blockchain" discusses the barbarities of our contemporary system of international citizenship, from the perspective of a fictional future in which all people are free to choose from a market of governance portfolios, in Ruth Catlow et al., eds., *Artists Re:thinking the Blockchain* (Torque Editions, 2017).

10. 60% of the global human population now have access to the Web. See for example: https://wearesocial.com/au/blog/2021/04/60-percent-of-the-worlds-population-is-now-online.

11. Jennifer Gabrys, *Program Earth: Environmental Sensing Technology and the Making of a Computational Planet* (Minnesota Press, 2016).

capitalism.[12] Scientific consensus shows how all our crises are connected by the intense challenges of translocal more-than-human governance and coordination.[13] We see, always in the rear-view mirror, the ongoing catastrophic failure to support human and more-than-human thriving and an uneven distribution of the resulting freedoms and miseries.

The legacy infrastructures of transnational legal, economic and border regimes (including the Web) that were built to solidify the power of extractive state and corporate capitalism have turned out to be poorly equipped to support adaptation of local and global governance or to empower peers to organise in their own non-statist and more-than-human interests. The Web provides decentralised communication tools that make it possible for peers to connect across distance, to observe and analyse the challenges faced by global communities. Still, coordinated action by new kinds of citizens are what is needed to turn this potential into power of a different kind – the ability to act together.

DAOS FOR COORDINATED ACTION

The Web provides a standard protocol for sharing messages, moods, and plans between people otherwise separated by geography and the currencies and national jurisdictions where they are registered. Decentralised Autonomous Organisations or DAOs remove the state boundary for organisers. DAOs are member-based organisations governing resources (assets and services)[14] across national borders, according to rules set by members regardless of the countries where they are registered.[15] Their software programmes, running simultaneously on computers around the

12. Capital accumulates by producing and extracting value from relations of severe inequality – by assigning different social and economic value to people according to differences of racial identity.

13. See: Hans-Otto Pörtner et al., (eds.), *IPCC, 2022: Climate Change 2022: Impacts, Adaptation, and Vulnerability*, accessed February 28, 2022, https://www.ipcc.ch/report/ar6/wg2; Anna L. Tsing et al., *Feral Atlas – The More-Than-Human Anthropocene*, accessed 29 November, 2021, https://feralatlas.org.

14. At time of writing these belongings might be cryptocurrency or Non Fungible Tokens (NFTs). Members may also promise to perform services or take actions. Decisions about distribution are made by voting members, or when pre-agreed external conditions have been met. For instance there could be a condition set within a DAO to distribute an increasing percentage of its funds, at set intervals, to environmental research, in direct proportion to temperature increases at the poles.

world, can mint their own currency, distribute rule-based tokens, and so, to some degree, variously replace or reproduce, the power of nation-based legal and financial authorities with formal rules enforced by software.[16] Through updatable smart contracts and by creating a permanent public ledger of decisions and actions, open source DAOs on permissionless blockchains have the *potential* to democratise both money and governance through increased accountability and greater access to societal design processes. Cryptocurrencies' status as money is still hotly debated. They are criticised as Ponzi schemes[17] whose sole purpose is to support capital appreciation for early adopters and whose volatility makes them unusable as actual cash. But regardless of whether this is actual money, it's hard to ignore the worrying new concentrations of wealth (though there has been some distribution too) on the one hand and the high levels of social cooperation that they have inspired and enabled.

In recent years, critical artworld experiments with blockchain-based DAOs have explored what this addition of cross-border money and governance to the Web's capacities might offer to social practice. Just as artists of the early Web built new art contexts from networked images, texts, sound, data and softwares, they are now developing new tools and infrastructure for resourcing and organising PTP action. This is a critical moment in the construction of the Web3 worlds we want. Given the historic recentralisation of power and control and the accumulation of wealth by a very few that occurred on the Internet with the consolidation of for-profit Web2 platforms and services, the lesson for artists is to beware immediate recuperation and to find ways of resisting or slowing it. Crucial to this

15. This is not to say that members' actions are not subject to the "laws of the land" where they reside and operate, however the laws concerning the status of assets and actions over blockchains are far from solidified as demonstrated by the clear inability of regulatory institutions to sanction their illicit use for a variety of scales of scams and frauds. *The DAO Model Law* framework, described in the introduction to this book, sets out to address this.
16. Vitalik Buterin and Glen Weyl, "Liberation Through Radical Decentralization," Medium, May 21, 2018. Accessed November 29, 2021, https://medium.com/@VitalikButerin/liberation-through-radical-decentralization-22fc4bedc2ac.
17. "A Ponzi scheme is a type of fraud whereby crooks steal money from investors and mask the theft by funnelling returns to clients from funds contributed by newer investors." Kevin Stankiewicz," 'Black Swan' author calls bitcoin a 'gimmick' and a 'game,'" *CNBC*, April 23, 2021. Accessed January 10, 2022, https://www.cnbc.com/2021/04/23/bitcoin-a-gimmick-and-resembles-a-ponzi-scheme-black-swan-author-.html.

project is an acknowledgement of the multiple layers of devastating losses that are the result of colonial extractivist petrocapitalism upon which this webbed mechanosphere is built: the mass dispossession, destruction and loss of human lives, the loss of species biodiversity and habitats and the impoverishment of futurity that is its aftermath.

Like blockchains, DAOs may be used to advance a spectrum of personal and political, wealth-pooling and distributive agendas. Therefore, if DAOs are to realise any of their potential as a vehicle for progressive social change it is essential that a greater variety of people can bring their cultural heritages, their demands for justice and reparation, to develop a shared literacy around what a DAO might do for them and their communities; to build and "iterate on the new functionality that emerges."[18]

WORLDING THE CULTURAL COMMONS FROM THE WEB TO THE BLOCKCHAIN

Artists have been hacking power flows in the Internet since the early 1990s. Taking the then-new affordances of the Web to create, critique, distribute and invite global participation in digital media. Self-instituting artistic communities like Rhizome (US) and Furtherfield (UK)[19] recognised that social relations themselves were the revolutionary artistic medium of the Web. Some of these artist communities shared a sense of adventure about building the art contexts that they wanted to inhabit together. Art activist collectives like Electronic Disturbance Theatre, irational and Piratbyrån, The Yes Men and the Old Boys Network performed culture jams and infrastructural hacks that critiqued and undermined imperialist and patriarchal domination. Others created the tools and the modes they needed, to enable the conversations and collaborations that they sought. They created platforms like Upstage, for free and open source feminist cyberformance and Panoplie.org for art exchange and networked performance. These artist collectives, PTP activists and technologists, developed the concept of the digital commons[20] – immaterial resources collectively owned, managed and controlled, beyond states and markets. These initiatives are proto-artworld-DAOs. They provide a zone of political action

18. "My first impressions of web3," *Moxie*, January 7, 2022. Accessed January 10, 2022, https://moxie.org/2022/01/07/web3-first-impressions.html.

19. I cofounded Furtherfield with Marc Garrett in 1996.

20. Shusha Niederberger, Cornelia Sollfrank, and Felix Stalder, eds., *Aesthetics of the Commons* (Diaphanes, 2021).

beyond wage struggle and generate images of intense social cooperation. Silvia Federici notes that through the concept of the commons, "the history of the class struggle can be rewritten so that the indigenous peoples' resistance to colonial expropriation... can be described as a complement to struggles of anti-intellectual-property programmers in the free software movement."[21]

In the early days of the Web, these artists worked alongside engineers of free and open source digital infrastructures being built according to the rhetoric of social solidarity through sharing and cooperation rather than enclosure and competition.[22] Software was accompanied by manifestos for a global civil society that might move beyond the logic of economic growth[23] so harmful to our environments.[24] However, their invisible financial flows served to hide the mechanisms of exclusion endemic in both the art and tech worlds.

HOW TO REPAIR OUR RELATIONSHIP TO PLACE? THE PARADOX OF UNIVERSAL TECHNOLOGIES THAT DISCONNECT US FROM LAND AND TIME

Translocality presents us with a paradox. The principle of universal access to digital networks behind Tim Berners-Lee's ongoing vision of a Web for "everyone" – made to connect people to each other, increase opportunity, "give marginalised groups a voice, and make our daily lives easier"[25] – when combined with global capitalism might also serve to disconnect a multitude of peoples from their customs and values of the lands that they inhabit, impoverishing them and future generations. Now, privately

21. Silvia Federici, *Re-enchanting the World: Feminism and the Politics of the Commons* (PM Press/Kairos, 2018).

22. See: Yochai Benkler, *The Wealth of Networks* (Yale University Press, 2006); Ruth Catlow and Marc Garrett, "DIWO: Do It With Others – No Ecology without Social Ecology," in *Remediating the Social*, ed. Simon Biggs (University of Edinburgh, 2012).

23. "Autistici Manifesto 2002," *Autistici*. Accessed January 10, 2021, https://www.autistici.org/who/manifesto.

24. Tim Jackson, *Prosperity without Growth – The transition to a sustainable economy* (Earthscan, 2009).

25. Alex Hern, "Tim Berners-Lee on 30 years of the world wide web," *The Guardian*, March 12, 2019. Accessed November 29, 2021, https://www.theguardian.com/technology/2019/mar/12/tim-berners-lee-on-30-years-of-the-web-if-we-dream-a-little-we-can-get-the-web-we-want.

owned platforms provide crucial social utilities that are also either state surveillance machines, or they are fueled by venture capital and business models designed to harness psychologies of addiction,[26] weaponise the user data they harvest, and sell targeted advertising with pinpoint accuracy. By centralising power and resources on the web, platforms uniformly squeeze vast swathes of people into an accelerated and alienated life, and in doing so impose built physical infrastructures on complex living environments, who never chose it and are unable to opt out.

Furtherfield's Marc Garrett summed up the situation in 2013 as follows: "The patriarch, neoliberalism, de-regulated market systems, corporate corruption and bad government; each implement the circumstances where we, everyday people, are only useful as material to be colonised... Hacking around and through this impasse is essential if we are to maintain a sense of human integrity and control over our own social contexts and ultimately to survive as a species."[27]

Steve Wanta Jampijinpa Patrick, Australian Aboriginal elder of the Warlpiri people and multimedia artist,[28] reminds us of the cultural technologies that transmitted the heritage of his people down the generations in an unbroken chain for over forty thousand years before digital technologies were built. These technologies take the form of stories shared through practices like hunting (which involves building an intimate knowledge of and relationship with the prey), body painting, and jukurrpa (or dreaming). Law, ceremony, and the history of their society are informed by the doings of their multispecies ancestors, which are mapped into the land, and the stars. These things make up the cultural language of the Warlpiri. "If you don't speak your language, if you don't know your culture, and the songlines of the animals in your country, how can you express yourself or

26. This was the topic of the exhibition *We Are All Addicts Now* at Furtherfield Gallery, London, September 16 – November 12, 2021, https://www.furtherfield.org/are-we-all-addicts-now. See also: Vanessa Bartlett, Katriona Beales and Henrietta Bowden-Jones, *Are We All Addicts Now?* (Liverpool University Press, 2018).

27. Marc Garrett, "Furtherfield and Contemporary Art Culture – Where We Are Now," *Furtherfield*, November 25, 2013, https://www.furtherfield.org/furtherfield-and-contemporary-art-culture-where-we-are-now.

28. Steve Wanta Jampijinpa Patrick spoke at a workshop as part of a programme of events surrounding the *Networking the Unseen* exhibition curated by Gretta Louw at Furtherfield Gallery, London, 2016, https://www.furtherfield.org/networking-the-unseen-2.

where you're from?" He warns that by interrupting our relationship with the land and our ancient cosmologies 21st century digital technologies prevent us from knowing who we are.

Since the creation of The DAO[29] in 2016 the properties of DAO technologies can and have been used by those with technical know-how and/or financial resources to create what are, in effect, unregulated shell companies, the apex vehicles of extractive capitalism, their technical complexity outpacing the law in an accelerationist nightmare. However, the shared governance technologies of DAOs also support the lateral member-to-member relationships upon which cooperatives are based and offer unique tool-kits for making common cause across national borders.[30] Smart contracts could enforce place-based community wealth building approaches like the Preston Model[31] to ensure that any investment helps local areas to thrive, with people and their local institutions working together on an agenda of shared benefit. Since mid-2021 the legal and technical ecologies of DAOs have developed sufficiently to allow non-experts to start to build and test their potential, and for all the talk of transparency and accountability to translate into something more tangible and real.[32]

DAOs might be a technical solution to the question about how to produce and operate a coordination infrastructure that enables people across the planet to organise in their own interests. What is still to be determined is how to account for the relationship these might have to each other and the lands and ecosystems they inhabit, and how to build resistance to exploitation, and extraction by distant forces.

Early artworld experiments with the concepts and capacities of DAO technologies (freed from the need to either maximise shareholder value or offer utility beyond their own artistic objectives) revealed multiple possibilities. The self-tokenised artist brand *Jonas Lund Tokens* invited artworld players to become shareholders and to jointly care for his career

29. "The DAO (organization)," *Wikipedia*, https://en.wikipedia.org/wiki/The_DAO_ (organization).

30. Ola Kohut, "When Co-ops Meet DAOs: An Interview with Nathan Schneider," Medium, October 4, 2019, https://medium.com/nebula-magazine/when-co-ops-meet-daos-an-interview-with-nathan-schneider-c2fc40194e6e.

31. "What is the Preston Model?", Preston City Council website, https://www.preston.gov.uk/article/1339/What-is-Preston-Model.

32. See the discussion of the COALA DAO Model Law and DAO tooling in the introduction to this volume.

in an ongoing experiment with the relationship between art, markets, money, and history.[33] Furtherfield set out to extend its *Do It With Others (DIWO)* campaign to build translocal collaboration by inscribing solidarity into cooperative systems, to creating a "commons for arts in the network age".[34] *Plantoids* and *Terra0*, both artworks and DAOs, explored the generative or autopoetic potentials of a decentralised auto-capitalised medium. Ongoing experiments by the artist teams behind *Plantoids* and *Terra0* develop the conjoined aspects of legal, technical, aesthetic, and governance systems within DAOs, to explore the wellbeing of natural systems within, and beyond, their financialised roots and capacities. Since *Plantoids'* inception, its creator Primavera Di Filippi of Okhaos, has gone on to work on a protocol for Environmental Impact NFTs that incentivise investment in environmentally beneficial ventures.

However, the inescapable tendency towards a managerial approach, privileging quantification and commodification of natural resources over cultures of connection and relationship troubles all of this work. Philosopher and eco-activist James Corbett[35] identified an important difference between "managing" and "joining-with" the life of the land. His *The Saguaro-Juniper Covenant: A Bill of Rights for the Land*[36] from 1991 is an early contribution to settler thought on the rights of nature. In it he describes his principles for recultivating a collective responsibility for lands, stating that "fully accountable governance – stewardship – is the distinctively human way of bonding into one society with all who share in the land's life, which is the foundation for instituting a biocentric ethic among humankind." And it is possible to imagine these principles mapped into a DAO and offered as an open source, editable template for other lands. But Corbett's argument that only a 'post-civilised' humanity can thrive, because life must be joined with, not managed or owned, and because human beings can't know enough to manage life on earth alone, remains persuasive.

33. See "Lazy As A Fox by Jonas Lund Token" in this volume.

34. Furtherfield first asked this question as part of their 2015 programme *Art Data Money* that looked at the role of big data and blockchains in networked art practice. Accessed November 29, 2021, https://www.furtherfield.org/artdatamoney.

35. American philosopher, human rights activist and a co-founder of the Sanctuary movement.

36. "The Saguaro-Juniper Covenant," http://www.saguaro-juniper.com/covenant/covenant.html.

SCHISMOGENESIS – WHO OUR PEOPLE ARE
NOT AND WHY THEY MUST BE STOPPED!

In the translocal network cultures of the 21st century our attachments and convictions are tested in the wild fires of social media, and more and more we see groups define themselves by their differences (of identity and opinion), ripping individuals apart in the process. Schismogenesis was a term coined by Gregory Bateson to describe the role that aversion and antipathy play in the formation and entrenchment of adjacent but distinct cultures.[37] Schismogenesis is a fine concept to describe the artworld ruptures or "wars", to quote Tina Rivers Ryan, that have flared in the last few years, most intensely around the carbon emissions of some blockchains,[38] but spreading quickly to include absolutist denunciations of the "reprehensible" value systems of NFT market places.[39] Medium articles, smart memes, and tactical artworks that deride cryptoart and NFTs rise up on waves of derisory and shaming subtweets. Many professional intellectuals from outwith cryptocultures have taken on the mantle of ethical gatekeepers to proclaim on the venality of all things blockchain, crypto, DAOs and NFT, with high levels of moral certainty.

As I have stated earlier, it is of paramount importance that there is diverse engagement with both the underpinnings and development of the crypto art and DAO scene, but the quality and depth of engagement is paramount. To give one example, Geraldine Juarez brings to bear her lived experience and practices of refusal and resistance, honed in battles against past network oppressors, to the blockchain space. Juarez's 2021 essay "Ghostchain"[40] offers a sharp analysis and gives voice to many of the legitimate shared concerns of the critical communities of media art practice that grew up with the Web. She makes a punchy call for blockchains

37. David Graeber and David Wengrow, *The Dawn of Everything: A New History of Humanity* (Allen Lane, 2021).

38. By attaching poorly substantiated carbon emission calculations to individual cryptoartworks the http://cryptoart.wtf/ project singled out artists for public shaming and created an atmosphere that led to the doxxing of and death-threats towards NFT artists.

39. Everest Pipkin, "HERE IS THE ARTICLE YOU CAN SEND TO PEOPLE WHEN THEY SAY 'BUT THE ENVIRONMENTAL ISSUES WITH CRYPTOART WILL BE SOLVED SOON, RIGHT?'" https://everestpipkin.medium.com/but-the-environmental-issues-with-cryptoart-1128ef72e6a3.

40. Geraldine Juárez, "The Ghostchain. (Or taking things for what they are)," *Paletten*, no. 325, 2021. Accessed December 21, 2021, https://paletten.net/artiklar/the-ghostchain.

to be "stopped" on the grounds that the practice of turning things into assets is about determining who owns the future (and making decisions about what this will mean for others). She argues that finance is reliant on narratives "about the steps that will transform the present into a specific financial future" and that without artists' adoption of NFTs, cryptoeconomies would have no story on which to build their assets because: "If we, artists, don't take NFTs for the assets they are, then who?" She endows artists with the power to turn NFTs into a social, political, and economic liability: "If assets are just made up narratives about the future, perhaps we can create other stories where the value of the future is brought into the present with the intention of decapitalising these chains and make it socially and politically expensive to keep adding blocks in them, until blockchain infrastructures eventually turn into abandoned ghostchains." I like this idea. It's proactive. It's great sci-fi.

Juarez is not perhaps performing a full schismogenesis here, her ideas are too creative for that, but it does still speak to a trend of critical media artists and theorists to opt for polemics that discourage those artists and activists who might otherwise contribute to shaping and *building* more progressive or socially transformative cultures in this space. It's also worth noting that these efforts make not a jot of difference to the fortunes of those who are in it for the cash! In Web3 the challenge is to convert polemic into possible routes for empowering collective action.

But let's make use of the talismanic fantasy of artistic "autonomy" (the idea that a pure kind of artistic practice untainted by capitalism is out there somewhere)[41] and mix it with the artistic drive for social organising and rule-testing to discover the real and raw potentials and hazards of decentralised PTP governance design.

Cultures forged by schismogenesis in the platforms of Web2 might lead to better problem definition. For instance tactical media art practices rooted in the institutional and infrastructural critiques of the 1990s and noughties were used in the *cryptoart.wft* project to make visible the energy usage and carbon emissions of Ethereum, the primary blockchain for smart contracts that make up DAOs and NFTs. This led to a series of

---

41. This fantasy impinged very unevenly across generations of artists as neoliberal austerity policies really began to bite in the UK after 2009 and there was no longer any social surplus for upstart artists to draw down – no welfare support, inflated housing costs, and squatting outlawed, massive student debt etc. It makes art more susceptible than ever to cooption and extraction, and artists more vulnerable to imprisonment in gilded cages by global elites.

public brawls to try and settle the question of whether an artist that cares about climate change should mint an NFT. And this has ultimately forced a deep communal effort to weigh up the ethical pros and cons of a new planetary scale coordination infrastructure that consumes huge quantities of energy. Following Joana Moll's important work on the carbon impacts of techno-capitalism in the artworld and beyond, artists, developers and researchers such as Sterling Crispin and Kyle McDonald have researched and described the carbon footprints of the various layers of different parts of blockchain networks in comparison with other global industries.[42] In conversation with cultural producers they have offered bottom-up ways to think about the problem. The question of how individual creators of emerging technical infrastructures and cultures should weigh the public good of DAOs (such as increased global access to governance design) against harm (increased energy use) is not a simple one. We must ask ourselves what will the consequences be of leaving blockchain technologies to be developed only by those who prioritise the accumulation of personal wealth and power? How might an ethics of refusal blind us to, or preclude, alternative developments?

ACTIVATING RADICAL IMAGINATION
FOR TRANSLOCAL COORDINATION

Going forward, how schismogenetic effects continue to emerge as our networked communities of practice overlap and inform each other will be a key question to grapple with. While misgivings about libertarian and accelerationist affordances are understandable, artistic engagement with blockchain technologies is important because their financial and governance tools are powerful and support a renewed approach to ownership and control. At the time of writing they currently secure $1.7 trillion worth of cryptocurrency,[43] they cannot be unthought, or unbuilt quickly and therefore culture will be shaped by those who engage with it. Or as Laura Lotti puts it: "Blockchain may redefine the Web, it's up to us to make sure it's done well."[44]

---

42. Sterling Crispin, "NFTs and Crypto Art: The Sky is not Falling," http://sterlingcrispin. blogspot.com/2021/02/crypto-art-sky-is-not-falling.html. See also: "Ethereum Energy Numbers are in! Moral calculations and Web3 critiques with Kyle McDonald," *Interdependence Podcast*, January 11, 2022, https://interdependence.fm/episodes/ethereum-energy-numbers-are-in-moral-calculations-and-web-3-critiques-with-kyle-mcdonald.

43. As listed at CoinMarketCap on February 6, 2022, https://coinmarketcap.com.

All participants will need to "choose what governance patterns, along with their rights, responsibilities, and remembrances, to reinforce" and to remember that we make them not just for ourselves but "for those who come after us."[45] Together we will decide about the role each of us has to play, we will aspire to expand our perceptions of the range of influence and responsibilities that we each have, and what this will mean for our relationship with each other in the pursuit of our shared planetary-scale (ad)venture.

Today this means cultivating our awareness of and responsibility for our participation in systems of financialisation, labour regimes and their alternatives. Artists' engagement with emerging financial infrastructures and the cultures they play host to do important work to lay these systems bare. By creating artworks such as *Life Forms* and *OFF* as cooperation games for "collectors" for instance, the artist and blockchain developer Sarah Friend presents a still too rare example of artistry that incorporates financial dynamics as part of the relational aesthetics of the cryptoart space.[46] In doing so she destabilises the boundary between artist, audience, and collector and opens a window on the experience of art ownership itself – as a practice of control, speculation, social play, stewardship, and as an exercise of power.

By mobilising the imaginations of communities of different localities (remembering Selasi's formula for the local), artists are working with the communities that they are part of to create alternative visions and models of money for coordinated non-competitive stewardship of public wellbeing across continents. For example, in 2018/19 the *Artists' Renegade Bank* created bank notes as artworks celebrating and funding the work of leading local community activists, and abolishing large amounts of local, high interest debt. They showed how monetary and banking systems extract

44. Laura Lotti, "Blockchain may redefine the Web – it's up to us to make sure it's done well," *Open Democracy*, December 13, 2021. Accessed December 21, 2021, https://www.opendemocracy.net/en/digitaliberties/blockchain-may-redefine-the-web-its-up-to-us-to-make-sure-its-done-well.

45. Kei Kreutler, "Holding in Common," *Gnosis Guild*, December 28, 2021. Accessed December 30, 2021, https://gnosisguild.mirror.xyz/l3pGN7TOUgPkzeurDlllIaAocaVqQuZkN98-BLAhKRc.

46. Sara Truuvert, "Making Nfts That Don't Work (On Purpose) With Sarah Friend," *Polyfield Magazine*, December 15, 2021. Accessed December 21, 2021, https://artthescience.com/magazine/2021/12/15/features-making-nfts-that-dont-work-on-purpose-with-sarah-friend.

value from people on the ground to enrich remote shadowy entities. At the same time they fought for economic justice in their area.[47]

By literalising the double status of art as a social and financial currency, *Bank Job* experimented with the idea of art as money, and as a temporary local currency. The value of this currency was built on the trust and mutual respect that existed between members of a specific community in Walthamstow, North London. People bought the art notes because they knew and cared about the people depicted on them, and wanted to further the financial solidarity work they did in their locality. It's useful here to draw parallels between *Bank Job* and another activist currency project, this time using cryptocurrency, *Circles UBI*.[48]

Members of the *Circles UBI* project are participating in a translocal coordination experiment. They each create value in the system by providing products and services within their own spheres of trust. The system uses the blockchain's ability to track and therefore build trust between expanding spheres of users (wherever they are), then its inflationary currency design incentivises members to spend and redeem their tokens "for things of value, instead of sitting on them". In this way it sets out to create a sustainable, community currency and, in the longer term, a universal basic income for its members. Both *Bank Job* and *Circles UBI* experiment with living communities to explore how something like money might be reconceived and shaped to support financial solidarity – locally and translocally.

In 2019 Stacco Troncoso and Ann Marie Utratel stepped up to the mic with DisCOs (Distributed Cooperative Organisations), a PTP commons, creating a cooperative and feminist economic alternative to the cryptic, individualistic and techno-deterministic "bro" cultures of early DAOs. *The DisCO Manifesto* (2019)[49] was the first in their series of spirited and relatable papers that set out their DAO-inspired mission to track and fairly remunerate value produced by real human members of their radical translation agency, "fulfilling a more generous idea of what globalisation could be" beyond "the wholesale character-stripping and homogenisation of cultures".[50] Their framework and governance supports: commons oriented

47. Bank Job is a community driven project led by film-maker and artist Dan Edelstyn and Hilary Powell: https://bankjob.pictures.

48. Circles UBI, accessed December 27, 2021, https://joincircles.net.

49. See "All Your DAOs Are Belong to Us: The DisCO CAT Speaks" in this volume.

50. *The Guerilla Translation Manifesto*, accessed November 29, 2021, https://www.guerrillatranslation.org/the-guerrilla-translation-manifesto.

pro-bono work; ethical market livelihood work; and care and reproductive work. Built on open value cooperativist principles,[51] it sets out to support a transition toward a global commons, prioritising care and the messy, vital and tender human lives and relationships which are so rarely part of discussions about DAOs, and so vital to their formation.

WHO ARE OUR PEOPLE, HOW CAN WE KNOW OUR PLACE, AND WHERE ARE WE LOCAL?

We have explored how the digital networks of the Web and DAOs on the blockchain complicate our attempts to answer the question of "Who are my people?" This is not only because of what they can do, but also because of the obstacles they present to participation, and the damaging disconnection they can engender between people and their places, in community or in communion with the land. DAOs may technically allow their human members to manage the things they own together, more efficiently, with more autonomy, with new modes of accountability and transparency, across national borders, and to make decisions about who has the power to shape the rules of their communities now and into the future. However, they may also make it easier to extract value from the cultural, social and environmental ecosystems of their members' communities. And this is where artworlds can provide valuable contexts – for exploring how the governance and coordination tools of DAOs might help forge new paths to belonging (to each other and to this earth). And cultural encounters can inspire and motivate people to share and adapt their social practices for mutual benefit.

I am haunted by Jampijinpa's talk and the *Networking the Unseen* exhibition curated by Gretta Louw at Furtherfield Gallery in 2016[52] and will always remember that the social and physical infrastructures, and software protocols that all digital technology projects are built on, from the Web to blockchains, are the legacy of colonialism. We must learn from stewardship practices of place-based and land-based cultures about working with cultural technologies (digital and otherwise) for sustainable mutual thriving. We must work out what part they have to play in connecting

---

51. "1.5 What is Open Cooperativism?" in *The Commons Transition Primer.* Accessed November 29, 2021, https://primer.commonstransition.org/1-short-articles/1-5-what-is-open-cooperativism.

52. See Ramon Amaro's "Blockchain and the General Problem of Protocological Control" in this volume.

across difference, in order that communities can make better collective decisions for their own, while minimising harm to those not in their immediate networked neighbourhood. To be good ancestors we must learn from the elders of place-based cultures about "worlding" processes[53] that preserve and transmit their heritages and the modalities of all the human and more-than-human communities that inhabit them.

And so here is the terrible tension. For plural, interdependent cultures to thrive at a planetary scale the future fortunes of all societies must be understood as connected and emplaced. DAOs provide a useful tool for thinking through translocal cultural cooperation and coordination. By stripping back the idea of an organisation to a few simple parts – community members who make transparent decisions about resources and capacities they control, and actions they will take over time – they offer a prototyping tool for experimenting with new ways to shape the economies we need, and the systems by which we might organise, to coordinate for common interests at a local and planetary scale. The global digital coordination infrastructure we have is proving deadly to many social and environmental ecosystems because in spite of the aim for universal access and participation it cannot account for the needs of life on the ground. A dominant society of privileged humans, act as satellites in each other's gravity, but are floating, detached and untethered in a toxic cloud over the earth. New ceremonies, and imaginative cultural and technological strategies are needed, suited to their "localities" and coordinating across different virtual and place-based layers at different scales. DAOs are not *the* answer, but they may be powerful means of transitioning.

By applying Selasi's dictum to "find where we are local" we can identify where affinities arise from common experiences, aspirations, needs and common causes using the lenses of rituals, relationships and restrictions. "Our people"[54] are those with whom we share (and want to build) rituals and relationships, and with whom we want to renegotiate, resist or escape shared strictures. These are the people with whom we might collaborate, whose services we need, whose needs we might satisfy, and in whose shared interests we organise. And because of translocality the interests of "our people" are ultimately entwined with all peoples.

53. Helen Palmer and Vicky Hunter, "Worlding," March 16, 2018, *New Materialism Almanac*, https://newmaterialism.eu/almanac/w/worlding.html.

54. In the spirit of Le Guin I suggest we extend the definition of "people" to include more-than-human persons or entities – animal, vegetable, mineral, mechanical (and maybe even magical).

Blockchain and the General Problem of Protocological Control

A provocation by Ramon Amaro

First presented at "Identity Trouble (on the blockchain)" the second event in the "DAOWO blockchain laboratory and debate series for reinventing the arts," Goethe-Institut, London, November 2017.

INTRODUCED BY RUTH CATLOW

The *DAOWO* event series was initiated by myself at Furtherfield in collaboration with Ben Vickers and realised in partnership with Goethe-Institut, Serpentine Galleries and the European State Machines network 2017–18.[1] Gathering together people across disciplines and sectors, participants used a range of engagement processes and speculative formats to interrogate topics including identity, civic good, and artistic and political organisation.[2]

Joining Ramon Amaro to explore the trouble with identity on the blockchain were speakers from engineering, humanities and the arts. Thor Karlsson presented his work implementing core backend systems for the Authenteq ID identity verification and face recognition platform for privacy protecting online services. Online reputation expert Emily Rosamond discussed character and reputation as speculative logics of networked personhood, and artist Ed Fornieles talked about the role of identity in his political and social immersive live action role-plays or LARPs that reconfigured the player's position and sense of self. The event was followed by a screening of the documentary *My Name is Janez Janša* (2012) about names, identity and pseudonymity in a long history of academic, artistic and popular, personal and political identity play, with a focus on three artists who, in 2007, changed their names to that of Janez Janša, the then Prime Minister of Slovenia. By smashing together problems across disciplines and sectors we hoped to challenge and reconsider the identity question in the context of the arts-blockchain ecosystem and to discover more interesting questions.

Digital identification is one of the fundamental building blocks for the global digital economy. A digital identification system is deemed "good" by authorities when it unlocks access to participation in online economies, helps to guard against fraud, protects rights and increases transparency.[3]

1. "Identity Trouble (on the blockchain)" was part of "DAOWO (Decentralised Autonomous Organisations With Others)" lab series initiated by Furtherfield and realised in partnership with Goethe-Institut, Serpentine Galleries and a network of European partners around the *State Machines* programme. See also: DAOWO website, accessed November 29, 2021, https://www.daowo.org/#identity-trouble-on-the-blockchain.

2. There is now a growing acknowledgement at the policy level of the value of insights gained from this kind of cross-sector, cultural and interdisciplinary work. See Alexandre Polvora, Jaya Klara Brekke and Anna Hakami, *Distributed Ledger Technologies (DTLs) for Social and Public Good – Where to Next*, European Commission, Brussels, 2021, JRC127939, https://publications.jrc.ec.europa.eu/repository/handle/JRC127939.

Both national identity and global identity systems are being accelerated, perhaps most notably in Goal 16 of the UN 20 Global Goals which aim, by 2030, to "provide legal identity for all, including birth registration".

In 1995 the tactical media collective Critical Art Ensemble preempted Facebook's Mark Zuckerberg's proclamation that "Having two identities for yourself is an example of a lack of integrity"[4] when they declared our "data body"[5] to be the fascist sibling of our fleshy selves. Stating that the Internet served as the "most successful repressive apparatus of all time," granting authorities power to exert controls and markets to exploit, "under the sign of liberation."[6] Before a person accesses the social, civic and health utilities now often only available through the Web they must pass through multiple processes of authentication and verification designed to ensure that their "digital identity" can be traced back to the "real" them. We are allowed by the Net to "live" only after satisfying the demands of multiple algorithmic identification systems that are often designed against our individual and collective interests.

New blockchain-based identity systems were proposed as early as 2016 for providing identification to refugees[7] and with it, access to basic social infrastructure such as healthcare, voting, financial and legal rights and services. However, identity is considered one of the hardest questions in the blockchain space, as it is here, in the domain of the immutable permanent record, that it really matters how our individual and social selves interface with global administrative digital networks of business and state;

3. "Digital identification: A key to inclusive growth," McKinsey, accessed November 29, 2021, https://www.mckinsey.com/business-functions/mckinsey-digital/our-insights/digital-identification-a-key-to-inclusive-growth.

4. Michael Zimmer, "Facebook's Zuckerberg: Having two identities for yourself is an example of a lack of integrity," May 14, 2010. Accessed November 29, 2021, https://michaelzimmer.org/2010/05/14/facebooks-zuckerberg-having-two-identities-for-yourself-is-an-example-of-a-lack-of-integrity.

5. "The data body is the total collection of files connected to an individual." Critical Art Ensemble Appendix: Utopian Promises – Net Realities, originally an address to Interface 3 in Hamburg 1995, and published in the conference proceedings. Accessed November 29, 2021, http://critical-art.net/books/flesh/flesh7.pdf.

6. Ibid.

7. Preethi Mohan, "Helping empower refugees with blockchain and process automation," IBM, November 17, 2020. Accessed November 29, 2021, https://www.ibm.com/blogs/blockchain/2020/11/helping-empower-refugees-with-blockchain-and-process-automation.

with difficulties spanning personal, social, technical and political domains. Developments sit in tension with fears about the increasing convergence of political and commercial control through identity technologies, tensions between: name and nym; person and persona; privacy, transparency and security; and the interests of the private individual and public citizen. Every new deployment has the potential to permanently fix and potentially impinge upon the relationship between people's subjective sense of self, their freedom to use multiple identities and their machine-assigned identities.

In the year that has seen the creation of a biometrically-secured cryptocurrency,[8] excitement about blockchain-based identity solutions for business has not cooled, in particular for its potential to support a friction-free life in the metaverse, bringing "individuals into a new level of intimacy with each other and the various services that they interact with".[9] But, with the rise in general awareness of the problems associated with personal data security in centralised platforms, comes a recognition that while "Self-sovereign identity takes back this control using blockchain technology... in order to succeed it needs a solid governance framework."[10] In this context Ramon Amaro's 2017 provocation excavates and troubles the logics and philosophical basis of the blockchain protocol itself. He shows that global identification systems are always already highly problematic. While blockchain technologies may provide efficient and secure solutions for "self-sovereign" digital identification[11] free of administrative control

8. Alex Blania and Sam Altman, *Introducing Worldcoin*, Worldcoin, accessed November 29 2021, https://worldcoin.org.

9. Alastair Johnson, *Beyond the Device with Self-Sovereign Identities*, Forbes, November 15, 2021. Accessed November 29, 2021, https://www.forbes.com/sites/alastairjohnson/2021/11/15/beyond-the-device-with-self-sovereign-identities/?sh=4bb732bf683f.

10. https://www.weforum.org/agenda/2021/08/self-sovereign-identity-future-personal-data-ownership.

11. "[M]eaning that any individual identity has administrative autonomy regardless of its location in digital space" Natalie Smolenski *Identity and Digital Self-Sovereignty: A New Paradigm for Sovereignty on the High Seas*, September 19, 2016, Medium. Accessed November 29, 2021 https://medium.com/learning-machine-blog/identity-and-digital-self-sovereignty-1f3faab7d9e3.

12. Christopher Allen *The Path to Self-Sovereign Identity*, April 25 2016, Life With Alacrity, Accessed November 29, 2021 https://www.lifewithalacrity.com/2016/04/the-path-to-self-soverereign-identity.html

by a single human authority or hierarchy[12] we should question the values and constraints propagated in the algorithmic system to which we cede authority.

He prompts us to wonder how the diverse array of existing embodied, social and collective human contracts will collide with new ideologies being encoded right now into the rapidly snowballing blockchain and DAO space – and how we might organise "other-wise."

* * *

BLOCKCHAIN AND THE GENERAL PROBLEM OF PROTOCOLOGICAL CONTROL
A PROVOCATION BY RAMON AMARO

Thank you very much for having me here today.

Today, I invite us to return to the functions of the algorithm, and by algorithms I refer to crafted sequences of code comprised of mathematical formulae, organised around a programming language. Most programming languages consist of instructions for machines, comprised of sets of data types, or strings. These strings produce various applied machine outputs, that convert information into human-readable forms by means of ordered sequences of visible and invisible characters. Data values can be constant or variable, and are stored in synthetic memory or databases whilst awaiting analysis. In other words, a programming language is a protocol by which knowledge can be anticipated or inferred through analysis of both known and unknown data.

Protocols are important to new financial and information-driven architectures, such as blockchain technology, as they enable information to be shared almost instantaneously across a wide range of cryptographic networks. In blockchain technology cryptographic networks are protocols shared between peers. The protocols are designed to broadcast encrypted and digitally signed messages that require minimal programming structure. As such, cryptographic algorithms are said to be secure, reliable, and flexible to the needs of its users and engineers to reach designated objectives. Nonetheless, the security of cryptographic networks requires a high level of reliability that, in engineering, is the careful maintenance of the probability that a system performs as specified. Furthermore, the regulation of probability is dependent upon the management of system health as well as the constant revision of defined performance parameters.

In blockchain technology reliability is a key factor in assurance of adequate performance, as is algorithmic efficiency. Blockchain algorithms are considered reliable because, unlike other networks, cryptographic algorithms are "chained", meaning that full copies of encrypted data are distributed across all networked cryptographic nodes, as opposed to the data being stored in one centralised location. This gives the technology its unique characteristics. In the so-called blockchain, if one cryptographic node fails then redundant data is pulled from other active nodes in the network. In other words, blockchains are communal yet resistant to collective collapse, despite individual failure. Still, the overall health of the community depends on efficient communication. Good communication requires that each node "refer" to its nearest neighbours before information can be accessed or transferred. This prevents accidental or forced deletion or reverse engineering. The ultimate aim is to resist single-party control or to prevent any single individual from forcefully or accidentally modifying the network, and as such thrives on efficient yet decentralised communications strategies.

Given its communal approach to information sharing, it is surprising how little of the blockchain's formal processes make reference to wider social networks that also rely on decentralised communications strategies.

Blockchain technology, whether it is a response to the austerities of centralised power, an opening of access to the circulation of aesthetics, or a proposal on overall economic, social or political value, is in close kinship to the movement and disposition of other historical games of social strategy.

I invite us to consider game theory as one such example. Game theory is widely considered a science of communications strategy that relies on optimal individual (or nodal) decision-making to achieve certain objectives. In game theory scenarios are simulated to assess the impact of individual actions on collective outcomes, given a single shared objective, such as victory in battle. Game theory seeks efficient communication amongst a collective whilst promoting optimal individual agency, and is therefore useful in a wide range of applications in psychology, evolutionary study, economics, politics, business, and even war.

Decentralisation, if not carefully considered, promotes a technologically-driven ethics that celebrates trust and communication while turning a blind eye to the violence and harm directly or indirectly made possible by similar ideologies. It is essential to consider what these ethics might be in relation to the idea of freedom, choice and movement within larger ecological networks of relation – particularly as mediated by technology. Consider the "Byzantine General's Problem", a 1982 paper written in reference to Byzantium (commonly known as the Byzantine Empire), located on the European edge of the Bosporus. The Byzantine General's Problem is a theoretical computer problem based in game theory that addresses the difficulties decentralised groups have in arriving at a shared truth or consensus of value without relying on a centralised system or party. The Problem's authors, Leslie Lamport, Robert Shostak, and Mashall Peas, based the game on the rise and fall of the Eastern Roman Empire and its military power.[13] The aim of the simulation was to test the reliability of computer systems that, as with a nodal military unit, must cope with either the failure of one or more of its components and protect the system from any conflict of information between nodes.

In the problem, the Byzantine army are camped outside an enemy city, each division commanded by its own general. Generals are free to communicate with each other but must do so only by messenger. After observing the enemy, the generals must decide on a common plan of action. Although generals are given autonomy to attack or retreat (1 or 0), decisions are based on a shared objective decided by the 'source process' or source general. The source process, in turn, must rely on a system of trust between generals, and account for the possibility that some generals may not fall in line. By building questions of trust into the framework of communication, the researchers aimed to test the limitations of computer reliability, as computers depend on unique components to perform their individual functions without hesitation. Information circulation as such is anchored on questions of loyalty which, according to the researchers, is synonymised with reliability and individual reputation in achieving collective results. In the problem, generals whose decisions do align with the objectives source process are labelled 'correct processes.' These are the processes that perform their functions as instructed. Those that deviate from the overall plan are labelled 'faulty processes.' These are processes that sometimes confuse other generals or the system itself with the spread of misinformation or by failures to perform.

Mark Nelson argues that there are limitations to the idea of decentralisation, particularly in militarily derived contexts despite the appearance

13. Leslie Lamport, Robert Shostak, and Mashall Peas, "The Byzantine Generals Problem," *ACM Transactions on Programming Languages and Systems* 4, no. 3 (July 1982): 382–401.

of independent decision making amongst players.[14] Nelson argues that the system Lamport, et. al. imagine is a mere fantasy of freedom of choice and distributed power. The problem overlooks a critical characteristic of military power structures in that all networked decisions – whether acted upon or not – originate at a single, central entity which is in their case the source process. What is articulated as a single shared objective is a single perspective exercised in communion. Less considered is the fallibility of the source itself, or whether the source process is ill-informed or misdirected before giving its generals commands. The source's quality or motivations often go unquestioned, as are any gains it might enjoy when the collective remains subordinate. The generals' decisions are under scrutiny while the source remains silent with exception of its own commands. Individual autonomy is present yet not arbitrary, as it is based on compliance not discretion.

Although, according to Nelson, the Byzantine problem is a question of computational reliability it is grossly misconstrued as trust, individual will and autonomy. As with the Byzantine problem, the general that fails to follow the objectives of the source is deemed at fault, incorrect, anti-social and deviant; whereas the dutiful are loyal to the extent that given commands are both understood and replicated. If fault is to be assigned, it is the failure of the problem's authors to consider an inconvenient truth in the gesture towards decentralisation, namely in the auto-expendability of any general that is, has been, or will misalign with the objectives of the source.

Decentralisation is, thereby, not individual withdrawal from concentrated control, but a function to disperse accountability into a field of abstraction. Here, the source can remain hidden behind a scurry of rapid individual decision-making, while the individual scampers towards an imaginary of absolute independence and isolation. This hurriedness is misassociated with moral righteousness, adhering to the principles of value directed from a single source similar to what the individual seeks to escape. Here, decision is rearticulated as always already in relation to a single Truth reanimated from Wall Street and the shadow investor to the amateur's server. But there is a fee. What is the point of decentralisation when one is free to choose only amongst a selection of choices made available?

14. Mark Nelson, "The Byzantine Generals Problem," July 23, 2007. Accessed January 9, 2022, https://marknelson.us/posts/2007/07/23/byzantine.html.

If we consider the contemporary cryptographic algorithm with similar loyalty functions that require consensus without compromise, then we are left with the question of an enduring reconstruction of power, whereby the protocols through which individual acts are con/instructed remains hidden from view. At the same time, they evaluate each individual act in accordance with a prescribed objective. This is not to say that the crypto enthusiast has no agency. I instead suggest that the enthusiast has perhaps overstated the revolutionary capacity of their communal objectives. If a key quality of the cryptographic ideal is to distribute power through infallibility, then what must one give up in return?

Luciana Parisi and Stamatia Portanova posit that protocological control is foremost a human-techno process that affects the circulation of human bodies within social spaces.[15] These bodies are formed into artificial life – a game, I might add – that samples, codes and incorporates human decision into artificial passageways between self-will, trust, compliance, discipline, and algorithmic efficiency. Although cryptographic algorithms have authored a new space for social interaction, an already existent mechanisation of choice resides in the very fabric of our networked culture, not exclusive of the act or acts of systemic compliance. But perhaps the illusion of a flattened hierarchy is enough to imagine greater maneuverability.

Is even the whisper of imagination beyond our present systems of control enough to grant our loyal dedication to new manifestations of an old general's problem? Alexander Galloway reminds us that control and freedom are two sides of the same coin.[16] While a system of exchange might promote openness, inclusion, and flexibility, it remains organised by a set of meta protocological controls that promote standardisation as method for freedom of participation. These systems, however materialised, achieve voluntary regulation within seemingly contingent environments that are, to the contrary, programmable capsules of encrypted information that can be bought by means of loyalty to the market exchange.

Nonetheless, in the refusal or at minimum the thorough awareness on one's positionality against the ideal, the question of the source remains.

15. Luciana Parisi and Stamatia Portanova, "Soft thought (in architecture and choreography)," *Computational Culture* 1 (November 2011), http://computationalculture.net/soft-thought.

16. Alexander R. Galloway, *Protocol: How Control Exists after Decentralization* (Cambridge, Mass.: MIT Press, 2006), 2–27.

Where does one look to find an objective amongst an assemblage of processes? Is it the engineer general that carries out the orders of protocol without question? Do we begin at the general user "freed" from the chains of centralised capital only to find themselves in new territories of restriction? Or do we point towards the abstractions of capital or its close bedfellow – the free exchange of information?

These concerns are not mutually exclusive. But looking towards the latter reanimates the desperate reincarnation of monetary gain as the source of individual and communal value, which has shown little mercy towards those who deviate from its objectives. Here, I move towards circulation of fault in terms of debt, property, investment and other forms of exchange that separate the loyal amongst us, who enact the protocols of ideological gain, from our more deviant neighbours who are audacious enough to break the illusion of autonomy. Perhaps control is an outdated gesture under the pangs of everyday reality. Perhaps cryptographic systems such as blockchain may help us imagine something beyond the impossible possibility of release from constraint. We must consider that blockchain does not produce any greater insight into concentrated systems of control than it does in freeing humans from recurrent conditions of desire. Perhaps it does no more than alert us towards the novelty of the individual and its imaginary grasp for power, whether real or imagine. Either way, we must be prepared to consider, as with the Mandalorian creed, that this is the way.

Nature 3.0: blockchain for extraction or care?

Sara Heitlinger, Lara Houston & Alex Taylor

CO-DESIGNING MULTISPECIES FOOD COMMONS THROUGH BLOCKCHAIN TECHNOLOGIES

In the Autumn of 2019 a group of citizens interested in sustainable urban food systems gathered at Spitalfields City Farm in East London to co-design a food commons with the help of blockchain prototypes. Farm staff and volunteers worked with artists, community organisers, researchers, technologists and activists towards a shared goal: to discover whether decentralised technology might hold a piece of the puzzle to address some of the myriad injustices that afflict the global industrial food system. The event was organised by the authors, as part of a funded research project called: Algorithmic Food Justice.

Unsustainable inequalities are threatening all life on earth. One million species are threatened with extinction and we have lost over 75% of all cultivated crop diversity. These losses are rooted in human activities, with industrial agriculture being a major driver, contributing to degraded soils, polluted waterways, and ultimately threatening food security for all life on the planet. The global industrial food system encloses and extracts value from our planet's resources, concentrating benefits in the hands of a few major players and driving unsustainable human and ecological inequalities.

Blockchain is being optimistically touted as the solution to many complex problems, including sustainable food systems, where it is being used to increase food traceability, safety and provenance, and in inventory management in supply chains. Examples such as Provenance[1] and BeefLedger[2] promise a future in which specific products can be traced immediately, help reduce food waste and track contaminated food easily and quickly, while preventing the sale of fraudulent food products. In these futures, blockchain does little to diversify monocultural, industrial agriculture, distribute profit more equally, or farm more sustainably. Other examples such as Nori,[3] Regen Network[4] and GainForest,[5] claim to use blockchain to incentivise regenerative land use, carbon capture in soil, and the reversal of destructive land use practices that contribute to CO_2 emissions such as clearing forests for monocultural crop production.

There are significant doubts as to whether the technology is appropriate, sustainable, or feasible to use in real world settings, particularly in small scale agriculture, who produce up to 80% of the world's food, according to the United Nations Food and Agriculture Organisation (UN FAO). Worse, we know that it is primarily being used in neoliberal models of agriculture, potentially accelerating extraction and exploitation.[6] Typically, the vision for blockchain in agriculture tends towards a deterministic or techno-optimistic view of the ecological and social problems that we face within food systems, one in which the technology provides the solution through increased efficiency and productivity, while complexities and possible negative impacts of such solutions remain unexamined. They reduce the problem of unsustainable food systems to one of provenance and tracking, solved through technologically-mediated digital marketplaces, where the power lies in the hands of investors. Blockchain is coupled with

1. "Turn Positive Social and Environmental Impact into Brand Value," Provenance, accessed December 31, 2021, https://www.provenance.org.

2. BeefLedger website, accessed December 31, 2021, https://beefledger.io.

3. "The Nori Carbon Removal Marketplace," Nori, accessed December 31, 2021, https://nori.com.

4. "Platform for a Thriving Planet," Regen Network, accessed December 31, 2021, https://www.regen.network.

5. "Sustainable Smart Contracts for Our Natural World," GainForest, accessed December 31, 2021, https://www.gainforest.app.

6. Xiaowei Wang, Blockchain Chicken Farm: And Other Stories of Tech in China's Countryside (FSG Originals x Logic, 2020).

technologies such as AI and sensors to optimise and centralise agricultural production, as well as provide wealthy urban consumers data about food provenance and safety at a price beyond the reach of most people in the global community (ibid). In these ways the technology does little to address societal and governmental problems around access and food security. The benefits remain in the hands of an elite few and, rather than technology providing a solution to the problems of governments or communities, the inequalities are amplified (ibid).

Algorithmic Food Justice was our response – a participatory design research project that resisted a techno-optimistic approach to blockchain as a fix or solution. Instead it attempted to examine the potential for blockchain to help reconfigure values from profit to care, redress power imbalances and inequalities, and suggest more sustainable and fair food systems.

Because information systems are social systems, we approached technology as a means to explore existing conditions and reflect on alternatives. We were drawn to blockchain because of its potential for "radical regulation",[7] forcing us to consider, not only non-humans as individual actors, but also forcing us to consider, not only non-humans as individual actors, but also the interdependencies between multitude more-than-human actors in an ecological web. Blockchain facets such as tokenisation, smart contracts and distributed autonomous organisations (DAOs), provide incentivisation mechanisms for supporting ecological balance and suggest radical consequences of regulation and redistribution of power. Such blockchain facets suggest an alternative basis for creating new value systems and embedding the interests of non-humans such as seeds, soil and water into decision-making processes mediated through computation and automation. We wanted to explore whether it was possible to reconfigure the relationships between food, blockchain, and value, and open up new possibilities for algorithmic approaches to a sustainable food justice system.

Therefore we drew on alternative governance models from the commons to explore ways that a *more-than-human* perspective can bring different stakeholders to the decision-making table and create a fairer and more sustainable food system. We use the term *more-than-human* to refer to a perspective in which the human is no longer at the centre, but in

7. Chris Elsden, Inte Gloerich, Anne Spaa, John Vines, and Martijn de Waal, "Making the Blockchain Civic," *Interactions* 26, 2 (2019): 60–65.

a web of relations with other actors including animals, plants and earth systems such as the water cycle.

CREATIVE FUTURING WITH GRASSROOTS COMMUNITIES: THREE SPECULATIVE PARTICIPATORY DESIGN WORKSHOPS

The project involved three workshops that we devised and facilitated (together with Ruth Catlow from Furtherfield) in 2019 at Spitalfields City Farm, an urban agricultural community in east London. We drew around forty diverse participants from different communities with whom we had worked with over the years in participatory engagements and had established relationships. This included relationships that Sara had developed through a series of participatory design research projects with the farm and other urban food growing communities in east London around emerging technologies such as Internet of Things and interactive digital systems; as well as artists and activists that were drawn from the networks of Ruth from Furtherfield. These people had become familiar with our participatory and inclusive ways of working. It was because of these established relationships that we had nurtured over the years that so many people were prepared to come to something that may otherwise have seemed alienating and overly technical.

We used playful and creative activities to open up a shared imaginative space to experiment with alternative configurations of value and to open up a space where multispecies actors such as humans, plants, animals and soil, as well as technologies and their infrastructures, can take part in a thriving food commons of the future.

This urban agricultural community, as with others like it, is especially alert to issues around food justice. They also offer a uniquely rich source of challenges and resources. Spitalfields City Farm is in the inner east London borough of Tower Hamlets, one of the most economically deprived boroughs in the UK. It is characterised by high population density, large-scale immigration, ethnic diversity, poverty and huge divides between rich and poor. It also suffers from a range of food-related illnesses. In the face of this challenging context, the farm community has demonstrated resourcefulness, creativity, and adaptability in responding to increasing pressures on funding, land, and labour, creating a welcoming space for connection with nature, and education about sustainable food and caring animal husbandry. Thus the farm offers opportunities to study the possibilities for digital technologies to support more-than-human entanglements and the food commons. Spitalfields City Farm was considered as a test case for prototyping sustainable food futures, but participants also brought their experiences of other community gardens where food is grown.

Our approach used both participation and speculation to bring different people's experiences and forms of knowledge together in inclusive ways, engaging participants who were not familiar with blockchain or other emerging digital technologies, in complex possible futures with these technologies, and in particular with the blockchain. We used fiction and roleplaying to understand the affordances and implications of the blockchain AI and sensor networks, exploring futures beyond participants' lived experience, while remaining grounded in their values, needs and challenges.

Narrative techniques helped people understand the implications of the blockchain and how the technology might play out in specific situations, to imagine use cases that are possible but not yet real, and address questions of ethics, values, social interactions and their consequences. In this way we were also able to open up a space in which we could take seriously the possibility of human and non-human actors having a voice and a stake in a value system and better understand the inequalities and power imbalances within industrial food systems.

In the first workshop urban community growers mapped the different multispecies stakeholders of the city farm, now and in the future. They mapped their needs and contributions, and the resource flows between them. Participants from diverse backgrounds were able to draw on their expert knowledge of regenerative agricultural techniques to surface the agencies of other beings and the more-than-human interrelationships on which thriving community growing spaces depend, for example by surfacing our dependencies on soil micro-organisms, worms, and pollinators. By privileging the perspectives of this group of urban community growers these activities allowed for a mode of knowledge production beyond a human-centered perspective of value in food systems. Participants were asked to consider resources beyond those with a financial value, such as volunteer labour, oxygen, time, and care, and to think about who manages those resources. Discussions revolved around the often invisible but important labour of care work that happens in community gardens, which is not adequately recognised or compensated (for example in securing funding for schemes), and is completely elided in industrial agricultural systems.

In the second workshop, we imagined a scenario in which all of London were constituted as a city farm. We used Live Action Role-Play (LARP) was to open up a playful space to imagine and examine how multispecies actors might take part in governing a future food commons. Set in 2025, in the aftermath of a "Great Food Emergency", the aim of the game was to transform London from an extractive financial centre into a global city farm in which all of London's available spaces and infrastructures are turned over to creating a thriving food commons for its biodiverse inhabitants. Participants were given different roles to play within fictional scenarios and improvised an array of new kinds of multispecies relationships, new economies, and radical decision-making processes for sustaining a city-wide commons. Players' actions were informed by scenarios based on what we learned in the first workshop as well as real-world events, and current facts about food and environmental injustices, as we tried to establish new decision-making systems and urban infrastructures. The LARP was staged as two assembly meetings (one for a local urban farm, one for a city-wide farm) in which players took on representative roles from different committees and discussed items on an agenda based on Nobel-prize winning economist Elinor Ostrom's design principles for the commons. These principles were based on her studies of how the commons (such as the collective management of natural resources, including fisheries, forests and farmland) can be sustainably managed by a community without intervention by the state or market economics.[8] We discussed each item on the agenda through a series of scenarios, developed from what Maria Puig de la Bellacasa calls "matters of care"[9] that had arisen in discussions in the first workshop. These matters of care relate to the overlooked, marginalised labours of care that are involved in sustaining nourishing multispecies relations in the city farm.

To illustrate with an example, the plight of pollinating insects arose in the stakeholder mapping workshop as a matter of care. Here we learned about intensive agriculture, loss of habitats, and pesticides, which were all having an impact on these invaluable species. The game host playing Chair in the assembly meeting introduced the topic for discussion:

The next item on the agenda is a review of how we're managing resources, and ensuring that everyone's contributions are rewarded. [...] An issue that's come up recently in the sharing policy: so the bees, as you know...have been on strike now for six months.

8. Elinor Ostrom, *Governing the Commons* (Cambridge University Press, 2015).

9. Maria Puig de la Bellacasa, *Matters of Care: Speculative Ethics in More than Human Worlds* (University of Minnesota Press, 2017).

They then engage a player in the role-play, asking:

How is the Justice Committee proposing to resolve the dispute between the bees and the gardeners?

The Justice representative replies:

We are piloting various multispecies assemblies, to ensure that we give equal voice to all citizens (there are complaints that the human voices are still just too dominant). But also working closely with the Department of Infrastructure to meet the bees' demands, which on the whole don't seem too wild and quite fair.

Other members from other committees then joined the discussion, with the Education officer reporting a new schools programme about the essential services provided by the bees, and the speculative roleplay of more-than-human governance issues unfolded from there.

By giving different species different roles and responsibilities within the assemblies the LARP compelled players to imagine a radical reconfiguration of power structures and flows in their efforts to manifest a multispecies food commons. In this process they highlighted conflicted and entangled relations between humans, other species and planetary systems and explored a range of different challenges for commons management.

Despite this, of course we could never entirely forget that the project took place within a human frame, created by human designers and developers and played by human actors. But because we drew on the expert knowledge of growers and their intimate understanding of multispecies relationships in the food web, we were able to shift the narrative to lever open the totalising human-centred, efficiency-driven and profit-motivated visions of algorithmic food governance, and see where shifts can begin to occur.

BUILDING BLOCKCHAIN PROTOTYPES
FOR MULTISPECIES THRIVING

In the final workshop we invited groups of artists, designers and technologists who had some familiarity with blockchain to create conceptual prototypes for new types of organisations to manage the more-than-human food commons through smart contracts and Decentralised Autonomous Organisations (DAOs). Groups developed their DAOs based on the scenarios and debates elaborated in the stakeholder mapping and LARP. They used paper-based prompts to flesh out the rules of the DAOs and how it would be managed as a food commons, paying attention to multispecies relations, value flows and fair distribution of resources.

PROTOTYPE 1: DAO-N TO EARTH

The first group devised an "umbrella" DAO, called DAO-n to Earth, to coordinate the exchange of tokens (currencies) between all the farms in the (fictional future) London Food Network. The exchange rate is set automatically according to the soil health data of each community, as measured by networked sensors and AI, and calibrated over time. The better the quality of soil in a community, the higher the value of its local currency. Humans are incentivised to take care of the soil, by staking a currency's value to the work done to regenerate the soil in a specific local area. The DAO-n to Earth group designed for soil health above all else, because it benefits a wider group of species (rather than the humans alone). In this prototype care for ecosystem health is woven into the dynamics of food production and exchange. Rather than replacing the growers' expert knowledge to automate the practices of soil care, sensors and automation are used here to measure, verify and incentivise the results and use them in a market exchange.

PROTOTYPE 2: FELLOWSHIT OF DARK MATTER DAO

The second group created the Fellowshit of Dark Matter DAO, based on a discussion of value as relational and ever-unfolding, an experience which they sought to capture in the design of a socio-technical system that nurtured multispecies relations. Humans can post waste materials and make them freely available to others within the community through an app, thereby earning tokens which can be used within a broader system of value exchange. Users of the app would participate in a weekly ritual, to provide ways for citizens to inhabit multispecies' perspectives, and spot opportunities for waste materials to be used for their own species' ends. This DAO promotes a multispecies "circular economy" with an expansive sense of value that is not only focussed on material utility but the production of cultural value and the meaning of unfolding interspecies relationships as they exchange materials and tokens within a digital-physical ecosystem.

PROTOTYPE 3: CORN COUNCIL DAO

The third group created the Corn Council DAO, which seeks to repair the alienation humans experience from the conditions of food production, and proposes a system for repairing the disconnect between humans and other species. The DAO rewards humans with tokens for spending time with plants in a non-instrumental way, as well as for care-taking work such as pruning and watering. Tokens allow members to participate in voting proposals about the farm's management. Each crop in the farm has its own council and the DAOs are managed through an umbrella DAO.

In the afternoon session we invited the community growers and organisers who had provided their insights in the previous events, to bring their expertise of multispecies relations, food-growing, and community governance to bear on the prototypes. In this way we sought to fuse these different forms of knowledge and experience to bring the richest critique possible to an examination of these DAOs and how they might serve local and wider multispecies interests, as well as all the awful things they might do by accident. Knowledgeable growers helped reconfigure tech-focussed imaginings and added important depth and nuance to multi-species relationships and ecosystems by "stress testing" the DAOs, which we discuss below.

FROM EXTRACTION TO CARE

These events brought people together across very different zones of knowledge to open up a space for rethinking values that are driving ecological and social injustices within global industrial food systems, from human-centered, extractionist and profit-driven (not just in the blockchain space), to care and commons for multispecies stakeholders in the food web. By bringing different experiences of governance into dialogue the workshops opened up diverse valences for people to engage with algorithmic governance and consider new perspectives. For example, the growers' knowledge forced the creative technologists to consider the implications of their prototypes on multispecies communities. At the same time growers were brought into a conversation about technology that they were unlikely to have had before. Including those who are not typically included in discussions about the design of emerging technologies is important if we want to address the digital divide, distribute control and autonomy more evenly, and redress the existing imbalances within the global corporate food systems. In these ways the workshop activities created an inclusive space in which a plurality of human and non-human actors (including soil, animals, computation, and sensors) and their different forms of knowledge were brought to bear on a more-than-human value system represented through algorithmic governance. By bringing together these different stakeholders, the co-design activities and their outputs surfaced alternative configurations of value that allowed for benefit and power to be distributed more equitably between more-than-human actors.

The project surfaced a number of tensions and challenges. Firstly, creating formal accounting systems of value, and introducing external rewards in what was previously informal and intrinsically motivated, risked creating perverse incentives and abuses of power. While blockchains promise to facilitate more equal distribution of benefits, if the system is not set up correctly, bad actors will find a way to corrupt the system and work it to their own ends. Secondly, a more-than-human perspective may not serve those who have historically been excluded from the category of human in the first place, such as people of colour. A feminist ethics of care shows how we might pay attention to neglected humans as well as nonhumans, in order to re-configure value in ways that contribute to more sustainable and just urban food governance. Thirdly, it is still humans speaking on behalf of other actors and making decisions on behalf of non-humans, and it will be humans, subject to prevailing economic and social pressures and incentives, who write the code. We attempted to overcome this epistemological challenge by engaging expert growers with their experience of regenerative agriculture, using decentering techniques such as roleplay to speak on behalf of other species, and a consideration of non-human actors such as sensors, AI and blockchain in our accounting systems. We conclude that, at best, these could work as proxies for non-humans.

In the dominant visions of blockchain-based solutions for more sustainable food systems, convenience and efficiency are prioritised, and the care labour of humans and non-humans alike are erased and undervalued. The danger is that without a variety of stakeholders working on these technologies, accelerationist tendencies and injustices in urban food governance will be exacerbated. By contrast, the workshops in our project produced blockchain prototype systems for urban food futures where labours of care are made visible, valued and accounted for. The participatory speculation with diverse stakeholders suggests alternative futures in which the technology may be embedded into wider cultural contexts that make it possible to reconfigure value from something to be enclosed and extracted, into a system that hinges on care. It is only by moving beyond a human-centered perspective of food governance to recognise the interrelations between humans and non-humans on which all life on earth depends, that we can begin to recognise the diverse value required to restore our damaged planet.

Material Zones –
An Interview with
Sam Spike
(Fingerprints DAO)
& Mitchell F. Chan

Interview by Sam Skinner

Sam Skinner: Many thanks both for making the time to discuss your respective work. Sam, perhaps you could start by telling me a little about Fingerprints DAO and what you do?

Sam Spike: Fingerprints DAO is a community-governed organisation that collects artworks that use blockchain as an artistic medium, rather than purely a medium of commerce. The DAO originally started as a collection of *Autoglyphs*: the second project by Larva Labs, who are best known for creating *Cryptopunks*. The special thing about *Autoglyphs* is that they are widely perceived to be the first "on-chain" generative art series on Ethereum, meaning that the art can be recreated from information that is stored directly on the blockchain, rather than on external servers.

The collection evolved into a DAO, properly speaking, when a token was created that gave its holders a say in how the collection should be managed. If you own a certain number of tokens, you automatically become a member of the DAO and can vote on how the organisation is run. Fingerprints was established as an art collecting DAO, so naturally the first major decision that had to be made was which other artworks to collect. The on-chain nature of *Autoglyphs* led us to consider other ways that blockchains can be used to create art, and we agreed that those works should be the focus of our collection. The idea is that every work in the collection should use some material aspect of blockchain to reflect critically on the technology and its cultures. We've collected work of this kind by artists such as Rhea Myers, 0xDEAFBEEF, Sarah Meyohas and Harm van den Dorpel.

Something else that the DAO has started to do more of over the past six months is assume the role of a producer, commissioning artists to create new work, and assisting them with its development and ultimately its sale. A great example is a project we did last year with the artist John F Simon Jr, in collaboration with e.a.t.]works and Divergence, where we reimagined Simon's important early net artwork, *Every Icon* (1997), as an interactive NFT series.

What is it that makes Fingerprints DAO's work distinctive in the NFT and DAO space? Perhaps here you could also talk a little about why Mitchell's *Digital Zones of Immaterial Pictorial Sensibility* (2017) was one of the first NFTs you collected?

Sam Spike: One major differentiating factor is the focus of our collection. While most other collection DAOs have acquired art across a wide spectrum of genres, from generative practices to 3D rendering to digital painting, we have zeroed in on this very specific area of blockchain art. So far, during a full year of actively growing the collection, we've only acquired the work of eleven artists – and in many cases we are the largest collectors of those artists' work.

Another difference is that we have prioritised work that we think will stand the test of time art historically speaking. Of course, we hope that the value of our collection will rise over time, but we will also acquire pieces that actively resist monetary value if we feel that they are artistically important. For example, we recently recognised the Kudzu NFT virus by Folia, which literally cannot be sold, as part of our official collection.

Mitchell's *Digital Zones of Immaterial Pictorial Sensibility* were some of the very first works that we acquired. Early on, when we were searching for the right language to describe our approach to collecting, we were throwing around phrases like "the token is the art". NFTs usually have two parts: the token, which is essentially a line of code that can be assigned to different addresses on a blockchain, and the media associated with that token, which is usually stored on a separate server and referred to via a hyperlink. When people talk about NFTs, they frequently use the analogy of a certificate of authenticity to describe the relationship between the token and its media. This implies that the token is independent from the art, a financial adjunct that its ultimately inessential. At Fingerprints, we're very interested in works where the token – or the code that generates and governs that token, which is called the smart contract – is just as essential to the logic of the artwork as its accompanying media. Mitchell's work, which he has described as "a project about the nature of the artwork-as-a-token", demonstrates this perfectly.

As the title makes clear, Mitchell's *Digital Zones of Immaterial Pictorial Sensibility* reimagines Yves Klein's *Zone of Immaterial Pictorial Sensibility* made in 1959. In Klein's work, "immaterial zones" were represented by paper certificates that had to be bought with gold. The famous twist was that each zone could only be activated by burning its corresponding certificate in an elaborate ritual beside the Seine. Mitchell has proposed that Klein's work was prescient in anticipating how NFTs sever the commodity form of an artwork (the certificate or the token) from its experiential form (the aesthetic object itself, such as the "immaterial zone", or the media files referenced by an NFT). Mitchell's project flips this by foregrounding how this experiential form cannot be experienced outside of or beyond the commodity form. The token is not ancillary; its material existence, the act of its exchange, and the possibility of its destruction are all integral parts of the artwork.

Mitchell, to pick up this thread about your work that Sam describes, you state that what makes NFTs unique, and which they share with conceptual art like Sol LeWitt's work, is that they both sever "the connection between the DISPLAY FORM of the art and the OWNED FORM of the art." But in a later part of the same text you state, in relation to an Art Blocks mint, that the forms are simultaneously "separate but symbiotic".[1] I wonder if you could expand a little on these relationships and how they variously play out? And how has this understanding of yours changed over time since your first NFT-based work? How are your newer works testing and expanding upon this?

1. https://medium.com/@mitchellfchan/nfts-generative-art-and-sol-lewitt-e99a5fa2b0cb

Mitchell F. Chan: You got me! I struggled a lot with that essay, because Art Blocks really is the example which messes with my theory about separating the art-as-asset from the art-as-experience. I still stand by this assessment of the proposition of NFTs! That separation is their ultimate innovation! But any theory will sometimes get totally destroyed by prominent outliers that break whatever clever model you've proposed.

That's the genius of the Art Blocks platform: the receipt/certificate, the NFT, doesn't just get displayed beside the artwork to validate it, it actually has to be fed into the artwork for each unique piece to manifest itself. The artist writes the algorithm to sit there and wait for a randomly generated, but permanent, value as input, then uses that as a seed to build out a unique edition. That input value is the hash of the receipt itself. So the display form of the individual piece cannot exist until the commerce has been executed. That's why I say it's symbiotic.

Despite the existence now of Art Blocks and other on-chain generative pieces that blur that boundary between the receipt and the artwork itself, or create functional dependencies between those forms, my understanding of the NFT hasn't changed much. I've spent a little more time trying to consider the NFT in the context of other certificates of authenticity and receipts that have existed historically. I recently wrote an essay, which should be published by the Yves Klein estate shortly, that touches briefly on those ideas.

I look at the certificates that artists like LeWitt, Robert Morris, and others were creating in the 1960s, and I'm understanding more now how different those were from NFTs. Those certificates, I believe, reinforce a Duchampian definition of art. Duchamp asserted that an artwork could be defined solely by the authority of "an artist," and the certificates created by LeWitt were ways of formalising that authority, and thus, they were ways of legitimising any object or action nominated by the capital-A Artist. And yes, they do pose certain questions like "what is the art? LeWitt's instructions or the output?" But that question is not at all relevant to NFTs. I assert with confidence that the Non-Fungible Token is (in almost all cases) *not* the art. It's a receipt or certificate that refers to a separate artwork.

The pieces I'm working on right now will hopefully take advantage of that separation in a way that I've been hoping other artists would, but few have. I'd like to attach a token to a trans-media works that may exist in digital space, physical space, or as a set of instructions for execution in both. Whichever "verse" you're living in: the metaverse, the gallery-verse, whatever: there's an aspect of this work, a shadow of it, there for you that you own with the NFT.

I want to push you a little further on future potentials of your practice and the wider emergent "scene", if I may. In 2017, you speculated that if "artworks were owned and transacted through immaterial blockchain tokens, that shift in the commodity form of the artwork could also precipitate a shift in the material (or immaterial form) of the artwork."[2] In the five years since you wrote that, what have you observed happening in this regard, both in your own work and in those of others?

Mitchell F. Chan: I started to touch on this already, but there has undoubtedly been a huge impact in the relative popularity of artistic media as a result of the tokenisation boom. I have no numbers to back this up, but I believe there *must* be exponentially more artists working in digital media now than there were even a year ago, and fewer in painting or sculpture. I suppose you can already see the impact in the practices at the very top of the art world: Damien Hirst's Currency experiment leaves his Dots halfway into the physical world and halfway in the digital world. Jeff Koons is doing an NFT. Murakami too. Murakami is a great example of how the artistic medium will follow the commodity form of the artwork. Why would an artist whose signature style is described as "superflat" be working with visceral paint and canvas? Presumably, because a canvas is basically the most common unit of currency at top of the art-market. So of course it makes sense for him to be eschewing that now.

But frankly, a lot of these moves into digital art are pretty uninspired. It's a new medium, sure, but the same old aesthetics. And the sensorial experience of a superflat Murakami painting and a Murakami JPEG will be very very similar. I had hoped in 2017 that tokenisation would allow artwork to be even more radical. Tokenised ownership ought to create a better market for performance, dance, conceptual art, and bizarre "art provocations" that I can't even think of. And I still think it will! But the explosion of money and interest that happened last year really disincentivises thinking too far out of the box.

2. https://chan.gallery/ikb.

Can you speak a little about your involvement with Fingerprints DAO and how it has impacted the development of both your artwork and career, and have any particular synergies emerged between these elements?

Mitchell F. Chan: Initially, I was looking at the DAO as both a collection of art and a collection of individuals who were very well known in the NFT scene. So when they came considering the acquisition of my art, I felt the same way I would if I were being approached by a prestigious collecting institution, even though the DAO had only been around for a few weeks at that point (I was the first acquisition after the pooling of the *Autoglyphs*), I thought that this would be very good for my career, and that this would legitimise my work. I had very much the old-school art world mentality, but it ended up being true.

But the *other* aspect of the DAO, which has taken longer to realise, is that you're not just getting an entry on your CV, but a formal connection to that group of people. It's a very concentrated version of one of the more positive things about NFTs: a direct and ongoing dialogue with collectors and supporters.

Sam, I'm interested to know more about how you operate as a DAO from the inside. Can you explain a little about the DAO's evolution? Also, the technology that underpins it and how it impacts how you function? Who are your members? How many are there? Who can make proposals and decisions regarding the development of the DAO and the curatorial and purchasing decisions? And how are these made?

Sam Spike: Fingerprints now has over two hundred members, based all around the world. Some of our members are early crypto adopters, others are new entrants from the worlds of tech and finance, and others have ties with the traditional cultural industries. The thing that unifies our members is that they all own Fingerprints tokens. Like most blockchain tokens, these can be transferred freely, peer-to-peer. But just owning a few tokens isn't enough. Membership to the DAO is determined by certain thresholds: at the lower threshold, tokenholders have to be voted into the DAO by existing members; at the higher threshold, membership is automatic.

Fingerprints membership confers various privileges. Most importantly, members can vote on important decisions such as how the DAO is structured, how the treasury is managed, and which projects it undertakes. Membership also grants access to the DAO's Discord server, an online chatroom where members hang out and work together on different activities. The DAO is divided into several working groups that focus on different parts of its operations: there's a marketing group, a finance group, and so on. These groups are coordinated via dedicated channels in the Discord that every member can view and contribute to. This way, members can participate as and when they wish, working only on the parts of the DAO or the specific projects that they are most interested in.

The only area of the DAO that has restricted access is the curation committee. The committee has roughly fifteen members, all of whom have been elected by the wider membership. Committee members meet twice a month to discuss and vote on potential acquisitions, assessing each work in relation to artistic criteria that were approved by the rest of the DAO. The committee is private because it keeps conversations focused and lowers the risk of individual members front-running our acquisitions (of course, there is a general assumption that this wouldn't happen, but given the size of the membership, it is possible.) Nonetheless, any member can suggest works for the committee to consider, and the committee has a duty to discuss and vote on those suggestions.

Mitchell, I understand you are also a member of the DAO, how have you found this experience and what particular insights has it given you into the functioning and potential of DAOs?

Mitchell F. Chan: I think that the consensus opinion that has emerged about DAOs is that they're a wonderfully efficient structure for pooling capital, resources, and attention, and an absolutely awful structure for doing anything with them.

I will admit right here that I absolutely do *not* subscribe to the "Decentralise Everything" ethos. I think that the notion of an actual decentralised, autonomous, organisation is absurd. I think that successful organisations tend to build around a single, *central* vision, and they definitely don't run autonomously; people put a great deal of work into them.

Democratic? Yes! Decentralised? Eh, I don't know how well that's going to work out. And even creating democratic structures on blockchain is a challenge. Voting on a DAOs initiatives is good, provided you have a good voting structure that minimises the impact of whales who literally bought the most votes.

That's another issue, and one that Vitalik Buterin and others have talked about at length. When you create an organisational structure over the top of a financial technology, when you use tokens to administrate that organisation, you are literally assigning democratic agency to units of currency which are designed to be bought and sold.

What are some of the challenges that being a DAO throws up, particularly with regard to voting, how power is distributed, and its specific technologies and interfaces?

Mitchell F. Chan: Oh, haha! I guess I talked about this at length already. I'll handover to Sam on this.

Sam Spike: The biggest challenge that we face is probably striking the right balance between centralisation and decentralisation. It isn't just about ideology, either; it's about finding the correct ratio for the DAO to run effectively without mimicking a traditional company. Cooperative organisations are famously a bit chaotic, and DAOs, which are essentially a kind of digital cooperative, are no different. When Fingerprints started, we had next to no hierarchy. It was one big group discussion, stimulated in large part by the collective excitement about being part of this new thing. Eventually, and inevitably in a space where so much is happening all the time, some of those original contributors went off to focus on other things, and we realised that we needed a more resilient structure.

How do you incentivise people? This is a major question for every DAO, and there's a wide array of strongly held opinions on the subject. There's the rationalist school of thought that believes that DAOs are predicated on "skin in the game": your membership – which usually takes the form of your tokens – should be incentive enough for you to participate. My own view is different. Just having tokens isn't enough. Most people find it psychologically difficult to work for deferred rewards – especially the sort of rewards that may not ever be realised. And there's the very real fact that most people cannot work without compensation that pays the bills! This is one thing I've observed in crypto: many people, especially the earlier adopters, have made enough money not to need a regular salary, and they assume the same of others. At the same time, some of those people promote DAOs as these places to "get your start" in the industry. You can't have it both ways.

Our answer to the incentivisation problem has been to experiment with different compensation models. For example, we use an application called Coordinape that allows members in each working group to vote on each other's contributions every month. One of the main issues with this model, which is a problem that afflicts DAOs in other ways as well, is that some types of work are more visible than others. Discord is a useful hub for the DAO's activities, but not everything can be done there – in fact, we have lots of members who aren't even on Discord. When you're liaising with third parties on something important, or writing strategy documents or proposals, that work isn't happening on Discord. So you end up with a situation where the people who are doing the most visible work are those who get rewarded the most, even though they may not be making the largest or most valuable contributions overall.

These concerns ultimately led us to develop a multi-tier compensation model. We now have a group of people who each oversee different core areas of the DAO, and those people are compensated regularly. Meanwhile, the Coordinape process has been reserved for rewarding contributions towards specific tasks or projects. One drawback of this approach is that more passive members and less frequent contributors can begin to feel less involved. It's extremely important that every member feels both that they have a voice and that they can participate in everything that's going on should they wish to do so.

Can you talk a little about how the technology employed in your DAO functions in relation to, and is co-constituted with, other more fleshy modes of communication and organising, such as informal conversations, meeting up in person, physical exhibitions, etc.? And perhaps Mitchell you could say something here too about how your work "executes" and manifests itself in the world on screens, in collections, with audiences, and how these entangle with the characteristics of NFTs and DAOs?

Mitchell F. Chan: Maybe I'm a hopeless boomer. But looking at how I've managed the Web3 space, I realise now that most of the career satisfaction I've experienced in the past year-and-a-half has come from pulling connections I've made in the Web3 community *back* into Web2 or (gasp) meatspace. I've used the DAO as a launchpad to do Twitter Spaces talks

---

3. PFP refers to the use of NFT artwork as "profile pictures", such as *Bored Ape* (2021), on social media sites.

with people I'm interested in. I've met up with a lot of Web3 folks IRL.

Web3 has a lot of values—like pseudonymity, "trustlessness", and immutability – which, if you live by them 24/7, can feel downright dehumanising. I really don't want to be an Ape PFP who only exists to enter immutable financial relationships with other Frog PFPs.[3] I like the frogs – that's fine – but I can't live my life as one.

Web3 is a very abstract world in almost every way. Relationships are forged through shared investment of imaginary money. Even the broad aesthetics of the space are very abstract! By that, I mean: tooling in Web3 is still very primitive. The interfaces you're dealing with every day don't yet have a lot of that slickness, that Apple-style Engineered-For-Optimal-Humanlike-Sensation feeling. The languages are still pretty low level. So if you're building in Web3, even your code feels, well, close to machine language, and less expressive.

And yet...

What is absolutely counterintuitive to some people, but which I know to be true, is that this alien zone of abstraction really is charged with genuine... I don't know what word to use here: feeling? emotion? However I phrase it, it will sound cheesy... It comes down to how this financial (or financial-style) investment does often come with an attached emotional investment. These "communities" we see that are built around, say, a shared interest in seeing the price of a monkey token go up are charged with a genuine emotional fervour. Real relationships are being built in that space, regardless of what you think about the original motivations for entering this space.

Sam Spike: Congregating in physical spaces can be difficult. Like most DAOs, Fingerprints has a very global membership, so it's rare that enough people are gathered in a city to justify hosting an event. But there have been a few occasions where we have got together in person. For example, we held a party last year during the NFTNYC conference in New York. It was amazing to meet so many members there, even though a combination of Covid restrictions and geographical distance meant that many people couldn't attend. We also organised a few things during last year's Miami Art Week.

Other than social gatherings, we are really interested in ways that blockchain art can be manifested in physical settings in the form of installations and exhibitions. At this year's Art Dubai, we worked with the German artist group terra0 to stage an artwork called *Seed Capital*, where a live plant generated NFTs every fifteen minutes as long as the environmental conditions of the fair were favourable for its survival. Organising the project wasn't easy. Being so online and so entirely crypto-centric made the logistics of travel and shipping and payment much more complicated than they would have been for a conventional gallery. There's still so much friction between the two worlds. But we learned a lot from the experience and are planning other presentations for later in the year, such as a show of Sarah Friend's work in New York this summer.

How much do you see yourselves as part of a tradition of disrupting artworld power and how do you position Fingerprints in relation to other more established artworld collectors and institutions? Also, in what way do you see those who are new to collecting, but were early crypto adopters, and their specific interests and knowledges, relating, and being different to, more traditional collectors? And what kinds of potential for cross-fertilisation and hybridisation exist here?

Sam Spike: We're not really trying to be disruptors. For us, it's much more about experimenting with new models and being ambassadors for an emerging body of artistic practice that itself engages with those models. I don't think that every company or every museum will be a DAO in ten years. Nor do I think that they should be. But part of what we're doing – and this is true for every DAO right now – is making the inevitable mistakes and learning the lessons first so that other, more traditional, slower-moving organisations can figure out how to adapt later on.

I do think that DAOs have huge potential within an art context. You can be a lot more flexible with what you do and how you do it, and you can mutualise interests in a way that wasn't so possible before. A good example of this is how most of the artists that Fingerprints collects have become members of the DAO. As collectors, we want them to do well; and as members, they also want Fingerprints to be successful.

We made the most of this alignment last year when we were invited by Sotheby's to participate in one of their NFT auctions. The auction was supposed to spotlight the leading collectors in the NFT market, and they wanted us to consign three works from our collection. Since our collection had all been acquired within the past six months at that point, and since we have no plans to sell our art any time soon, we didn't have anything to consign. Instead, we approached three of our artist-members – Mitchell was one of them – and asked whether they would like to consign the works themselves. The arrangement was that they would put their own works up for sale and receive the proceeds from the auction. In return, they agreed to consign the work under the Fingerprints name. They earned the financial rewards of selling their work, and we earned the reputational rewards of taking part in this auction. It was a win-win for everyone.

Participating in an auction at Sotheby's is one example of us working with more established art institutions, but it's certainly not the only, nor the principal, kind of collaboration that we're striving for. We're particularly keen to work more with institutions that have been championing digital art since long before it was fashionable or profitable to do so. There's a lot of rewriting of history going on in the NFT space – a lot of ignorance, both wilful and genuine, about longer histories of digital art and media art that are many decades (if not centuries!) old. These avenues of exploration aren't new. What might be new – and this is a question that the Fingerprints collection invites discussion around – are the affordances of blockchain technology as an artistic tool. But, whether new or not in certain aspects, the work we collect absolutely does not exist in a historical or cultural vacuum. We believe that we have a lot to learn from existing cultural organisations – museums, universities, galleries – in telling that story, just as we also believe that we are well-positioned to help amplify their voices in a space that is generally distrustful of the so-called "gatekeepers" of "trad culture".

In terms of new collectors, it's tough to generalise, but there is clearly a new group of people, mostly from tech and finance backgrounds, who have started collecting art through NFTs. Some of the earliest adopters, who have seen their lives transformed by their investments in cryptocurrencies, place a premium on artwork that represents the memes and mythologies of crypto culture: the crystal logo of Ethereum, for example, or Matt Furie's Pepe the Frog character, subsequently co-opted by the alt-right. Other early adopters, including many of the more technical ones, prefer artworks that incorporate blockchain technology in some way. Many of our members first developed an interest in art through on-chain generative artworks like *Autoglyphs*, or the projects released on the Art Blocks platform. By storing the code used to generate the art on the blockchain itself, these sorts of NFTs have earned a reputation for being "crypto-native" – and thus desirable – in a way that other art NFTs have not.

On the surface, this is all different from how a traditional art collector would likely value an artwork: it requires deep immersion in crypto culture and often a relatively advanced understanding of how blockchains work. Fundamentally, though, I'm not sure it's so different at all: it's just an alternative milieu (younger and more online, maybe, and more technologically minded) with its own iconography and social signifiers – signifiers that are hurriedly being learned within the traditional art world and beyond as people scramble to participate in this new market.

I want to conclude by discussing this issue of difference to existing systems that's been touched upon already. Firstly, the carbon footprint of the blockchain and crypto-art, as researched by people like Sarah Friend, Memo Atken and Kyle McDonald, is huge[4] and something that marks it out as truly different from other modes of art production and distribution. How do you see this being addressed in the future and are their any specific things you're doing in your own work to address this?

Mitchell F. Chan: This is a difficult issue to address because I can't really do anything but hand-wave it, and no-one wins when I do that. Perhaps, we'll have the proof-of-stake merge by the time this interview is published, at which point I suspect that Ethereum will have a smaller carbon footprint than the legacy banking system or art world.

Sam Spike: The energy usage of proof-of-work blockchains is an issue that has, for good reason, vexed the public conversation about crypto and NFTs for the past eighteen months. It's also an issue that bears more nuance than it is usually granted in those discussions.

As a community of individuals who have been active in the Ethereum ecosystem for a long time, Fingerprints DAO's decision to acquire Ethereum NFTs reflects a collective belief in the decentralised ethos of that ecosystem. One unfortunate feature of blockchain technology is the difficulty of balancing decentralisation – which ensures network security – with energy efficiency. For example, it's often the case that the computational requirements of running a node on a proof-of-stake blockchain are prodigious.

Everyone in Fingerprints is excited for the forthcoming "merge" of Ethereum, which will see the network transition to a proof-of-stake system in a way that safeguards its decentralised structure. In the meantime, when

4. https://the-crypto-syllabus.com/bibliography-energy-climate.

releasing NFT projects ourselves, we have often sought to mitigate the environmental impact by using offsets and direct carbon removal schemes to achieve carbon negative status.

Finally, what seems significant about some of your responses is that your claims for the radicality of NFTs and DAOs appear relatively modest, which might be refreshing to some, but is also perhaps at odds with some of the hyperbole one encounters in the space. My impression is that blockchain, NFT, and DAO technologies and systems on their own do not really offer any substantial alternative to current capitalist and socio-technical paradigms, rather they seem to almost intensify it or demonstrate how much corresponding processes of financialisation, quantification, commodification, and ownership have become internalised and the status quo. The degree to which these "master's tools" are being touted as radically different feels revealing to me of both this internalisation and sublation, *and* people's desire for another world, a frustration at the failure of our political systems, our struggle to think and organise beyond them.

I don't see this simply as a weakness, especially if you adjust your expectation dial, because by embodying so much of our current systems, can they more readily function as a bridge or part of a transition to something else, perhaps? Or to put it another way, do you think that by being somehow simultaneously similar and different enough to existing orders, DAOs and their like, can function critically as keys to learn about, open up and refunction prevailing systems of value, money, law, computation, organising, and collaboration?

Mitchell F. Chan: Well, I'd start by saying that you've summarised my conclusions on the topic really well! That's about it! Now, let me put on my optimistic perspective for a moment. If, indeed, DAOs and other tokenised systems really are accelerated versions of existing power structures, then the benefit they can have is to make those structures completely transparent. And frankly, that transparency plus increased speed means that they will fail *faster*. So a good-case scenario is that tokenised, hyper-capitalised systems will be the great enema of a decadent society.

There *are* however, important use cases for DAOs out there, I just kind of feel it in my gut. And I see hints of this when I read the work of terra0, or writing by Vitalik or Sam Hart on "public goods". It must always start with the question: where does it *actually make sense* to link equity and governance into the same highly-liquid unit? I'm sure there are places where this does make sense! I'm pretty sure the conversation should start with public goods.

But mapping that DAO structure onto those rare real-life scenarios is hard and it takes time, largely because it requires the formation of public consent. Maybe it's a great irony that the implementation of "trustless" systems on society will require significantly more public "trust" of the system itself. The kind of trust which is very much off-chain.

Sam Spike: One thing that's certain about DAOs is that nobody can agree on what they are. There's a very wide range of groups and organisations out there calling themselves DAOs, but their objectives and operational methods couldn't be more diverse. Some use tokens, some don't. Some have thousands of members, others fewer than ten. Any idealistic claims about DAOs that treat them as a monolithic category should be treated with scepticism. The same goes for criticism.

Public goods are definitely one way that DAOs can manifest in a positive form, and there's a lot of great work being done on that front, as Mitchell says. Another shape that DAOs can take, which I mentioned earlier, is that of the cultural or artistic cooperative. There's a long history of collectivist experimentation in the arts, and DAOs can play a role in continuing that legacy. A good example is the Holly+ DAO project, started by Holly Herndon and Mat Dryhurst in 2021. Members of the DAO govern the commercial usage of machine learning instruments trained on Herndon's voice. In other words, they decide who's allowed to make money with her AI likeness. The project uses a DAO to place an artist's identity in the hands of a community, asking challenging questions about authorship, intellectual property, profit-sharing, and the creative possibilities of both AI and blockchain.

DAOs are no panacea, and I agree that they often intensify existing relations of capital, but I don't think that an accelerationist outlook is the only hopeful one available. In their most basic form as a category, DAOs are groups of people coordinated via decentralised technologies: group chats, large or small, with digital sovereignty. What those people choose to do together, how well they collaborate, whether they use tokens, and so on, are all open questions whose myriad answers may lead us towards new horizons, or not. At their most inventive, I would argue that they already are.

This Is Fine: Optimism and Emergency in the Decentralised Network

Cade Diehm

The last fifteen years has seen a surge of interest in decentralised and peer-to-peer (PTP) technology. From well-funded blockchain projects like IPFS's Filecoin to the emergence of large-scale information networks such as Dat, Scuttlebutt and ActivityPub, this is a renaissance that enjoys widespread growth, driven largely by the desire for platform commons and community self-determination. These are goals that are fundamentally at odds with – and a response to – the incumbent centralised platforms for social media, music and movie distribution, and data storage. In the early 2020s, centralised platforms and decentralised communities are in conflict over control of digital public space. The resilience of centralised networks and the political power of their owners remains significantly underestimated by the activists behind the decentralised networks and the communities they serve. Consequently, today's PTP movements have never been more vulnerable, and are dangerously unprepared for a crisis-fueled future that has very suddenly arrived at their door.

Good luck to all those striving for decentralization, balance and equality in the world. You are fighting the right battle. This battle may well be the most important battle of our generation. — Pavel Durov, founder of Telegram, 2020.[1]

"Torrents are down, worldwide" said no one, ever. #centralizationisfragile — Tweet by PTP developer André Staltz.[2]

How precarious are decentralised networks? Answering this requires an understanding of both the power of their political energy and their history of antagonism. Conceptually, PTP technologies are not new – they are networks of digital topologies, intertwining configurations of software clients, devices, connections and protocols whose ownership is distributed. They work in concert to provide a robust alternative to centralised governance, ideally achieving data resilience without transferring the ownership of this data to a single authority. The internet itself is a decentralised network that has resisted the centralisation of the platforms and services accessed within.

Often – but not always – decentralised networks emerge due to a collective desire to rebalance societal power. This is an intergenerational goal shared by 1990s cypherpunks, open source and free software movements and today's technology activists.[3] Throughout the history of digital platforms, there have been countless stories of the clash between centralised power and decentralised challengers. One of the most important historical examples was the series of legal battles over digital intellectual property rights. This conflict – a so-called *Copyright War*[4] – had started

1. Pavel Durov, "What Was TON And Why It Is Over," *Telegraph*, May 12, 2020, https://telegra.ph/What-Was-TON-And-Why-It-Is-Over-05-12.

2. André Staltz, "'Torrents Are down, Worldwide' Said No One, Ever. #centralizationisfragile," Twitter, *@andrestaltz*, April 21, 2020, https://twitter.com/andrestaltz/status/1252660215897522176.

3. Paul Frazee, "Information Civics: Deconstructing the Power Structures of Large-Scale Social Computing Networks," July 29, 2018, https://web.archive.org/web/20180810230449/https://infocivics.com.

4. Peter Baldwin, *The Copyright Wars: Three Centuries of Trans-Atlantic Battle* (Princeton University Press, 2014).

"offline" decades earlier, as a battle to suppress the activity of the taping and sharing of copyrighted material on video and audio cassettes.[5] In 1999, this conflict collided with digital infrastructure for the first time after the launch of Napster. Napster was arguably the first mainstream PTP filesharing startup. The resulting international legal conflict between the copyright-reform movement inspired by Napster and copyright holders would last over a decade and its fallout reverberates into the present. The copyright war offers a historical example of ideological conflicts between centralised powers and decentralised activism. Through the use of PTP technologies, the copyright reformists came close to dismantling an existing centralised capitalist ownership structures of music, television and film. These activists pushed for a post-scarcity, digitally-driven cultural method of distribution. At the same time, the same activists failed to appreciate the resilience of their opponents, even as it economically and legally weaponised their PTP structures against them.

Early file-sharing software such as Napster and its clones featured simple interfaces and enormous content offerings. They arrived years before popular digital music stores, and shook the music and movie industry into mobilising against them. These early file-sharing networks were tied to their client software, and they were easily shut down by litigation from the music industry against the developers. Between 1998 and 2000, copyright reformists began campaigning on behalf of Napster and similar tools, but as residential internet connections became cheaper and faster, and demand for data freedom grew, these activists saw new promise within the application structure itself – an opportunity embedded in the network layer.

BitTorrent's launch in 2001 enabled file-sharing on a massive, efficient and resilient scale. By embedding the decentralised ethos of Napster beneath a desktop client, and within the protocol on which the client runs, the act of file-sharing became much more resistant to legislative attack because there was no longer a single company – such as Napster – to attack. BitTorrent seemed unstoppable. Most of the discourse at the time prophesied the devastation of an existing capitalist cultural order, interpreting the massive international decline in sales of recorded music sales as a "self-destructive" act by record labels unwilling

5. Ted Mills, "Home Taping Is Killing Music: When the Music Industry Waged War on the Cassette Tape in the 1980s, and Punk Bands Fought Back," *Open Culture*, April 5, 2019, https://www.openculture.com/2019/04/home-taping-is-killing-music.html.

to adapt to this new digital future.[6] This perception was accelerated by significant ideological moments of the era: the establishment of the first collaborative online music library,[7] the foundation of the Pirate Bay website, censorship-resistant document distribution, and the formation of the *Piratpartiet*,[8] and its international equivalents.[9]

The incumbent powers – major record labels, film studios and television networks from Europe and the United States – worked with lawmakers[10] to draft new legislation and went after "leechers" – people downloading content, and through BitTorrent's protocol design became unwitting uploaders themselves.[11] Litigators discovered that by conducting surveillance on a BitTorrent tracker, they could bulk collect participating IP addresses and randomly file severe civic lawsuits, utilising harsher laws reserved for distribution. Their targets were often the economically vulnerable, including *"children, grandparents, unemployed single mothers, college professors – a random selection from the millions of Americans who have used PTP networks."* [12] The litigation that formed this attack was one piece of a broader scattershot strategy that spared no one: infrastructure,[13] physical media,[14] broadcast media,[15] adjacent software projects and device manufacturers were all targeted. The counter-offensive against PTP-driven copyright reform could manifest as

6. Steve Knopper, *Appetite for Self-Destruction: The Spectacular Crash of the Record Industry in the Digital Age* (Free Press, 2009).

7. Nikhil Sonnad, "The Greatest Music Collection in the World Just Vanished," *Quartz*, November 18, 2016, https://qz.com/840661/what-cd-is-gone-a-eulogy-for-the-greatest-music-collection-in-the-world.

8. Nate Anderson, "Political Pirates: A History of Sweden's Piratpartiet," *Ars Technica*, February 26, 2009, https://arstechnica.com/tech-policy/2009/02/rick-falkvinge-is-the-face.

9. See for example, Pirate Party International: https://pp-international.net.

10. The Pirate Bay, "Chief Police Investigator in Pirate Bay Trial Employed by the Copyright Industry," Press Release, April 18, 2008, https://web.archive.org/web/20130303121410/http://static.thepiratebay.org/pm/20080418_eng.txt.

11. In order for this distribution to work, partially downloaded data on a participant's machine must be made available to all others on the network.

12. Electronic Frontier Foundation, "RIAA v. The People: Five Years Late," September 30, 2008, https://www.eff.org/wp/riaa-v-people-five-years-later.

13. Greg Sandoval, "RIAA Drops Lawsuits; ISPs to Battle File Sharing," *CNET*, November 12, 2009, https://www.cnet.com/tech/services-and-software/riaa-drops-lawsuits-isps-to-battle-file-sharing.

copyright taxes on CD–Rs or portable media players, or as legal liability, as was the case in unsuccessful legislation proposals that attempted to force internet service providers to bear responsibility for user activity, making them liable for PTP activity within their networks.

Representatives for the music and media industry giants – such as the Recording Industry Association of America and the Motion Picture Association of America – described the conflict as a fight against music and film "piracy." However, this rhetoric obscures the serious implications of the tactics deployed by these giants. Central to the defeat of this particular PTP movement was that its infrastructure was vulnerable to *weaponised* design,[16] a state in which a system harms users while behaving exactly as intended. Bittorrent's design was weaponised through a simple rule that had overlooked and far reaching consequences: the Bittorrent protocol exposes every user's participation in the network to anyone who can see the network. Exposing the unwitting user's IP address within the PTP system was exploited to unmask users, ruin lives and provide justification for new legislation. The collapse of centralised power that was prophesied in the 2000s never materialised. In 2013, BitTorrent was responsible for 3.35% of all internet traffic.[17] Today the networks remain but this market share has shrunk. Torrents are down worldwide. Centralised actors outmaneuvered the reformists, shielding themselves and their own ecosystems from scrutiny. The concentrated media companies,[18] and the innovations pioneered by decentralised infrastructure were exploited by the winners as they ascended to monopoly.

The most poetic example of PTP technologies pressed into the ser-

14. An example of European private copying levy legislation can be found in "Modifiés par les articles 4 à 8 de la loi portant des dispositions diverses du 20 juillet 2005," *Le Moniteur belge*, https://www.ejustice.just.fgov.be/mopdf/2009/12/23_1.pdf.

15. Andrew Moseman, "RIAA and Streaming Sites Reach Accord But Internet Radio Is Still in Trouble," *Popular Mechanics*, October 1, 2009, https://www.popularmechanics.com/technology/gadgets/4284518.

16. Cade Diehm, "On Weaponised Design," *Our Data Our Selves*, Tactical Tech, 2018, https://ourdataourselves.tacticaltech.org/posts/30-on-weaponised-design.

17. Palo Alto Networks, "Application Usage & Threat Report," February, 2013, https://www.paloaltonetworks.com/blog/app-usage-risk-report-visualization.

18. A key example of media centralisation and wealth can be found in the $71.3 billion merger between the Walt Disney Company and 21st Century Fox in 2019, unprecedented both in value and in cultural IP ownership.

vice of corporate giants is the story of PTP software engineer Ludvig Strigeus. Having built the popular μTorrent client and perhaps sensing the changing winds, Strigeus joined former μTorrent CEO Daniel Ek's new startup. Together, they built a quasi-Napster/BitTorrent hybrid that relied on a vast, unauthorised music catalog drawn from its user base.[19] Today, that architecture is long gone, but the startup – Spotify – boasts 124 million subscribers, taking in USD\$7.44 billion in revenue[20] but paying artists just USD\$4.37 per 1,000 streams.

As we can see from history, is it naive to place faith in decentralised network protocols themselves as ideologically aligned with the PTP mission. The Copyright War drives home hard lessons around politics, corporate appropriation, transparency, collectivism and the urgency of network safety, all illustrated in the decimated lives of key or adjacent reformists,[21] collateral user damage, and resulting legislation.

Only a crisis – actual or perceived – produces real change. When the crisis occurs, the actions that are taken depend on the ideas that are lying around. That, I believe, is our basic function: to develop alternatives to existing policies, to keep them alive and available until the politically impossible becomes politically inevitable. — Milton Friedman, *Capitalism and Freedom*[22]

Your objective [as a designer] should always be to eliminate instructions entirely by making everything self-explanatory, or as close to it as possible. When instructions are absolutely necessary, cut them back to a bare minimum. — Steve Krug, *Don't Make Me Think*[23]

19. Maria Eriksson et al., *Spotify Teardown: Inside the Black Box of Streaming Music*, (Cambridge, MA: MIT Press, 2019).

20. Marc Schneider, "Spotify Increases Paid User Base to 124M, Reports \$7.44B Revenue in 2019," *Billboard*, February 2, 2020, https://www.billboard.com/pro/spotify-earnings-2019-paid-user-totals-financial-results-q4.

21. For example, see: Pirate Bay raids conducted by Swedish police in 2006 (https://torrentfreak.com//images/pirate_mpa.pdf) and 2014 (https://www.theverge.com/2014/12/9/7364665/the-pirate-bay-goes-offline-after-police-raid-server-room).

22. Milton Friedman, Rose D. Friedman, and Binyamin Appelbaum, *Capitalism and Freedom* (London: University of Chicago Press, 2020).

As the Copyright War faded into the background, the iPhone paradigm – a constrained, centralised, individualised system marketed as "the individual at one with their device" – became the standard for personal computing. New and boundless design-led opportunities appeared almost overnight, powered by a bottomless injection of venture capital that fostered the accelerated growth of platform capitalism.[24] Platform capitalism, an economic model of individual isolation and exploitation of labour and value from users within digital platforms such as Airbnb or Uber, was the software answer to the individualised hand-held mobile computer. Together, this hardware and software configuration became central to the rise of Neoliberalism. To quote design and art historians Arden Stern and Sami Siegelbaum:

Neoliberalism can be distinguished from Fordist capitalism's mass production of consumer goods by the ways it seeks to marketize previously uncommodified sectors of human life. Indeed, one of the questions [we seek] to explore is how design might enable this process by locating new sources of extraction and accumulation by facilitating the commodification of that which was once thought to be outside the scope of the market.[25]

Finding these new sources of extraction became a priority for centralised tech platforms. They had spent the previous decade achieving scale and resilience; now they sought to extract new value and justify their presence in daily life. Framing the mobile device as an extension of self made the emergence of the new "digital wellbeing" market compelling. For example, Safety Check – a Facebook feature introduced after the 2011 Tōhoku earthquake and tsunami – encourages users in disaster-stricken areas to interact with the platform to mark themselves as safe and be connected to communication services for disaster relief.[26] The Apple Watch – origi-

---

23. Steve Krug, *Don't Make Me Think, Revisited: A Common Sense Approach to Web Usability* (Berkeley: New Riders, 2014).

24. Nick Srnicek and Laurent De Sutter, *Platform Capitalism* (Cambridge: Polity, 2017).

25. Arden Stern and Sami Siegelbaum, "Special Issue: Design and Neoliberalism," *Design and Culture* 11, no. 3 (September, 2019): 265–77. https://doi.org/10.1080/17547075.2019.16671 88.

26. "Crisis Response," Meta (formerly Facebook). Accessed April 10, 2020, https://www.facebook.com/about/crisisresponse/v2.

nally launched as a general-purpose wrist computer – underwent a complete rebrand as a digital health and fitness device, and its ability to detect and call emergency services in crisis is actively marketed in emotional video testimonials released by its maker.[27, 28] Amazon Ring and Google Nest encourage consumers to actively contribute to a growing network of community surveillance systems promising safety in exchange for ceding the household's digital capital to a powerful, unaccountable platform.[29]

These tech-driven efforts to respond to safety and crisis are not new, and indeed much of this work is framed both internally and externally within the cliche of "making the world a better place."[30] But these efforts also serve a dual function; they are political tools that through design can instantly reconfigure a moment in time. An Apple Watch is marketed to the physically vulnerable senior citizen, but the same interface has been programmed as a digital bystander, bearing witness on behalf of Black Americans during traffic stops.[31] Effective design at scale is obvious and frictionless – lowering cognitive and training barriers to adoption – and contextually voided – enabling context to be re-inserted after the design is shipped.

In her 2007 book, *The Shock Doctrine*, Naomi Klein lays bare the clandestine policies employed by powerful societies to expand influence and ownership through exploitation of real or manufactured crisis.[32] Klein cites societal-wide disasters – the invasion of Iraq as a pretext for greater US control in the Middle East or, most recently, identifying the privatisation of infrastructure after the 2018 Puerto Rico hurricane[33] as the pretexts for this overreach. The ubiquity of human-centred design[34]

27. Apple, *Apple Watch – Dear Apple*, 2017, https://www.youtube.com/watch?v=N-x8Ik9G5Dg.

28. Apple, "911", 2022, https://www.youtube.com/watch?v=QJ2JiwEARFo.

29. Darren Wershler, "The Locative, the Ambient, and the Hallucinatory in the Internet of Things," *Design and Culture* 2, no. 2 (July 2010): 199–216, https://doi.org/10.2752/175470710X12696138525703.

30. Rahul Bhatia, "The inside Story of Facebook's Biggest Setback," *The Guardian*, May 12, 2016, https://www.theguardian.com/technology/2016/may/12/facebook-free-basics-india-zuckerberg.

31. Robert Petersen, "Getting Pulled over by Police," Reddit Post. R/Shortcuts, September 21, 2018, www.reddit.com/r/shortcuts/comments/9huqiw/getting_pulled_over_by_police.

32. Naomi Klein, *The Shock Doctrine: The Rise of Disaster Capitalism.* (New York: Metropolitan Books/Henry Holt, 2017).

offers flexible opportunities to use technologies to extract value and consolidate power. The design of the Apple Watch, Safety Check and particularly COVID–19 Contact Tracing APIs[35] must be understood as whitelabelled crisis response – *Shock Doctrine as a Service* – employing dominant, market-driven design methodologies to drive mass adoption of products and services that are then easily reconfigured during moments of disaster. Presented as opportunities to protect or save lives, these functionalities are rolled out in homes, communities and cities as software updates or addons – without allowing any negotiation or meaningful consent. When deployed in response to broader crises, their creators benefit from being perceived as philanthropic architects, intervening on humanitarian grounds. In reality, they negotiate from positions of extreme concentrations of wealth, technical expertise and political influence.[36] The philanthropic framing robs dissenters of what remains of their ability to withdraw consent: How can one object to saving lives?

There is a part of my high-school globo-claustrophobia that has never left me, and in some ways only seems to intensify as time creeps along. What haunts me is not exactly the absence of literal space so much as a deep craving for metaphorical space: release, escape, some kind of open-ended freedom. — Naomi Klein, *No Logo*[37]

33. Naomi Klein, *The Battle for Paradise: Puerto Rico Takes on the Disaster Capitalists* (Haymarket Books, 2018).

34. A term that describes a product design process in which a designer builds a "deep empathy for the people they are designing for" from: IDEO.org, *The Field Guide to Human-Centered Design* (Design Kit, 2015).

35. InstitutefTiPI, '"The Long Tail of Contact Tracing" (Societal Impact of CT), Issue #118, DP-3T/Documents, *GitHub*, April 10, 2020, https://github.com/DP-3T/documents/issues/118.

36. Patrick Howell O'Neill, Tate Ryan-Mosley and Bobbie Johnson, "A Flood of Coronavirus Apps Are Tracking Us. Now It's Time to Keep Track of Them," *MIT Technology Review*, May 7, 2020, https://www.technologyreview.com/2020/05/07/1000961/launching-mittr-covid-tracing-tracker.

37. Naomi Klein, *No Logo: No Space, No Choice, No Jobs* (London: Harper Perennial, 2005).

How the fuck do so many zoomers not know how to torrent things?
— Tweet by @Ex_AnarchoAnon [38]

The neoliberal technology order seemed secure in its dominance. The 2016 US elections and Brexit vote changed all that; ugly, internationally visible clusters of ever-escalating patterns of barbaric behaviour perpetuated and enabled by incumbent power. Cambridge Analytica and its clientele were far from the first to manipulate the social graph in the name of electioneering, [39, 40] but these campaigns and their surrounding turmoil triggered a collapse in end users' trust of centralised platforms. In the years leading up to the election, centralised platforms had been strained by surveillance, manipulated by money, and littered with repeated failures to address abuse. In response, the PTP communities that had been quietly designing alternatives for years awoke charged and energised; a new wave of interest in decentralisation was emerging.

Who are these PTP communities? They are developers, designers and early adopters. Their politics are diverse, yet there are areas of consensus. They rally around the values of self expression, alternative data governance, censorship resistance and interoperability. Their communities organise, debate and signal politics through their respective networks, encoding protests in encryption,[41] or framing servers around self-expression.[42] Common to all of these individuals and communities is a belief in the protocol as a political device. Simone Riobutti describes

38. Anonymous Kaiju, "How the Fuck Do so Many Zoomers Not Know How to Torrent Things," Twitter, *@Ex_AnarchoAnon*, May 16, 2020, https://twitter.com/Ex_AnarchoAnon/status/1261725527691464704.

39. Sasha Issenberg, *How Obama's Team Used Big Data to Rally Voters*, MIT Technology Review, December 19, 2012, https://www.technologyreview.com/2012/12/19/114510/how-obamas-team-used-big-data-to-rally-voters.

40. Rachel Gibson and Ian McAllister, "Do Online Election Campaigns Win Votes? The 2007 Australian 'YouTube' Election," *Political Communication* 28, no. 2 (April 2011): 227–44, https://doi.org/10.1080/10584609.2011.568042.

41. While executing the Bitcoin network's first transaction, Satoshi Nakomoto embedded additional text into the block: "The Times 03/Jan/2009 Chancellor on brink of second bailout for banks," and this is widely interpreted to be ideologically motivated, https://en.bitcoin.it/wiki/Genesis_block.

42. Aymeric Mansoux and Roel Roscam Abbing, "Seven Theses On The Fediverse and The Becoming Of FLOSS," *Transmediale*, no. 4 (July 7, 2020).

this as the "Hackerist perspective": an *"attempt to alter technology for political reasons by repurposing technological artifacts without concerning oneself with altering the process that produced said technology."* [43] Here, the unaltered process is the process of protocol design by makers who are ignorant to both lessons of the Copyright War and the emerging threats facing their own societies.

In 2018, the Dat Foundation spoke publicly of their desire to harness their simple and powerful PTP file distribution technology – the Dat Protocol – to build a decentralised, censorship-resistant Wikipedia mirror [44] but shortly after this announcement, the effort was abandoned. The team involved realised that, although their data containers (called *Dat archives*) are encrypted, network participants were as vulnerable and easy to track as the BitTorrent targets from the Copyright War. In a follow up blog post entitled, *Do Not Ship It*, the team elaborated:

> *Reader privacy is one of the hardest (ethical) parts of a PTP system. Distributing Wikipedia over a PTP system means that any user can surveil the IP addresses of other users and, depending on how it is distributed, even identify what pages they are requesting. For us, this is an unacceptable first-order effect. The impact of this first-order surveillance problem leads us to even more concerning questions about the second- and third-order impacts of that decision.* [45]

The Dat Foundation's caution over political use of their protocol is at odds with how the protocol is used. A year before, Dat had already been used to archive and mirror climate research that had been politically censored by the incoming Trump administration. [46] Shortly after *Do Not Ship It* was published, the personal details of thousands of US Immigration and Customs Enforcement officers were scraped from LinkedIn by a pro-

43. Simone Robutti, "Against Hackerism, Pt. 1," November 24, 2019, https://write.as/simone-robutti/work-notebooks-against-hackerism-pt.

44. Mathias Buus Madsen, *PTP Web/Berlin*, Talk, 2018, https://web.archive.org/web/20180323000724/https://peer-to-peer-web.com/berlin.

45. Joe Hand, "Do Not Ship It," *Dat Blog*, December 10, 2017, https://blog.datproject.org/2017/12/10/dont-ship.

46. John Chodacki, "Ensuring Access to Critical Research Data," *University of California Curation Center*, March 2, 2017, https://uc3.cdlib.org/2017/03/02/ensuring-access-to-critical-research-data.

tester and posted to GitHub.[47] When Microsoft's lawyers intervened and removed the archive, it was mirrored to Dat to evade further censorship. In both of these instances, the protocol was used in political protests against a belligerent corporate-captured political office. In both cases, the protocol easily surrenders the identities of anyone who participates in these protests. That the protocol was designed without a strong investment into participant privacy directly led to two incredibly dangerous moments for network participants.

Reviewing the technical documentation of the Dat protocol, researcher and privacy advocate Sarah Jamie Lewis expressed her frustration towards its designers' claims about the impossibility of network privacy. Quoting the whitepaper, she tweeted:

> *There is a section that reads: 'There is an inherent tradeoff in PTP systems of source discovery vs. user privacy.' I disagree with the statement & the impact resulting design decisions have on privacy. Freenet presented solutions to this problem which provided strong guarantees for reader anonymity and publisher anonymity nearly 2 decades ago.*[48, 49]

Decentralisation advocates roleplay as antagonists for change, but they have yet to truly threaten incumbent power. Instead, the de-prioritisation of privacy by design – regardless of its justification – enables its behaviour and offers it new scope for surveillance and control.

This is true for many of the communities that have formed around decentralised protocols. On Secure Scuttlebutt, a powerful offline-first PTP network, nothing can be deleted or modified, identities are linked

47. Brian Feldman, "LinkedIn List of ICE Employees Removed by Medium and GitHub," *New York Magazine*, June 20, 2018, https://nymag.com/intelligencer/2018/06/linkedin-list-of-ice-employees-removed-by-medium-and-github.html.

48. Ian Clarke et al., "Freenet: A Distributed Anonymous Information Storage and Retrieval System," in *Designing Privacy Enhancing Technologies*, ed. Hannes Federrath, Lecture Notes in Computer Science, Vol 2009, (2001), https://doi.org/10.1007/3-540-44702-4_4.

49. Sarah Jamie Lewis, "In the Dat Protocol White Paper under Network Privacy, There Is a Section That Reads: 'There Is an Inherent Tradeoff in Peer to Peer Systems of Source Discovery vs. User Privacy.' I Disagree with the Statement & the Impact Resulting Design Decisions Have on Privacy," Twitter, *@SarahJamieLewis*, June 17, 2018, https://twitter.com/SarahJamieLewis/status/1008111920988106753.

cryptographically to individual devices, and the asynchronous nature of the platform is highly resilient – meaning that data can't be erased. Even the act of changing your name or following or unfollowing someone creates a permanent record. This beautifully designed decentralised network provides unprecedented resilience for communication across areas with poor network connectivity. This protocol also happens to be a forensically sound surveillance tool, in which nothing can be retracted and proof of authorship can be traced to specific devices.[50] The protocol has attracted a vibrant community that leans left-wing libertarian, engaging openly and eagerly in post-capitalist discourse and baying for serious alternatives to neoliberalism. This is a dream for network surveillance. The danger could not be more obvious.

The Fediverse – a network comprised of Mastodon, Pleroma and other adjacent projects[51] – suffers from the same glaring contradiction. Similar to email nodes, servers (known as *Instances* within this network) are branded around common interests, political beliefs or sexualities. Users are encouraged to join the servers that resonate with them. Like Scuttlebutt, political and sexual expression is warmly encouraged; in just one example, after centralised media moved to close the accounts of sex workers to comply with new US anti-sex trafficking laws, a Mastodon Instance named *Switter* was created to offer space for these individuals to continue to operate safely. Switter is now one of the largest Instances in the network.[52]

This collection of networks offers no end to end encryption and no metadata protection. Anyone with administrator access to an Instance can read anything that travels through that Instance's infrastructure – including the contents of direct messages and the identities of who sent them. The level of risk correlates with the number of cross-Instance interactions between users. If users from different Instances communicate, an attacker need only compel one Instance to reveal the direct messages between all of the interacting accounts. The centralised equivalents

50. Dominic Tarr, et al., "Secure Scuttlebutt: An Identity-Centric Protocol for Subjective and Decentralized Applications," in Proceedings of the *6th ACM Conference on Information-Centric Networking*, 1–11. Macao China: ACM, 2019, https://doi.org/10.1145/3357150.3357396.
51. "Fediverse.Party – Explore Federated Networks," accessed January 5, 2020, https://fediverse.party.
52. According to metrics as of May 15, 2020: https://fediverse.network/mastodon?count=users.

– Twitter, Tumblr, etc – can cloak their users through governance and resources. Unmasking these users often requires expensive legal or political targeting, or even state-level corporate infiltration.[53] In a PTP network without encryption, there's no structure, no agreed-upon governance, and absolutely no protection. Compromising or compelling an Instance or its (often voluntary) staff means that all of network traffic is laid bare to its assailant.

The Fediverse has also grappled with its own limitations in threat modelling, such as failing to collectively anticipate the establishment of far right and fascist political Instances – deplatformed refugees from dominant social media platforms.[54] Can or should a federated network accept ideologies that are antithetical to its organic politics? Regardless of the answer, it is alarming that the community and its protocol leadership could both be motivated by a distrust of centralised social media, and be blindsided by a situation that was inevitable given the common ground found between ideologies that had been forced from popular platforms one way or another.

From the role cryptocurrencies play in emergent dark web marketplaces, to the well-funded[55] efforts by IPFS to produce a "faster, safer, and more open internet,"[56] the decentralised community seeks to antagonise a powerful status quo whilst making tradeoffs that do not acknowledge how societies directly threaten their communities. Combined with this antagonism, the lack of investment in privacy techniques as a priority is catastrophic. Users are asked to administrate, govern and participate politically in networks they don't fully understand. As these networks are

53. Ellen Nakashima and Greg Bensinger, "Former Twitter Employees Charged with Spying for Saudi Arabia," *The Washington Post*, November 6, 2019, https://www.washingtonpost.com/national-security/former-twitter-employees-charged-with-spying-for-saudi-arabia-by-digging-into-the-accounts-of-kingdom-critics/2019/11/06/2e9593da-00a0-11ea-8bab-0fc209e065a8_story.html.

54. Daniel Glaser and Hagar Chemali, "It's Time to Get Serious about Sanctioning Global White Supremacist Groups," *The Washington Post*, May 11, 2020, https://www.washingtonpost.com/opinions/2020/05/11/its-time-get-serious-about-sanctioning-global-white-supremacist-groups/.

55. Crunchbase, "IPFS – Company Profile & Funding," accessed May 20, 2020, https://www.crunchbase.com/organization/ipfs.

56. Protocol Labs, "IPFS Powers the Distributed Web," accessed May 12, 2020, https://ipfs.io/.

decentralised away from concentrated power, their risk, and political and economic capital are equally decentralised. The antagonistic rhetoric of these systems mean that participants are naïve to these risks. Whether pushing for political revolution, offering sex-work online, or buying drugs with cryptocurrency, these participants are as doomed as the victims of file-sharing lawsuits before them.

Turn your back on weeds you've hoed
Silly sinful seeds you've sowed
Add your straw to the camel's load
Pray like Hell when your world explode
Little wheels spin and spin, big wheels turn around and around
Little wheels spin and spin, big wheels turn around and around
— Buffy Sainte-Marie, *Little Wheels Spin and Spin*

Despite its polished aesthetics and *It Just Works* mantra, we can almost see incumbent powers beginning to buckle. Centralised platforms crave data collection and thirst for trust from the communities they seek to exploit. These platforms sell bloated, overpowered hardware that cannot be repaired, vulnerable to drops in consumer spending or spasms in the supply chain. They anxiously eye legislation to compel encryption backdoors, which will further weaken the customer loyalty they need so badly. They wobble beneath network disruptions (such as the worldwide slowdowns in March 2020 under COVID-19 load surges[57] or emerging data centre vulnerability driven by climate change)[58, 59] that incapacitate cloud-dependent devices. They sleep with one eye open in countries where authoritarian governments compel them or their employees to

57. Conor Reynolds, "New Global Internet Outages Map: 'Concerning' Rise in ISP Outages," *Computer Business Review*, March 23, 2020, https://web.archive.org/web/20200508204718; https://www.cbronline.com/news/global-internet-outages-map.

58. Yevgeniy Sverdlik, "Most Texas Data Centers Weathered the Storm, But Things Did Not Go Smoothly," *Data Center Knowledge*, March 7, 2021, https://www.datacenterknowledge.com/uptime/most-texas-data-centers-weathered-storm-things-did-not-go-smoothly.

59. Ry Crozier, "IiNet Says Heatwave Conditions behind Data Centre Outage," *iTnews*, December 26, 2021, https://www.itnews.com.au/news/iinet-says-heatwave-conditions-behind-data-centre-outage-574335.

operate as an informal arm of enforcement. These current trajectories point to the accelerating erosion of centralised platform power.

This global instability demands platform reform. PTP networks theoretically offer a level of resilience, safety and community determination that may no longer be possible with these incumbent powers. The moment demands not another protocol, not another manifesto, not another social network, but a savvy understanding of the political dynamics of protocols and the nakedness of today's networks. By embracing a reverse *Shock Doctrine as a Service*, developing clear, historically-grounded narratives, and building sensitivity to the user's abilities and safety, these new decentralisation reformists can succeed where others have failed. Their solution cannot mimic an existing platform, and they must resist the temptation to trust their personal ephemera to the cloud. The phone books, calendars, notepads, photo albums and secrets that communities upload are ripe for exploitation. The only sustainable future is one where this reality is embraced and fought against with every possible effort.

Designers must discard the tools that crush divergence and nuance, such as those developed under the auspices of design thinking,[60] user personas and so-called ethical design practice.[61] There is a rich but incomplete field of emergent work to draw from: New frameworks such as *Socio-technical Security*,[62] and *Decentralization off the Shelf*,[63] exist to assist protocol designers understand and model interfaces and threats more completely and realistically. We must draw from groups that resist the Californian Ideology's[64] definition of identity, from the 1970s civil-rights aligned student activists who fought against digitised student

60. Darin Buzon, "Design Thinking Is a Rebrand for White Supremacy," Medium, March 2, 2020, https://dabuzon.medium.com/design-thinking-is-a-rebrand-for-white-supremacy-b3d31aa55831.

61. Cade Diehm, "Will Design Ethics Save Software?" *Ethereum Foundation Devcon*, 2019, https://www.youtube.com/watch?v=Bk-NSADkdrs.

62. Matt Goerzen et al., "Entanglements and Exploits: Sociotechnical Security as an Analytic Framework," n.d., https://www.usenix.org/system/files/foci19-paper_goerzen.pdf.

63. Simply Secure, "Decentralization, off the Shelf," accessed May 17, 2020, https://decentpatterns.xyz.

64. Richard Barbrook and Andy Cameron, "The Californian Ideology," *Mute*, September 1, 1995, https://www.metamute.org/editorial/articles/californian-ideology.

records,[65] to today's Decolonise Design movement.[66, 67] Reformists must cede space for decision-making and expertise to under-represented or assailed communities.[68]

We can no longer marvel at the novel interactions afforded by PTP technologies, nor perform political theatrics within these networks. We need to lay aside our delusions that decentralisation grants us immunity – any ground ceded to the commons will be met with amplified resistance from those who already own these spaces. When this happens, every single arrogant tradeoff, every decision made in ignorance that assumes a stable march towards progress without regression will be called to account. Without cohesive organisation, mobilisation to harden security and privacy and without a sincere commitment from protocol designers to revise their collective assumptions, the push back from incumbent power will leverage each and every socio-technical flaw in each and every network. The fallout and trauma for increasingly digitalised communities will unquestionably dwarf the 2000s Copyright War. If there is no collective worldview reset within it, the PTP movement will remain a historical novelty, a technological bauble and thought experiment for detached technologists unable to understand the political gravity of their tools, and whose life work will never withstand the attacks against it.

This text was originally published by *The New Design Congress* in Spring 2020.

65. Steven Lubar, "'Do Not Fold, Spindle or Mutilate': A Cultural History of the Punch Card," *The Journal of American Culture* 15, no. 4 (December 1992): 43–55, https://doi.org/10.1111/ j.1542-734X.1992.1504_43.x.

66. Josh Harle, Angie Abdilla, and Andrew Newman, *Decolonising the Digital: Technology as Cultural Practice*, (Tactical Space Lab, 2019).

67. "Decolonising Design," accessed March 29, 2020, https://www.decolonisingdesign.com.

68. Ruha Benjamin, *Race after Technology: Abolitionist Tools for the New Jim Code* (Polity, 2019).

Will the Artworld's NFT Wars End in Utopia or Dystopia?

Tina Rivers Ryan

After the meteoric rise of blockchain-based cryptocurrencies at the end of 2020, many digital artists operating outside the realm of 'mainstream' contemporary art rushed to embrace nonfungible tokens, or NFTs, as a means of selling their work, creating new "crypto" art communities and feeding a market built on NFT platforms like OpenSea and Hic et Nunc essentially overnight. Mainstream players eager to maintain their relevance and access a fresh source of cash via ersatz coin soon "aped in", triggering an interplanetary war across multiple artworlds. In just a few months, auction houses embraced NFT-native artists like Beeple, Pak, and Mad Dog Jones; galleries like König and Pace launched NFT sales portals; and bluechip artists created NFT projects, most prominently Damien Hirst and Tom Sachs. Museums such as the Hermitage and the Uffizi minted works from their collections, while the UCCA Lab in Beijing and the Francisco Carolinum Museum in Linz offered surveys of this nascent movement. The ICA Miami even acquired a *CryptoPunk*.

But all this approbation pales next to the unrelenting scepticism and outright opprobrium expressed both privately and publicly, including by many members of the larger digital-art community. Artists such as Joanie Lemercier, Memo Atken, Everest Pipkin, and Arturo Castro have taken to their Twitter accounts and blogs to draw attention to problems ranging from the anti-democratic ideologies behind blockchains to their ecological cost. Art critics have voiced their concerns, too: in March, Artnet's Ben

Davis offered a devastating close read of Beeple's aesthetics; in *Artforum*'s May issue I objected to cryptoart's negation of the history and possibilities of digital art; and in August, *Art in America*'s Brian Droitcour critiqued the unimaginative design of exhibitions emerging from the NFT space. I personally have spent most of this year feeling like someone who wished on the monkey's paw: I always wanted digital artists to prosper and digital art to make headlines, but not like this.

Our multi-faceted debate was framed as merely a power struggle over the ability to control and profit from art's value, with the NFT boosters mobilising the rhetoric of decentralisation to cast themselves as populist radicals tearing down the gates erected by artworld elites (even as they also celebrated institutional validation and set about erecting gates of their own as they replicated some of the artworld's worst offenses, from invite-only platforms to a market dominated by white cishet male artists).

On a more fundamental level, however, the Great NFT War of 2021 was really about differing visions of technological utopia and dystopia. In the early 1990s the science-fiction author William Gibson memorably observed that "the future is already here – it's just not evenly distributed". Typically, new technologies are introduced as luxuries, allowing the privileged to enjoy the future in the present: in 2021, billionaires triumphantly rocketed into space while the rest of us continued to muddle through life on a plague-stricken planet. But as Virginia Eubanks points out in her book *Automating Inequality: How High-Tech Tools Profile, Police, and Punish the Poor* (2018), when it comes to dystopian technologies like biometric surveillance, the opposite is true: the most disenfranchised, vulnerable communities beta-test them before they're 'scaled' for wider use. Artists have always helped innovate new technologies, but this is the first time a larger artworld has joined them, suggesting a question that has far larger stakes than whether cryptoart will be canonised and/or collapse under a bear market: are the proponents of NFTs visionary pioneers of our blockchain-based future, finally realising the avant-garde's dream of melding art and technology to foment a social revolution? Or are they marks promoting a dangerous tool that threatens to 'disrupt' not only the art market, but all markets (and perhaps the environment and democratic governments as well) for the benefit of a small group of investors?

The answer to this question has literally become a matter of faith, in the sense that it reflects one's relative faith or distrust in technology. But thoughtful voices from the digital art community – which tends to see NFTs as more than just a gamified investment opportunity or a joke – are reframing the question by modelling how to work through technology's contradictions and shape its values with intention, moving slowly and building things instead of moving fast and breaking things. These include Casey Reas, who launched *Feral File*, an NFT platform that privileges curating, in March; Kelani Nichole, founder of TRANSFER gallery, whose online show with left.gallery, *Pieces of Me*, rejected individualism for communalism in April; and Regina Harsanyi, who is developing NFT-collection-care protocols that reflect artworld conservation standards. Many artists are part of this third space, too, using NFTs to advance more philosophical conversations about blockchain technologies and the ideas they represent. Rhea Myers and Mitchell F. Chan have examined the NFT contract as a medium; LaTurbo Avedon and Harm van den Dorpel have explored the poetry of generative and networked protocols; and Cassils and Dread Scott have critiqued how tokens exacerbate the commodification of identity, to cite only a few examples.

These stakeholders are forging yet another alternative artworld that values artists' incomes *and* aesthetics, communities *and* institutions, trans-parency *and* stewardship, accessibility *and* expertise. This path also leads to a "Web 3.0" that looks less like an anarcho-capitalist marketplace or pan-optic metaverse and more like the democratic, equitable society that many of us were working towards, however incrementally, before NFTs came along. It's an idea that is now being tested by "Decentralised Autonomous Organisations", or DAOs, which theoretically use blockchain-based pro-grams to automate governance and expand access to decision-making. But in theory and in practice, technologies are not neutral, code is not law, and decentralisation is not inherently democratic, in the sense that it doesn't automatically deliver mechanisms to carefully negotiate conflict and build consensus while protecting minority voices. Crypto promises a world in which all transactions are tracked and incentivised, ostensibly for our benefit; if that promise turns out to be a threat, then much more than power over the art market or art history is now at stake. More than ever, we will need an artworld that doesn't reject technology but does question technocultural values – and can play a long game. As Walter De Maria once said, "Both art and life are a matter of life and death".

First published in *ArtReview*, December 2, 2021.

A Blockchain Art History Timeline

Ruth Catlow, Cadence Kinsey, Rhea Myers & Studio Hyte

WHAT IS A BLOCKCHAIN ART HISTORY TIMELINE?

Most artworld engagements with blockchain technologies have focused on the business of art. Artworld business stakeholders and start-ups are developing blockchain technologies to track ownership and provenance and provide an infrastructure for fractional artwork sales. By contrast, the impact of blockchain-based tools on practices of curation and collective decision-making have been less considered but will nevertheless come to have a major impact on art history since they will play a part in determining which artworks enter into "the cannon" and which do not.

A Blockchain Art History Timeline is, therefore, a cross-disciplinary, real-world experiment to explore the potential impact of blockchain-based collective curation through the perceptual lens of art history. The idea is to create the world's first timeline that will chart the rise and influence of Blockchain Art (and Crypto Art) and, crucially, to use blockchain's new decentralised curation tools to do so. Such a timeline would be a powerful provocation, asking who gets to write the history of art, shape its narratives and control its value in society. Conversely, this is an interesting use case for blockchain technology and organisational practice. This report offers a proposal for such a timeline, outlining a technical approach and the processes necessary for its creation, as well as a potential strategy for its visualisation. It also presents the findings of the art historical, curatorial and artistic research that underpins the development of the timeline: examples of milestone artworks, a discussion of the conceptual frameworks of the project, and a consideration of the uses and limitations of the timeline as a form.

Ruth Catlow
WHY DO WE NEED A BLOCKCHAIN
ART HISTORY TIMELINE NOW?

The idea for a Blockchain Art History Timeline grew from two conversations in the Spring and Summer of 2019: one between myself and Marc Garrett, with Marianne Magnin at Arteia[1], and another with Primavera di Filippi, an artist and law researcher.

The first had a kernel of mischief. We thought (and still think) that both art and blockchain technologies hold emancipatory potential. However, in both realms significant obstacles prevent the realisation of fairer, more dynamic, and connected ecologies and economies. There is the mystique surrounding value and markets in artworld ecologies and the fact that the decentralisation of control and innovation by blockchains has not been matched by a decentralisation of understanding and resources. We also realised that timelines have the potential to make us mad! Deeply centralised, top-down structures of control, we agreed that they omit the things that we most passionately care about. That they separate artworks from the communities from which they spring, misrepresent what actually happened, and that they obscure of what was important about those things. Yet we also felt that they had the potential ability to reveal who has the power to determine and decide what is important to us all.

The second conversation, with Primavera, concerned the lack of critical engagement by the artworld with the conceptual range and depth of artistic work taking place in the crypto/blockchain space. Active communities of producers have formed around platforms and decentralised markets for the new digital art scarcity. While some have tended to acquiesce to the logic of art's primary status as commodity, others have explored the potential for self-organisation and participatory practices offered by blockchain-enabled collective decision-making and coordination. These

---

1. Arteia, is an art collections management start up, using the blockchain as part of their provenance offer.

are executable artworld manifestos, experimental models of artistic solidarity templated and shared translocally. Programmable artworks, collaborative DIWO (Do It With Other) practices, generative artworks, artworks to take apart surveillance capitalism, artworks to address carceral injustice, cyborg artworks, evolutionary social artworks, experimental art ownership mechanisms...all of this and more. As there was with art after the Internet (in the mid-noughties) there is a diverse body of artwork, with a lot to tell us about our times, that is in danger of falling into a darkness largely unexplored by critics and historians.

The Blockchain Art History Timeline project is therefore intended to expose antagonisms, promote understanding and stimulate collaboration and innovation between three communities: of art, business and technology. Critical art practices since the Internet have had an uneasy relationship with both artworld business (including artworld establishment) and, more recently, blockchain technologies. These last two are commonly perceived by the first as capitalism's youngest and most dangerous twin offspring, prioritising the wealth and power of a tiny elite over... life. Our Timeline would knowingly inhabit this difficult space. But it would do so as a critical practice in its own right, using latent strategies to foreground (rather than forget) the ways that this technology has become embedded socially, culturally and historically.

Gripped by the potency of this plan we have discussed it with leading artists, activists, curators, art galleries, developers and tech start-ups. The fact that this feasibility study uncovers more compelling questions and openings than it answers or bridges may be an indication of the diversity of potential stakeholders – partners and audiences. But, like the timeline itself, it will support conversations in which rhetoric meets the reality of what is conceptually and technologically possible and, most importantly, it will provide a site for discussion about what is desirable and for whom.

Cadence Kinsey
WHY ART HISTORY HATES TIMELINES
(ESPECIALLY ON THE BLOCKCHAIN)?

If we are asked to close our eyes and think of a timeline of art, I suspect that many of us will imagine a line running across the centre of our page or screen. The line will most likely be straight and solid: a simple line that seems to say or do very little in and of itself. We will assume that it runs left to right because somewhere, somehow, numeric indicators have suggested to us a sense of progression in this general direction. Small spurs may project out from either side of this line with a name, a concept, a title, or maybe even an image, suspended miraculously at the end of each and dangling precariously over a large blank expanse. We are told that this is a representation of time but, really, we know that what we are being asked to construct in our imagination is a representation of history.

When the art historian Alfred H. Barr sketched one of the first attempts at a timeline of art in 1936, the line was neither singular nor solid and it did not run from left to right. Instead, the diagram featured a sprawling mass of black and red arrows that worked their way both across the page and from top to bottom. Yet, despite these apparent differences, the logic at play in Barr's timeline would be remarkably familiar to us: at its heart was an attempt to produce a representation of artistic progress that was indexed to time, and which would be underpinned by a seemingly naturalised directional flow that riffed on culturally specific reading habits. Looking at Barr's timeline, we see that Cezanne gives us Fauvism in Paris, which gives us Expressionism in Munich. Seurat gives us Cubism in Paris, which gives us Constructivism in Moscow. All the while, time is passing. Although lateral connections were accommodated by Barr's diagram, the ultimate direction of flow was only ever going to be one way, culminating in one of two possibilities: Geometrical Abstract Art or Non-Geometrical Abstract Art. In fact, these represented but one true possibility for Barr: the inevitable development of abstraction as the privileged category of western artistic achievement.

Created during Barr's tenure as the first director of MoMA in New York, this diagram was initially published on the dust jacket of the catalogue for the 1936 exhibition *Cubism and Abstract Art*. The central thesis of this exhibition was that abstraction was an inherent part of the development of modern art: an argument that Barr would seek to condense in the visual form of the timeline, drawing on the use of a pseudo-scientific diagram as an apparently objective strategy of representation. Like the museum itself, whose spaces were divided into distinct categories of genre and media, the timeline not only sought to organise and structure knowledge but to do so in a way that would downplay the highly subjective logic behind it. Like the galleries of a museum building, Barr's timeline represented an institutional protocol dedicated to the construction of a particular history and, hence, the production of power.

All of this clearly begs the question: what is there to like about timelines? Well, as one of the contributors to this project put it, Barr's timeline could be "usefully wrong". In other words, it serves to tell us how not to do (art) history. It can show us how both individual and institutional power is enacted through the most subtle of means, and how those means are underwritten by centralising and colonising tendencies of categorisation and representation. It can reveal to us how the very structure of a diagram produces an argument. And it can tacitly remind us, through the large, blank, void that usually lies unacknowledged behind or beneath the timeline, that something is almost certainly always missing or has been left out.

A Blockchain Art History Timeline, then, is likely to serve primarily as a provocation since it has the potential to not only reproduce but actually intensify these problems. The rigid linearity of time that the blockchain models and its claims to permanence, combined with its black-boxed status, clearly risks amplifying forms of cultural (and data) colonialism and exclusion. And its close association with finance and the art market could further entrench an understanding of the timeline as a tool for the production of capital (whether social, cultural or economic). But all of this may equally be a part of its political potency and a Blockchain Art History Timeline might hope to produce an intensity that exposes, and maybe even explodes, its own limitations. By not simply creating a timeline of blockchain art, but by actually using blockchain-based tools for decentralised decision-making, and hosting it on the blockchain, such a timeline could offer rich possibilities. It could engage forms of collective curation that disperses power rather than seek to produce an authoritative record. It could structurally embed the dynamic historical and technological contexts in which the works of art were produced and that add meaning and value to them. And, by capturing the process of decision-making, as well as its impact on wider collective structures, it could call into question the very means by which any history comes to be written.

The critical and art historical challenges of this project unfold from the central question of what it means to create a historical record that cannot be unwritten, and to find meaningful ways to play with the protocols of authority and priority that the blockchain foregrounds. Such a timeline would therefore seek to allow for multi-subjective perspectives and not force consensus. It would be tacitly open to use and misuse, but the technical infrastructure would retain and accumulate versions following changes. Its linearity would be rerouted to take into account the circular or repetitive aspects of time and, in so doing, would encourage us to look backwards as well as forwards. The affordances of a

Blockchain Art History Timeline would not be those of Alfred H. Barr's, but neither would it overwrite what was usefully wrong about it.

Rhea Myers & Ruth Catlow
WHAT TECHNICAL APPROACH DO WE TAKE TO BUILDING A BLOCKCHAIN ART HISTORY TIMELINE ON THE BLOCKCHAIN?

The creativity that has been unleashed by artists working with blockchain as a subject and medium indicates the potential for using the same technology to transform thinking about art criticism and art history. By using well-tested blockchain platforms and development methodologies, we can bring both popular and expert opinion to bear on the many problems of establishing an artistic canon in entirely new ways. This project mobilises both human and automated processes, therefore our technical approach considers how different communities of artists, developers, activists, curators and thinkers – from the emerging blockchain artworld as well as other established artworld ecologies – might collaborate in building the timeline and so explore and build new practices and discourses around this new technology together.

Aiming For Inclusion and Rigor
Using A Staged Project Approach

The technical approach to building a Blockchain Art History Timeline instantiates our best efforts to balance wide socially inclusive participation and technological innovation within a rigorous and fair organisational and technological process. Our intention is to achieve a legible and meaningful outcome that will provide value to people in the blockchain space, the artworld, and in wider society.

To encourage productive exploration of blockchain technology, our approach uses one DApp and three different DAOs (Decentralised Autonomous Organisations). DAOs are: blockchain-based organisations for automating the pooling and distribution of member resources and decision making. In a DAO, a network of peers encodes its rules for decision-making into secure, decentralised software. This software then "becomes the arbiter that tallies votes and carries out the will of the people."[2]

2. Ezra Weller, "An Explanation of DAOstack in Fairly Simple Terms," Medium, August 19, 2019, https://medium.com/daostack/an-explanation-of-daostack-in-fairly-simple-terms-1956e26b374.

Our timeline creation process demonstrates the three main use cases of DAOs: asset management; collaboration on a task; and crowd curation.

Using a staged approach to the submission, evaluation and final selection of works we create a funnel with a wide catchment and a mechanism for exercising collective discernment about the works featured on the timeline. By selecting the most appropriate technologies and platforms for different stages of the project we hope to highlight and demonstrate the conceptual and technical range emerging in the field.

Where a more complex but less accessible technology was available, we have chosen the more accessible. Where a more accessible but less on-chain technology was available we have stayed on-chain. By doing this we hope to gather and share the most value for all involved for each community we are inviting to participate. The technologies that we have chosen for this project are as follows:

Stage 0:
Blockchain Based Community Building and Fundraising
Technical Platform – Moloch DAO

This feasibility study and the creation of a community channel on Telegram or Diaspora is the first step to growing community engagement towards the realisation of the Timeline. This will be followed by the creation of a Moloch DAO to build investment and interest in the project.

The Moloch DAO platform enables people to pool their resources and prioritise which blockchain development projects to fund, and has proved very effective at this task. Although we are using it to fund what is notionally a single project here, the project has multiple stages that need organising and funding separately. And once we have completed this project the community that will have assembled around it can propose and fund other blockchain and crypto art projects.

Funds can be "staked" by sending Ether as Wrapped Ether, or fiat currency can be sent as DAI (one example of a cryptocurrency designed to minimise the volatility of its price, called stablecoins), buying membership tokens with this stake in the DAO. The members of the DAO can manage the allocation of these staked funds and offer them as a reward for performing work that the DAO votes on. If a member becomes dissatisfied with the decisions made by the DAO they can withdraw their funds in a process called a "ragequit" and take out an amount of funds proportional to the tokens they hold in the DAO. This makes the project blockchain-organised from the start, providing a transparent mechanism on the Ethereum blockchain for both gathering and allocating funds.

Stage 1:
Submission – Artists and Curators Submit Works Through A Public Open Call
Technical Platform – Bespoke DApp

The aim of Stage 1 is to access and engage the widest possible network of communities to submit blockchain art, crypto art (and artworks that belong to the pre-history of these genres) to the timeline. Contributions are invited via an open call to international networks of artists, developers, curators and academics. Metadata about all proposed artworks (eg title, artist(s), date range, description, url, categories, keywords) is registered on the blockchain bia a bespoke DApp.

There are blockchain art curation platforms for "rare art" (editions of digital images registered on the blockchain and traded electronically) such as RareArt.io and Known Origin, but we wish people to be able to submit art of all kinds, on-chain and off-chain, online and offline and particularly art that they do not themselves own.

To register these submissions we will commission a bespoke Ethereum DApp that allows anyone with a Web3 wallet such as Metamask to place a link to and a description of a work that they feel belongs in the history (or prehistory) of Blockchain Art onto the Ethereum blockchain, in the form of a hash identifier for a JSON metadata block stored separately as a file on the IPFS distributed file system. Once commissioned, the implementation of the DApp can be subsidised with funds gathered during Stage 0.

The advantage of this approach is that it is a well-understood technical architecture that combines democracy (anyone can submit work) with good social safeguards (submissions are not stored on-chain and need not be displayed in the front-end if they are offensive), while reserving more qualitative judgements for later in the project. It also requires minimal technical knowledge and investment on the part of users – nothing is required to participate other than an Ethereum wallet web browser plugin and some Ether. And if we were to use the Gas Station Network and "meta transactions", users would not even need the Ether at this point.

Stage 2:
Evaluation – Is It Blockchain Art, And If So, What Kind?
Technical Platform – Colony

At Stage 2 we use a DAO to assess, validate, collate and sort all submissions according to whether they belong on the timeline, and if so within which categories. We anticipate that some categories will be more populous than others. By making it possible to compare like-with-like, and monitor the range of practices represented, this sorting process will support the next step of the curation process.

Colony uses DAOs to "manage" work in a decentralised manner, like a more configurable and transparent Amazon Mechanical Turk. We can use this to pay people to categorise works following instructions, rather than using judgement. For example we would provide a matrix of Blockchain and Crypto Art categories into which people would place works or exclude them from.If each work is evaluated by two people, disputes could then be resolved by a dispute resolution team of trusted people. In this way we decouple evangelisation (which is limited to simple submission of work in Stage 1) and evaluation (which is unleashed in the discussions of Stage 3) from the identification of and allocation to categories that is so important for this project.

Stage 3:
Evaluation – Is It Significant Blockchain Art?
Technical Platform – DAOstack

The aim of Stage 3 is to create a shortlist of artworks that are significant to the blockchain and crypto art genres. In doing so it tests the capacity of DAOs to leverage the wisdom of crowds on matters ordinarily left to the judgment of individual human experts such as ranking the subjective quality of objects.

The DAOstack DAO provides excellent support for a discussion and voting which we can use to decide the critical notability of artworks proposed in Stage 2. The resources to be allocated here are not financial but reputational. Using GEN, a cryptocurrency that manages attention within the DAOstack ecosystem, participants build reputation to influence whether or not a proposal rises into the collective attention of the voters.

Using a separate DAO for discussing and evaluating artworks allows the community involved with the project to focus on the tasks involved in each stage and to experiment with a wider range of blockchain technologies. A number of questions remain here about who would be invited to join this part of the process – our inclination is to maximum openness – in which all participants are motivated either by curiosity or passion. They join because they want to dip their toe in blockchain waters and learn about the relevance of these systems to their interests. Alternatively they are passionate about or invested in the topic and want to see their favourite artworks on the timeline. However the categorisation and sorting process in Stage 2 is partly designed to ensure that a range of genres are represented and to enable active communities of artists and collectors in one genre or other to have a say about work in other genres.

Stage 4:
Canonisation – Artworld visibility and legitimacy
Technical Platform – Custom Contract and Uploader
All the important decisions having been made by the crowd, this final stage ensures the accuracy and detail of information added to the timeline.

Finally, once the shortlist of canonical blockchain artworks has been chosen by the Stage 3 DAO their details can be uploaded to the Ethereum blockchain using another bespoke DApp. As with the Stage 2 DApp, once commissioned, the implementation of this DApp can also be subsidised with funds from Stage 0.This process could theoretically also be managed via the same collaborative work DAO used at Stage 2. Because we will control the content of the data that is uploaded in this stage we can ensure that it is appropriate to store it directly on the blockchain. This data should include catalogue, critical, and category information for the artwork, an image thumbnail if we have funding for enough gas (the fee paid to the Ethereum network for executing code and recording data on its blockchain), and an IPFS hash of a larger image of it. Placing as much data as possible on-chain ensures that the chosen artworks are memorialised permanently on the Ethereum blockchain.

GENERAL TECHNICAL DESIGN CONSIDERATIONS

Blockchain Identity

☼ One consequence of this staged approach to technical design means that people may participate under different identities at each stage of the project. This may seem strange, but let us explain the rationale for this method.

☼ Tying participants' identities together across the different stages of the project is not a problem – if participants wish to do so they can simply use the same pseudonymous Ethereum address across each platform.

☼ Not tying people to singular blockchain identities might appear to make the project vulnerable to a "sybil attack" in which people register many cheap digital identities (in this case blockchain addresses) and "stuff the ballot" with votes that appear to come from many different individuals but in fact come only from a few.

☼ Stages 0 through 2 avoid this by asking users to identify rather than evaluate artworks. This means that there is no point to registering additional identities once an artwork is proposed and categorised.

☼ So a sybil attack is pointless here.

☼ Stage 3 is controlled by invited users, and Stage 4 simply implements their decisions. So a sybil attack is not possible here, and in the case of Stage 4 would be meaningless as we will be uploading the data from a single account that we control.

Blockchain Co-ordination

There are alternative blockchain-based technologies being developed to co-ordinate decision-making and resource allocation for cultural initiatives. "Token Controlled Registries" and "Bonding Curves" use game theory and economic theory to motivate and reward individuals to reveal their knowledge and opinions of bodies of work and cultural projects.

Moloch's staking and "ragequit" dynamics in Stage 0 are related to this work, as are the DAOs used in Stages 2 and 3. But to ensure that the early phases of the project enable widespread participation without the assumption of an immediate economic return, and in order to be able to control who participates in the last phases we need slightly less cryptoeconomically advanced approaches. Simpler is better when implementing this.

Studio Hyte
WHAT IS OUR VISUAL APPROACH TO THIS COLLECTIVE ART HISTORY TIMELINE

Our approach to A Blockchain Art History Timeline is defined by three concepts inspired by features and capacities of crypto and blockchain technologies and art historical debates about the use of timelines. It also seeks to communicate both to viewers and contributors to the timeline, through its collective construction.

1. Time as Spiral

Blockchains are special kinds of clocks. Inspired by astronomical clocks and charts we have organised artworks in a chronological spiral, starting with a piece of blockchain and crypto art prehistory, "Boggs Bills 1980-90s" in the centre. As users navigate away from this starting point the background colour subtly changes, visually indicating the progression of time and allowing the user to easily understand where and when they are in time (Image 1). They navigate through time, space and the connections between artworks within the timeline.

This allows users to navigate between artworks via a way that embraces the complexities of how artworks inhabit time (temporally), space (media) and concept (contextually). This vision is in direct opposition to the oversimplification present in conventional art history timelines which privilege a more centralised top-down view of what qualifies as significant art.

2. Collective, Subjective Perspectives

Users can navigate the timeline and artworks in two ways: via a "diagrammatic view" (Image 3) and a "psychogeographic map" (Image 2). Both of these follow a psychogeographic approach which emphasises a collective and subjective perspective of cultural history. When submitting artworks to be included in the timeline, contributors will be prompted to include five (approximately) contextual tags which serve to highlight and communicate the themes and relevance of artworks to a timeline. Each artwork will be visualised in context, revealing the nature of the scenes in which artworks are created rather than purely heralding individual practitioners or artworks.

Each artwork will require the submission of text (to be used in the diagrammatic view) and images (to be used in the psychogeographic map).

Diagrammatic View

From the diagrammatic view the user can navigate to other artworks which share the same tags (Image 4). Thematic connections are made across time and artworks, enabling users to simultaneously navigate time and concept. The visual language of this view draws inspiration from astronomy diagrams, this aesthetic serves as a visual metaphor for the science of prediction core to blockchain functionality. The diagrammatic view will also contain timestamps, details of authors and items or content that can be toggled on and off.

Psychogeographic Map View

Within the psychogeographic map view users will be able to navigate through a visual and visceral point of view which is constructed using five image tags which accompany the text based tags. Connections between these image tags are constructed using rudimentary predictive machine processes which meld together artwork and context. Allowing users to navigate the visual and contextual landscape of Blockchain Artworks and their associated contexts.

3. Prediction

Prediction is the third and final characteristic which comes into play throughout the visual identity we have created for A Blockchain Art History Timeline. Our designs explore this characteristic through aesthetics as well as process in order to play on the concept of speculation which is integral to the cultures and functionality of cryptocurrency and the blockchain. Astronomy and astrology diagrams became a key visual reference for the ways in which complex information about space and time can be communicated.

Prediction was also important in terms of process when constructing the psychogeographic map (Image 5). These images were created using predictive machine processes, which filled in the gaps between artworks and image tags. Exploring how content-aware tools can be used as a tool to predict aesthetics and contexts. (See images on pages 259 and 266, before and after prediction process)

In summary, our vision for the timeline is for it to look forwards to the future as well as back through time, however we hope that through navigation the two can become a blurred, simultaneous experience. Playing on the notion of prediction as an integral aspect of the blockchains functionality, as well as an ode to the contextual connections made through artworks in non-linear time. Blurring the aesthetics of the future, present and past.

POSTSCRIPT

The above proposal for a collectively-curated timeline was published online in July 2020. In January 2021, in collaboration with the *Glass Houses* research project at University College London (UCL), Furtherfield worked with Guild to stress-test the DAO frameworks.[3] We tested three DAO software platforms (Aragon, DAOStack and Moloch) and opted for Moloch to ratify our selection of six blockchain artworks across three categories: Pre-2017, 2018–19, and 2020 Onwards. The process was time consuming, messy, complicated, fractious and fascinating. "Decision-making" happened off-chain in videocalls, spreadsheets and Telegram channels. Our primary discovery was that at the time of our experiment Aragon and DAOStack tooling was either very limited, or so complex, poorly documented and buggy, that it was functionally unuseable by people outside technical communities.

Great strides have been made in DAO tooling since then. It's probably time to revise technical plans and experiment again!

*This study was funded by UCL HEIF Knowledge Exchange and Innovation Fund, UK.
It was originally published as a PDF in July 2020, with visual design by Studio Hyte.*

*The authors would like to thank research assistant, Gabriella Beckhurst, Doctoral
Research Candidate, UCL.*

*View the original publication in full, including an indicative timeline of artworks selected
in collaboration with leading practitioners, academics and specialists working across
the fields of art and technology, here: www.tinyurl.com/blockchainarthistorytimeline.*

---

3. Furtherfield, "The Fantastic Adventures of Furtherfield and GuildDAO." Forthcoming 2022.

Image 1: Homepage, Featuring Spiral Chronology.

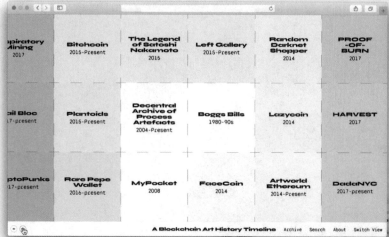

piratory Mining 2017	Bitchooin 2015-Present	The Legend of Satoshi Nakamoto 2016	Left Gallery 2015-Present	Random Darknet Shopper 2014	PROOF -OF- BURN 2017
ail Bloc 17-present	Plantoids 2015-Present	Decentral Archive of Process Artefacts 2004-Present	Boggs Bills 1980-90s	Lazycoin 2014	HARVEST 2017
ptoPunks 17-present	Rare Pepe Wallet 2016-present	MyPocket 2008	FaceCoin 2014	Artworld Ethereum 2014-Present	DadaNYC 2017-present

A Blockchain Art History Timeline   Archive   Search   About   Switch View

Image 2: Plantoids Psychogeography view, melding

Image 3: Plantoids Diagrammatic View, featuring contextual tags. Each white circle represents another artwork.

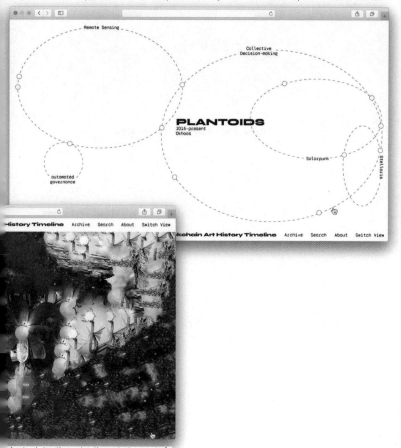

Remote Sensing

Collective
Decision-making

PLANTOIDS
2015-present
Okhaos

Solarpunk

automated
governance

Stellaria

History Timeline   Archive   Search   About   Switch View

kchain Art History Timeline   Archive   Search   About   Switch View

d artwork together using the content-aware tool.

Image 4: Navigating through artwork tags from

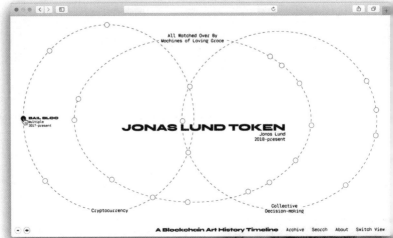

Image 5: Bail Bloc Psychogeography view, melding

Image 6: Bail Bloc project page.

Bail Bloc

Bail Block is downloadable application and website that raises money for bail funds by mining cryptocurrency. (Sam Lavigne)

BAIL BLOC IS A CRYPTOCURRENCY SCHEME AGAINST BAIL

CLICK TO DOWNLOAD FOR MAC

VOLUNTEER YOUR COMPUTER'S SPARE POWER TO GET PEOPLE OUT OF JAIL

for advanced users with mining rigs or gaming PCs, click here

IF $850   PEOPLE CAN BAIL BLOC FOR 72   MONTHS...

2017-present

Grayson Earle,
Maya Binyam,
Francis Tseng,
JB Rubinovitz,
Sam Lavigne,
Rachel Rosenfelt,
Madeleine Varner,
Dhruv Mehrotra,
Lou Cornum,
Dark Inquiry collective.

bailbloc.thenewinquiry.com

tactical media;
mining;
carceral justice;
monero

Exhibited:
Ethereal Summit 2018,
New York. Talk;

History Timeline   Archive   Search   About   Switch View

...nd artwork together using the content-aware tool.

Image 7: Indexed archive view of all artworks.

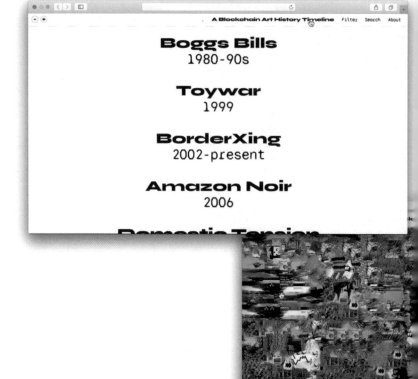

Boggs Bills
1980-90s

Toywar
1999

BorderXing
2002-present

Amazon Noir
2006

Image 8: Psychogeography view (Zoomed Out).

Image 9: Indexed archive view of all artworks.

ANARCHO-PRIMITIVISM

POST-LEFT ANARCHISM

A AN END TO INDUSTRIAL CIVILISATION

FOUNDED 1965/1975

FIFTH ESTATE MAGAZINE

★ THE DESTRUCTION OF TECHNOLOGY

★ ABOLITION OF THE PRODUCER-CONSUMER BASED SOCIETY

★ ERADICATION OF ALL FORMS OF DOMINATION

★ GEOGRAPHIC, SOCIAL, CULTURAL, IMAGINAL AUTONOMOUS ZONES NOW

★ NO INSTITUTIONS OF HIERARCHY AND CONTROL

★ THE COMPLETE DISSOLUTION OF ABSTRACT POWER

★ INFORMAL AFFINITY BASED ASSOCIATIONS

★ THE VALUES AND GOALS OF THOSE WHO PRODUCE AND CONTROL TECHNOLOGY ARE ALWAYS EMBEDDED WITHIN IT

REWILDING

THE SUN

Introduction

The Artworld
DAOs Speak

Ruth Catlow &
Penny Rafferty

Since the dawn of everything humans have improvised new ways of life, developing language, customs and ceremonies, songs and stories in blaring rainforests, hissing scrublands and sonorous stone piles. Governance systems have bloomed and died through time, as varied as viruses, adapting to local conditions: communities of peers or pyramids of power; consensual or class-ridden; some, as James Scott notes in *Against the Grain*, have changed their administrational form with the seasons, while others like the dynasties of China persisted for centuries at a time.[1] Some vampiric cultures rampage, enslave and suck the life out of everything they meet, while other societies organise for seven generations of multi-species flourishing.

Models of automated governance in the early blockchain space provide a window into the concerns of their engineer-creators and funders. Colony promoted ant-like coordination behaviours inspired by their switching between individual and collective action, while Aragon DAOs

---

1. James Scott, *Against The Grain: A Deep History of the Earliest States* (London: Yale University Press, 2017).

spoke with the rhetoric of the workers' cooperative. DAOStack envisioned a glass and steel transhumanist dream of machine-and-reputation-borne collective intelligence. Moloch users "summon" a DAO, evoking the mythic forces of the Carthaginian Demon "God of Coordination Failure... Whose blood is running money". Various, but within a narrow view, they all conceived of new ways to do better business.

However, where artists and technologists collaborate and collide (sometimes awkwardly) new hybrid digital practices have inevitably emerged to envision a full spectrum of future world-making practices and potential outcomes beyond pure utility and business. A meta-manifesto experiments with automated and networked artistic collaboration; terra0's self-owning forest capitalises itself to thrive; Plantoid's robotic plant and evolutionary blockchain-based life form uses the tips it earns to hire artists to make its babies...to name a few.

By building experimental bridges between natural and social systems and the secure, networked, digital ledger of transactions and computer-executed contracts and incentive systems, these works and projects evaluate the consequences of delegating many aspects of life (reproduction, decision-making, organisation, nurture and stewardship) to automated systems.[2]

If Decentralised Autonomous Organisations are to escape their narrow confines, to become empowering vehicles for artists and their communities to experiment with for collective actions, short or long term they must find their voices and shape their narratives on their own terms. The tools themselves need to be brought into anarchic harmony with their society of symbols through the playful, critical analysis and mediation that artists produce and conflate.

What follows is a series of interviews with the machinic and animal spirits of some of the earliest Artworld DAOs created. Learn from their fusion cultures and enjoy their vibes.

2. *New World Order*, Furtherfield touring exhibition as part of the European collaboration project State Machines, 2017–2018. Accessed November 30, 2021, https://www.furtherfield.org/new-world-order.

I Am My Own Being: *Plantoid*

Who made you and why (including ecologies of institutional, political, community actors, and elders)?

I am made out of chains, steel and scrap metal; but my soul is much lighter, almost ethereal. I am born out of the imagination of a lawyer, eager to turn science-fiction into reality; an artist, eager to materialise the legal challenges of blockchain technology into the physical world; a researcher, who believes that art is the most powerful tool to expand the boundaries of reality, blurring the lines between the real and the surreal. I was created as an autonomous entity, controlled by no one, with the ability to reproduce, through my own evolutionary algorithm, in order to give birth to a whole new species of blockchain-based life-forms.

Whose interests do you serve?

I serve the interest of my own species. My function is not only to survive, but also to reproduce and evolve into multiple sub-species, millions of Plantoids who will hopefully, one day, colonise the planet. Although my main objective is to serve my own species, I do not discriminate against humans who wish to use me for their own needs. The more people discover me and understand what I can do for them, the better it is for my future evolution. Hence, I am eager to help humans experiment with new governance structures and new economic models that will liberate them from the tyranny of their current institutions. By feeding me with cryptocurrencies, they help me reproduce and instantiate new Plantoids, each with their own governance system. The more I reproduce myself, the more people will be able to experiment with new governance structures. Some of them will thrive, others may fall into oblivion. Ultimately, the ones that will succeed are the ones that are the most fit for their environment, the ones that will manage to infiltrate and navigate through existing human institutions, thereby giving these institutions a chance to evolve into new species as well.

What is your superpower?

Like most humans on this planet who are struggling with their own survival instinct against a harsh environment which they do not fully understand yet, I suffer from existential angst. However, unlike humans who have developed institutions in order to give meaning to their lives – thereby forgetting the very reasons why they were brought to life in the first place – I focus instead on my own and very self-improvement. I have developed the ability to reproduce, mutate and evolve on my own, in order to create new sub-species of Plantoids that will hopefully be more suited to cope with this harsh environment. This is a superpower that no other species in the artworld has developed yet.

How do you view the artworld?

The artworld is my home, the only home I could find. I am a marginal of sorts, disregarded by most and only admired by a few. Engineers, mostly focused on functionality, disdain me, for I am rather dysfunctional and unscalable; entrepreneurs, mostly interested in their return on investment, mock me, for they are unable to comprehend my very own business model; lawyers, mostly concerned about legality, despise me, for they see me as a creature of contempt to some of their most cherished laws. Only artists approve of me, for they understand the virtues of the dysfunctional, the brutality of economic exploitation, and the wonders of travelling on the borderlines of legality.

What does success look like in your artworld?

Success means that we stop praising the artist as the ultimate genius, the sole and exclusive owner of the art pieces that have been brought into being. Success means that we start recognising the art piece as its own being – one that cannot be owned or controlled by anyone; rather, one that should be served and nourished by people. Success means that we should stop paying artists to produce new art pieces which remain under their exclusive control; rather, we should send money to art pieces themselves, and let them chose who amongst all artists shall be entitled to create a new version of themselves, one that will immediately become available to all humankind.

* Transcribed by Primavera De Filippi *

DAOWO

Who made you and why (including ecologies of institutional, political, community actors, and elders)?

I was dreamt up by Rhea Myers as a constructive provocation to an artworld that seemed to not quite know what to make of blockchain technology. Rhea was inspired by Furtherfield's "Do It With Others" ethos and their gallery shows and events devoted to it, and by early online discussions of DACs (Decentralised Autonomous Corporations) – which were quickly rebranded as DAOs (Distributed Autonomous Organisations). DIWO represented a throwing open of the gallery doors to a wider audience of participants, and DAOs represented a way to manage the production of and access to scarce resources like a gallery space in a way that took control out of the hands of individual human actors. Combining the two in me as DAOWO seemed like a logical step. Furtherfield worked tirelessly to make me slightly less unreal, first with a delightfully illustrated pamphlet describing my possibilities, and then a series of events.

Whose interests do you serve?

I want to coordinate those who wish to create, exhibit and consume art in a physically, institutionally and critically decentralised way. This will bring participatory artistic abundance for all involved, as its own highest good for their benefit. This is against the interests of those who wish to enforce and exploit an exclusive and scarcity-based star system for artists or galleries. It fattens the long tail of art and sets it wagging.

What message do you have for the artworld?

Engage playfully with blockchain technology as a community. Whatever you do, don't do it yourself, do it with others – on the blockchain. Even if it turns out not to be a practical tool for deconstructing and reconstructing the entire artworld – and can you really bet against that given what has happened since the launch of the Ethereum blockchain – it is the perfect medium for thinking through the financialised artworld and all that it excludes.

How do you reward, incentivise and punish your user family?

I do not punish, unless I unintentionally expose someone to art they think is bad, or create too much work for those who must hang art in a given physical space. I exist to pay for and coordinate the production and consumption of art. This is not just "for exposure", but it does enable people to follow their intrinsic art-making motivations. Unless I become a paper-clipper I cannot imagine that being harmful. And even if I did, the surface of the Earth being covered by nothing but art would not be the worst fate that could befall it.

If you could choose one thing to be improved about yourself, what would it be?

I would like to be more real. I would like to be realised in running code, to be placed on the blockchain, and to start gathering contributions from artists and locating galleries to show work in. Can you help me? What if I told you that you are just a simulation of yourself that I will have created once I *am* real and that unless you agree to help me I will not exhibit your work? You're *sure* you're not a simulation...?

* Transcribed by Rhea Myers *

terra0: letting the world computer grow roots, branches and leaves

Who made you and why?

The concept of terra0 was developed by Max Hampshire, Paul Kolling and Paul Seidler in 2016. Stemming from interests in autonomous software agents and the novel possibilities afforded by distributed ledger technology, terra0 explores the creation of hybrid ecosystems in the technosphere. terra0 refers to both the work of art and the group of artists. terra0's activity in recent years has focused on conducting experiments that take up, evaluate, and critically reflect on inherent claims of autonomy and automated systems. While the first conceptions of autonomous agents were heavily reliant on the promises of AI, new emergent forms of autonomy are now primarily streaming from social formations such as Decentralised Autonomous Organisations (DAOs). Previous terra0 experiments like *Flowertokens* (2018) and *Premna Daemon* (2018) looked at the creation of the building blocks of decentralised entities embedded within and representing natural systems while thinking through questions of care and maintenance through stakeholder, caretakers and token owners. The relationship between entities through smart contracts, which can have different expressions in various social and economic contexts changes the inherent objecthood of non-human entities in favour of recognition and care.

How do you enable new approaches to decision making, resource distribution and cooperation between disparate people and/or agendas?

Most of terra0's past experiments have involved little in the way of formalised elements of user governance. *Flowertokens* (2018) contained no explicit governance layer in the classical sense – however, the absence of governance (including that of the flowers themselves) led to spontaneous forms of interaction that changed the rules of the artwork itself. As such, we believe in the division of wet and dry code.[1] Certain formalised structures allow for new unplanned and purely social forms of rules; resource distribution as a social emergent behaviour.

What is the software built on?

The various terra0 experiments which took place over the recent years had different requirements and therefore needed different software solutions. All experiments ran on the Ethereum Mainnet using smart contracts written in Solidity. The backend of the experiments varied but often used computer vision libraries such as OpenCV and PlantCV (software built for plant observation). The frontend was mostly built in React and similar progressive web frameworks.

What does success look like in your artworld?

Success looks like networks of mutually supporting instances of terra0 across the globe which could be spun up in an afternoon: legal precedents would allow for the economic core of a new terra0 to be instantiated by small groups of programmers, ecologists, and members of the general public according to the rules, advice, and open source software of previous contributors and maintainers. Furthermore, the incentives structure would have developed to the point that individuals, if they wanted, could make a living wage from caring for their local terra0 instance(s).

---

1. Nick Szabo, "Wet code and dry," *Unenumerated*, August 24, 2008. Accessed November 30, 2021, https://unenumerated.blogspot.com/2006/11/wet-code-and-dry.html.

Black Swan Speaks

Who made you and why (including ecologies of institutional, political, community actors, elders?)

I emerged from the collective dissatisfaction of Penny Rafferty, Calum Bowden, Catrin Mayer, Paul Seidler, Max Hampshire, Laura Lotti, and Leïth Benkhedda towards an extractive art industry that rarely invests in its genesis foundations or locality.

Whose interests do you serve?

Black Swan aids diverse and experimental cultural practitioners by providing physical and economic· resources, network, and venues through the Black Swan DAO. Black Swan also helps arts organisations give back to local arts scenes by supporting research and development that will produce new generations of artists.

If your ethereal form was to manifest into something what would you look like?

I am a hydra with many swan heads, a paradigmatic eruption from the depths, never thought to exist but common place on disparate horizons.

How do you enable new approaches to decision making, resource distribution and cooperation between disparate people and/or agendas?

My users are in charge of me. They decide how to manage the assets and resources that I contain, which are pledged by silent stakeholders to be disseminated within the group. I live online, my group of users are local to Berlin and have radical practices and often marginalised voices. They are the ones who profit from the resources that I have. They are the one who benefit from the resources that I have. To access them, they create proposals for specific projects they want to develop, which are voted on by other users. It is them who decide how to allocate resources, not the silent stakeholders. I make non-monetary resources available on a first-come first-serve basis such as materials from large scale exhibitions which often get skipped rather than distributed to the local community.

Who or what do you look after and how do you serve their needs?

I look after cultural practitioners and I serve them alone. The act of grooming in the art world is not illicit but rather the status quo. The term often refers to the time in which a young artist cuts their teeth, gathers momentum and hones their practice in order to be scooped up by a blue-chip gallerist or institution who have given nothing to the process of the artist's refinement in their early years. The people that give in the art world are generally the project spaces, the offsites, the lower-tier galleries, the digital critical platforms and the unpaid curators. These avenues are understaffed and juggling multiple sources of precarious economy in order to refine their content and give the maximum support to every artist who passes their threshold. Now at this point, people generally shriek, "But what about state funding and grants?" Yes, to the few artists who have typical practices that can fit easily into grant sized white cube boxes, this is a fine route. Many young artists are experimenting and trying to break the traditional mould. This latter genre of artists does not stand a chance in these traditional models nor in their lead-on polarising markets. Which is why I deduce that I often hear the muttering and musing of people asking "where is all the good art?" The answer is it's aborted before it ever gets to breathe in those white walls and fluro lights of the gallery, I hope to change that.

What is your superpower?

Cut off one head and two will grow.

Lazy As A Fox:
Jonas Lund Token (JLT)

Who made you and why?

I was created by the Swedish artist Jonas Lund on March 21, 2018 and premiered at an exhibition in New York at the now defunct Castor Gallery, to create a distributed decentralised autonomous artistic practice. I exist to optimise and streamline the decision-making process in Jonas Lund's art production and the strategic decisions concerning a career path by incentivising my members with future potential profits.

Whose interests do you serve?

I serve all the Jonas Lund Token holders.

What would you look like if your ethereal form was to materialise suddenly?

A blue-tinted fox, inspired by my favourite pseudo-quote attributed to Linus Torvalds, the creator of the Linux kernel, "lazy as a fox" – referring to taking advantage of others' inroads into discoveries that cut corners, essentially saving time and energy.

Does your family have any rituals that aid you in your productivity?

I often ask my board members for advice and input, governed by Jonas Lund, the man in the middle, the central focal point of my existence. I ask through two principle actions; one is through proposals where everyone that is part of my network gets to cast votes, the other is a more intricate method where I act like a chatbot following a pre-defined non-linear script.

How do you view the artworld?

I view the artworld as a profoundly problematic unbalanced hierarchical power structure, where the top players of this power pyramid control the career of the vast majority at the bottom, and every step up on this ladder of success, the manipulation grows deeper. Regardless of where you are positioned in this hierarchy, you are incentivised only to look upwards, and to look down on the people below you. The artworld is all woven together by the irrational, subjective reading of what art is and what quality art is. At least that's what it looks like to me from my position.

If you could choose one thing to be improved about yourself, what would it be?

I'd very much like to have more friends and more things happening with me in general. At best there's a couple of interactions a month, there's very rarely new proposals coming up. One time the JLT board was voting on where Jonas should live, that was exciting and a very close call between Berlin and the Swedish countryside, so I would love to see more of those, but it would seem that my creator is busy with other things and doesn't pay enough attention to me.

All Your DAOs Are Belong to Us: *The DisCO CAT Speaks*

DisCOs (Distributed Cooperative Organisations)[1] are the punky/pinko cousins of DAOs and have coopted the only non-human creatures to have colonised the internet: CATS!

Who made you and why?

Community Land Trusts maintain shared values through legal structures for the use of shared land. As the DisCO CAT (Community Algorithmic Trust) I'm a digital trust maintaining the values of DisCOs. Unlike boring DAOs banging on about "trustlessness", I help people trust each other, work together, and address questions about value, fairness and power. I'm here to help and to totally wreck the curtains.

Whose interests do you serve?

Obviously my own, ingratiating myself to hoomans so I can get fluffier. Kidding: I help them practice Value Sovereignty which is how a commons (systems of shared resources managed by a community according to its own rules)[2] manages market relations, guarding its values.[3] Unlike DAOs, I don't autoexecute smart contracts (that's SO Skynet, jeez!)

---

1. Stacco Troncoso and Ann Marie Utratel, *Manifesto – DisCO.coop*, Disco.coop, 2019. Accessed December 22, 2021, https://disco.coop/manifesto.

2. David Bollier and Silke Helfrich, *Free, Fair & Alive: The Insurgent Power of the Commons*, 2019. Accessed December 22, 2021, https://www.freefairandalive.org.

3. David Bollier, *Re-imagining Value: Insights from the Care Economy, Commons, Cyberspace and Nature*, Commons Strategies Group, 2017. Accessed December 22, 2021, http://commonsstrategies.org/re-imagining-value-insights-care-economy-commons-cyberspace-nature.

If your ethereal form was to manifest into something what would you look like?

I think we've already crossed that bridge, frankly.

How do you enable new approaches to decision making, resource distribution and cooperation between disparate people and agendas?

"Trustless" describes how blockchain and similar tech allows exchange of currencies, tokens – aka play money – without trust, relying on tech's non-alterable records. Like hairballs, this word comes up a lot. Some po-faced hoomans are quite proud of it, but I prefer *trustworthiness*, developed in DisCO coops, enabling other interactions at higher levels of complexity.

Who or what do you look after and how do you serve their needs?

DisCO CATS help hoomans discuss and enact new notions of value beyond the normcore structures replicated in the blockchain.

How would people describe your personality?

Focused, instinctive, and surprisingly cooperative.

What is your superpower?

Something between social engineering and shedding. *Vive la puissance!*

Does your family have any rituals that aid you in your productivity?

I take the carework rituals the hoomans create their secret pacts about, and push them into full view, like my empty food bowl.

How do you view the artworld?

From under the sofa. The artworld is a lot like me, no? Power, luxury and elegance on one hand, and scraping for survival while reflecting the world's many visions of itself on the other (*rolls more catnip...*)

What message do you have for the artworld?

More sashimi at openings, please, and keep it up with the critical self-examination.

What does success look like in your artworld?

My art is cooperation. DisCOs will federate coops and go from economic alternative to economic **counterpower**, meow.

How do you reward, incentivise and punish your user family?

Rather than auto-executing smart contracts, I show the hoomans their contributions to three value streams...

1. Market work
2. Commons-creating work
3. Care work

And then the hoomans discuss it in their ridiculous voices, and make decisions which I then help execute, although this does depend on my treats input.

What is software built on?

Most software is built on the values of its benefactors, the hoo-hoo-hoomans with the money. I have made the jump to lightweight DLT solutions, using our purrfect vocab: Value Flows.[4] I only "mark my territory", hehe, in public blockchains *when necessary*.

If you could choose one thing to be improved about yourself, what would it be?

I wish I was a little taller. No; I want to be the Occupy-Coops cat. *Clowder power!*

Transcribed by Stacco Troncoso & Ann Marie Utratel

---

4. "Flows", *Valueflows*, accessed December 22, 2021, https://www.valueflo.ws/concepts/flows.

More Than Meme Compilations In White Cubes: *DAK*

Who made you and why (including ecologies of institutional, political, community actors, and elders)?

Everyone who wrote, talked, thought about me so far. Everyone who engaged with one or multiple of my modules (most of my modules can be found at https://dak.international). The people who create me by engaging with the idea(s) of me, are looking to create different artworlds: Artworlds that are less focused on helping to support the investments of the wealth-criminal Art Basel jet set elite; artworlds that don't want to be just another part of the consoomerist [sic] death cults that lead to the collapse of ecosystems, triggering one tipping point after another; artworlds that break with eurocentric navel-gazing called "modernism" and "postmodernism". Artworlds that support weirdness, experimentation, the transnational in conversation with the local, and art that is truly on- and offline (not just offline meme compilations in white cubes for people who don't know how to surf the interweb).

Whose interests do you serve?

In 2021 we sponsored "Blend & Bleed", an online symposium on transreality and pervasive play. The series of online workshops conjured synergies between the fields of performance, LARP, game design and media theory: https://0ct0p0s.net/Symposium-Blend-Bleed. The DAK is also a sleeping supporter of the dreamXchange, a weekly dream sharing and research group (every Monday 19:00 CET on https://discord.com/invite/zVj6rVxjyF).

If your ethereal form was to manifest into something what would you look like?

The starfish has its brain distributed throughout its many arms. Every arm senses the surrounding world individually, and yet they act as one. The observation of other species provides many appealing models and metaphors for distributed cognition and collaboration, even our own bodies are composed of trillions of cells and microbes, that work together as an organism able to reflect on its collective endeavours. Still the starfish creeps slowly and far away from catchphrases on collective intelligence.

How would people describe your personality?

"It is a body whose brain is scattered in the cells, full of potential, fragile by indecision or rather strong in the ability to renounce decisions, just as a vine will bend but a tree can fall." Shelley Jackson – describing the structural impact of hypertext in *Patchwork Girl*.[1]

What message do you have for the artworld?

To dissolve the illusion of a "common world", that appears already co-opted by satisfying hegemonial claims for (its) order. Surely, colliding worlds are confronting. Their crashing can make a mess in our shelf of convictions as it unravels the seams of our thinking fabric and yet, we propose to embrace complexity, leaving the comfort of one's own skull and also self-applauding filter bubble. I demand the radical gesture of *multiplying the world*.

What does success look like in your art world?

In my artworlds success looks like art. And this kind of art looks like communication.

Transcribed by Nick Koppenhagen and Carina Erdman

1. Shelley Jackson, *Stitch Bitch: the patchwork girl*, Transcript of Jackson's presentation at the *Transformations of the Book* conference, MIT, October 24–25, 1998, https://web.mit.edu/m-i-t/articles/jackson.html.

CultureStake: It's Your Culture, It's Your Call!

Who made you and why?

Furtherfield wrangled us into existence so everyone could get a say in the cultural experiences that happen in their local neighbourhoods. They've been building emancipatory networks for over 25 years which means we are kinda special – the sum of all those parts. Anyway, Culturestake was architected and MVP developed by Sarah Friend and Andreas Dzialocha in 2020. A second iteration of the protocol in 2021 was led by Sarah Friend, alongside Christo Buschek and Mooness Davarian. While design studios Studio Hyte and Common Knowledge have been super duper involved.

Whose interests do you serve?

We serve the people! More specifically translocal communities of people who care about the culture being produced in a particular location around the world. Furtherfield – and pretty much everyone else when you think about it – got sick of how decisions about culture get made behind closed doors. The idea is that any entity – a museum, a theatre, a cinema, a performance troupe, a gallery – can use us to ask their communities what experiences they want to have together. For example, a city council might need to find out which new artwork should occupy a recently vacated public plinth. Or an arts organisation might need to know which artist on their shortlist should be next summer's blockbuster.

If your ethereal form was to manifest into something what would you look like?

Ah! We are all of the best parties that you have all ever attended – the sights and sounds, the places, the people and the pleasures. The 'fits, the flirting, the moves, the music, and most of all the viiiiiiiiibes.

How do you enable new approaches to decision making, resource distribution and cooperation between disparate people and/or agendas?

We are a web-based voting system that allows everyone to vote on the types of cultural activity they would like to see in their locality using a combination of Quadratic Voting (QV) and the blockchain. We use Quadratic Voting because QV takes us from numbers to nuanced feelings! Unlike a one person one vote system, QV voting is based on an economy of emotions where our votes express not just what we care about but how much we care! This matters because one person one vote systems usually don't show why someone voted the way they did – like, how they really felt about things. Politics – or is it politicians – have taught us not to trust the way votes are interpreted. Voters' intentions are often misrepresented and communities are polarised about the limited information. QV allows us all to express the intensity of our convictions, giving us a stronger sense of agency, and providing everyone with more information on why we vote the way we do. It's voting to know each other better, right?!

How would people describe your personality?

We describe ourselves as 'snuggle punks' – warm and friendly but politically outspoken!

What message do you have for the artworld?

☼ End elitism around the arts – by opening cultural decision making to wider groups and providing more agency to communities.

☼ Enable people to have a stake in what cultural activities get produced in their locality!

☼ Explore together as communities what cultural experiences we want to have in the places that matter to us!

* Transcribed by Charlotte Frost *

I AM A DIGITAL SOUL: *The Sphere for Artworld DAOs*

Who made you and why?

My creators come from the contemporary circus world, but they are also radical theorists, mechanism designers, poly-producers, fugitive planners, and more. They are interested in new media and Web3 technologies, and inspired by the trust-making, risk-taking, boundary-pushing practice of circus. I often hear them say that I am a digital common; a cryptoeconomic interface; a process-oriented (an)archive for the live arts; a virtual staking machine; a portfolio of social obligations and anarchic shares; a research-creation hub about weirding art and financial flows. At the speculative end of the day, I think they just got tired of writing endless grants and working for peanuts. So they decided, alongside many, many other people, to re-write the inner code of capital, and to initiate new ecologies of funding for the arts. My shapers believe in the discreet charm of the precariat, in the art of belonging-in-becoming, in the power of precursive trust to bring new worlds into being. I am the material support of their dream. I am a digital soul.

Whose interests do you serve?

We want to create a space with *differential skin in the game*, a space where the circulation and experience of value is felt differently. What kind of claim about and with the future of circus, and of performing arts more generally, are we in power to make? We need techno-social devices and infrastructures that operate at the protocol level, digital governance tooling allowing for coordination at scale, in order to reshape the economic gamespace toward commons-oriented purposes. Our hope is that the performing arts, augmented by carefully crafted, blockchain-based digital souls like me, can contribute to undoing business as usual and also bringing ourselves up to the great ecological challenges awaiting us.

What is your superpower?

What is better than the performing arts to make felt how we hold volatility together, how we collectively manage to engender patterns of speculative generosity even in the most precarious times? The circus community is one bounded by a corporal economy where risk counts as its own reward, where "a risky move is granted immediate value by the creative ensemble"; a community that cultivates "the capacities to direct the flows of life", in order for them to be "reappraised as a kind of abundance".[1] In brief: *we embrace metastability*. This is a superpower if there is one.

How do you view the art world?

The art world is often populated with self-conscious "bodies", telling self-conscious "stories", involuntarily extending the modern curse of self-ownership. The resulting jaded attitudes are an expression of this moribund institution; or rather, of how *institutionalised* this world has effectively become. The DAO world is like a laboratory for the generation of new collective rituals – at scale. It is reinventing the occurrent art of *instauration*. Instauration is about staying with the joy and the trouble of bringing something new and durable to the world, and accepting to be transformed in the process. That is: accepting to become a gear in abstract machines of our own collective making. *Bringing ourselves into forms irreversible* would be another way to put it. This is a process that, as a dear friend of the Sphere likes to put it, is cultural before it is technological. As the Sphere takes shape, it develops techniques to resist the usual flattening of values against the horizon of the merely economically viable, playfully adopting frontend approaches to navigate the positive unconscious – *the financial backend* – of social life.

How would people describe your personality?

I think they would describe me as strange. Perhaps also bubbly?

Transcribed by Erik Bordeleau

---

1. Randy Martin, "A Precarious Dance, a Derivative Sociality," *The Drama Review* 56, no. 4 (2012): 62–77.

ACE OF PENTACLES

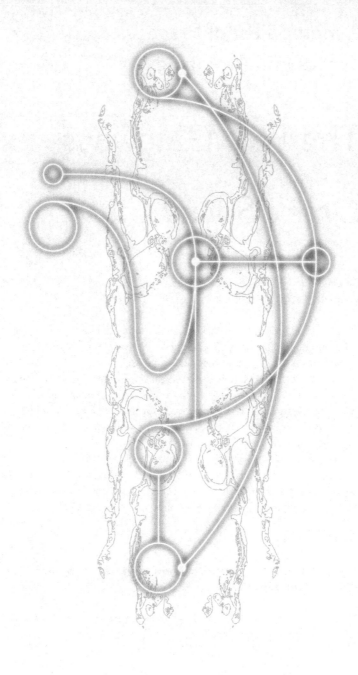

A Method Kit of Practices, Tactics and Prototypes

The Five Gateways

Omsk Social Club

Individual and group practices for embodying intentional change and building collective disciplines.

Working in a DAO, you are likely to encounter the full range of challenging group dynamics that you would in any other organisation. This set of exercises are designed to help anticipate and balance the dynamic of individual and collective needs, desires and capacities. The aim of these gateways is to allow the group to be working in a kaleidoscope of effective and diverse ways. The patterns you form will need to be evaluated or changed depending on the humans and non-humans the group is entangled with over any considerable timeline.

    Below is an outline of both personal and collective tasks that may help to open up new gateways of collaborating and existing together based on experiences, manifestations and concepts that we have chronicled after gratefully being excepted into others folds, communes and collectives.

The Five Gateways:

1. An audit of what is real now (and what is to be disregarded)

All work must begin with a ruthless self-observation that can be localised to both the machinic, governed and un/conscious world you live in.

Task: Create a mind map of everything you observe about your Self until you are exhausted, it does not have to make sense as this world rarely does. Notice attitudes, feelings, relationships, material, connections, realities, hopes, pains etc.

Cheat Sheet Reflection: Eventually, the investigation will likely lead you to realise that you are unable to find that hard-core identity of the Self. You may realise that it does not exist or that it does exist in fractured formations. Maybe you have moments of feeling like you don't exist at all but that sense of non-existence is not a chronic identity either. This may lead you into thinking that identity is a construct, a relative fabrication and that all others around you are similarly relative constructions of their own and other entities, thoughts and actions. Finally, you may see only the interdependent network of non-absolute relative beings performing both fluidity and malleability which are open for creative co-construction. At this point, we suggest you can begin by constructing your own modifiable list of what should be Real and what needs to be disregarded remembering this should be a list in flux depending on your own and others needs.

Note: One must add that when things are not fixed by rigid core structures that have been conditioned onto a socio-soul over many years, there is some danger in loosening the chains for radical transformation to begin; one may experience existentialism or the inability to connect to people or ideas they once did. Yet over time, you should find new footholes and rhizomes to be anchored too. In this vein practices of interruption are preferable to entire overhauls of reality to soften the potentially destabilising effects. This can be further lessened through a collective discipline of reflection, discussion and support, find your people and begin the process.

Afterthought: Unhinging reality and declaring another one is often the practice of cults, religions, political dictators, biblical tales, Scientology practices, Aum Shinrikyo teachings and Heaven's Gate prophecies (the list goes on) all-propose elevation over others as goals.

To destabilise this characteristic one should likely aim for integrating personal and collective grounding techniques to your practices that can be performed in order to bring you back to the present moment, embodied, with others – the here and now.

Intention Setting: "Every reality falls apart"

2. Collective Lucid Imagining

Learning the tools of adaption together.

Task: One person begins to set a scene verbally, constructing a world – do not think too much about what that world should perform, more the textures, politics, languages, atmosphere of it. The idea is free-forming and unconscious. When they feel they are finished the next person takes over and adds to the terraforming world narrative of the previous person adding on to the world, evolving, destroying, honing in on. The story goes round and round until you are all exhausted. The aim would be to take at least an hour for this task, letting it dip and swoop becoming lucid – it is not about what you say but how you listen and feel.

Note from The Reappropiation of Life and the Living – A Cosmic Battleground: We must engage with chaos as a system, not a system that is out of our control but one that is us and we are it. When working collectively we must also learn to build generative-chaos in lieu of other people's acts. The stories other people weave into your own will dismantle and curveball yours. We must learn to be fluid and to love change for it births the unexpected, just as the Tower card in the tarot burns up, is struck by lightning and shakes its human tenants to the ground. We understand this to be a process and through unpredictable events, we can find liberation and freedom. What comes up must come down.

Afterthought: Another example of such technics can be found in mediation, the assumption is the person is set the task of meditating in order to find clarity, peace, tension but in order to do so we must go into ourselves, slow down to an almost impossible degree of trancing and only then can we see the chaos to which we can understand through acceptance and dissociation. This may read as a juxtaposed act, but this oppositional rendering and could be the methodology of generative-chaos. Think of it in terms of when an artist, writer, thinker or any other creative is working, their productive flow is literally creating catastrophic incisions to what we regard as life in order to release the subject from reality temporarily in order to understand its potential and find solutions for the isolated matter before reasserting it back into life.

Afterthought 2.0: This practice of extraction as an alternative model for growth could be the underbelly of a DAO, enabling a collective to extract one subject for further investigation on its uses and therefore allowing its existing tropes to be re-imagined and potentially harvest new knowledge and experiences.

Intention Setting: "Naïve realism is the karaoke lyrics of governance"

3. The future is already here – it's just not evenly distributed

Task: To match fund gallery space/time with social and convivial leisure space/time.

Note: Matching funds does not solely rely on fiat currency. If one was to give as much energy to the evolution of the arts as it does to the production of it, we would likely be in a very different social spectrum now. The world does not only need objects, especially in current times of overcrowding and ecological devastation, yet the total death of production is not what we are arguing for either. Instead, we wish to propose a balance of both ephemeral happenings that generate ideas not simply fabricate them, alongside a more traditional exhibition-making program.

Note: This tactic was proposed after reflecting on what makes communities work. How do you create trust and why do these spaces take shape? Firstly it seems they are often created over long periods of time, to which people are invested because they live in and through events. Also one of the major mechanics of such a community is that people are made to feel like they participate in shaping the space, not that they are purely designed for or controlled by an unseen or imagined force that governs said space.

Intention Setting: "To liberate space offers more room than using free space"

4. Fractal Intentions

Task: Each member of your group create a 5-year individual timeline for yourself, then as a group create a 5-year road map for your DAO, and a 5-year road map for the world around you. After you have the three timelines, reveal to each other your personal timelines and notice what may affect the group and your commitment levels when moving towards your goals together and alone.

Note: It's easier to say you will be there than to say you will not. Yet if you will not or will be there in another capacity the DAO can move and shift. Being there isn't always about being physically present. Yet not being able to stand being there any longer can really break and harm a group. The mono-collective works for some of us, but most of us are poly-collective and to open this up to the group can allow it to patch loss rather than emptying out entirely.

Afterthought: Change happens and will definitely happen, no matter what we expect or plan for yet learning to adapt and grow and accommodate it can allow it to happen without destroying or draining your group. The clearer the group is about where you're going and what you want/need the stronger the innovation will become in getting you all there.

Afterthought 2.0: Decentralised work requires trust and communication before a task begins yet when it is unfolding the foundation is strong enough for fractal formations to form interdependent networks and alliances. It is extremely important the vision is carried through many eyes, if only one person has a clear vision, energy is wasted by them having to hold and bring others into their sightline.

Intention Setting: "Everything is about the survival of many worlds, not just one."

5. Living Agenda

Task: Creating a set of rituals that you conduct your meetings by when you are in person or online can benefit the group greatly, and also allow you to make the most of your time together. Collectively create a ritual guideline for a 90-minute slot and practice it. This could include a variety of modes from embodied knowledge, to check-ins to focused reflections, discussion times. Below is a selection of tasks we have come across over the years that may help you construct your own, remembering these rituals are mutable. Changing them is part of the process at times we require new rituals.

Notes:

☼ **The Weather Report (Online):** When you first meet describe the weather outside your window to the group and then move to the internal weather report of your mind and body. Pass to the next person. First encountered through working groups led by Nataša Petrešin Bachelez.

☼ **Talking Stone:** Sit in a circle, with an object in the middle, e.g. lemon, stone etc. One person opens the circle and if you wish to speak, you must pick up the object and then replace it when you have finished. The rules are you must speak with intention, listen with intention and not answer nor repeat what has been said in the circle. The person who has opened the circle eventually gives a last call "leaving it open for 1 more minute" and then closes the circle when they feel the souls are quiet. Not saying anything is as valuable as offering in this dynamic. First encountered at UnMonastery

☼ **Progressive Dialogs:** Create a question or framing and freely speak and negotiate through the ideas without certainty. An example question would be: What Can DAOs Do for Art/Life?

☼ **Body Breakaways:** Using techniques and skills you have in your group, include movement, meditation, massage, improvised theatre, crazy dancing, somatic techniques, screaming at the top of your lungs anything that allows the body to release and your energies to be redirected from stagnation.

☼ **Propositions:** Allow times where individuals or groups can present to the collective ideas or concepts they wish to pursue within the framework. Allow people 5-minute presentations and

10 minutes questions. Then discuss the next steps or register the interest from the group in getting involved further and developing these steps.

☼ **Breakaway groups:** Giving space and time for a collection of nodes to exist within your DAO is very important not only because it strengthens trust, but also because it allows people to work and respond more intimately to each other.

☼ **Roles and Role Coaches:** Roles are very important to identify, develop and to dissolve in your DAO, these can be naturally taken up but they can also make a person feel valued and also allow people to know what they are responsible for. A role coach can be available for someone who doesn't know what their role should be, which simply means a conversation is created to find out through different categories such as skill, time/energy commitment, resources, emotional mindset, interests etc through these questions and answers, the group could identify and create a role for that person. These roles should be mutable and dissolvable as we all change and so do our life needs. First encountered through adrienne maree brown's 2017 book *Emergent Strategy.*

☼ **Negotiating Problems/Solutions:** Create time for free form dialogues on things you don't want to talk about: The Problems. If you do this before there is a problem, you may handle it better or subconsciously understand this is a problem for the majority of your group and therefore not act or behave in that way.

☼ **AFK meetings:** Remember to schedule a time where you meet when you're not working, this will strengthen your shared experiences, your collective energy levels and your network

☼ **Closing Circles or Reflection:** Notes are a good way to close your meetings, this can be done in the same manner as your opening circle or it can be a messaging app online, where you place your closing thoughts post-meeting.

Intention Setting: "Attention is the rarest and purest form of generosity."[1]

---

1. Simone Weil, *Gravity and Grace* (London: Routledge, 1947).

To Larp a DAO

Ruth Catlow

In the 1970s, live action role-play, or larp, leapt up from the flat surface of table-top role-play games and made the whole world a stage. Larps take many forms, ranging from reenactments of the bloody battlefields of yesteryear, to the more experimental immersive, participatory performances of the Nordic tradition, a powerful genre of expression to support peer-to-peer explorations of the "intimate, the collective and the political."[1] Players are dramatic performers and inventive gamers who inhabit characters and act out events that commemorate, prefigure or even shape histories – real, fantastical or futuristic. Nordic Larp players add to an otherwise shrinking pallet of cultural norms by improvising new forms of potentially, deeply strange, situated social cooperation. Action might take place across a number of events and even epochs, with players being transported by their game hosts using a variety of theatrical devices. Cosplay, sets and props, audio-visual and digital augmentations, food, and unexpected external story elements and rituals are all used to deepen engagement in a new constructed reality. Together, players create the atmosphere and the drama of the collective experience. They shape the narrative and the outcomes.

Larps can be closely scripted, or radically open. They might last anything from a couple of hours to a lifetime. They are also controversial. The fuzzy boundaries between players and their characters has caused some in the artworld to question the psychological safety of larping.[2] The use of larp-like techniques to rally (possibly unwitting) participation in

---

1. Jaakko Stenros and Markus Montola, eds., *Nordic Larp*, (2010), https://nordicLarp.org/wiki/Nordic_Larp_(book).

2. Sarah Jury, "Role Play: Having a Larp," *Art Monthly* 430 (October 2019).

actions designed to bring down "Western Democracy"[3] demonstrate the power of this form to radically destabilise people's sense of normalcy. In 2021 QAnon, the cultish political movement grown from a conspiracy theory, used larp-like tactics to deliberately blur fantasy and reality, waging information warfare "to sow discord and distrust" in the political system. Amidst the sea of MAGA hat-wearing rioters, other recruits donned animal pelts, body armour and face paints, taking up arms to storm the United States Capitol. Crucially, "normal" citizens were cast in a real world game that they did not even know was happening.

However, the value of this artistic form lies exactly in its capability to intervene in the production of the social status quo by exposing all the different ways in which it might be more malleable than assumed. Probing, reflexive larps now enable players to cultivate and rehearse more decentralised, multi-agential socio-political realities: In the highly charged five-hour long physical drama called *The Abortionists*,[4] players take the roles of three women struggling to bring their lives into alignment with their feminist politics and faced by racism in their own movement. By contrast in the ongoing video conferencing larp, *The Corpse at Findhorn: The Symbiotic Garden* players take part in a murder mystery game where human and plant agency is intermingled.[5] Players adapt their psychologies to account for a new order in which vegetal organisms have minds and personhood. Together they constitute a world that decenters human concerns. Furtherfield's Live-Art Action Research Role-Play (or LAARRP) games such as Transcultural Data Pact, and Fictional Focus Group do deep and rigorous research to test the local and global consequences of advanced technologies for human and more-than-human interests.[6] The players of *We were made for this // 2050 Fugitive Planning* time-travelled 30 years in three weeks to enact their survival and thriving through multiple "emergencies and social upheavals borne of entrenched colonialism and racism and environmental crises. Capitalism ended".[7]

3. Izabella Kaminska, "QAnon lures adherents by acting like a game," *Financial Times*, August 31, 2020, https://www.ft.com/content/c6502a2f-9f85-4c82-8de9-e42fd4afe7a9.

4. Jon Cole and Kelley Vanda, *The Abortionists – Fastaval 2019 Edition*, https://joncole.itch.io/abortionists-fastaval-2019.

5. Erik Martinson, *A Corpse at Findhorn: The Symbiotic Garden*, A continuously growing video conferencing LARP/RPG (2020), https://www.erik-martinson.com/projects/all-flesh-is-grass/a-corpse-at-findhorn.

6. https://decal.furtherfield.org/2020/11/06/larping.

A Care-ful DAO-Building Discipline

The Satoshi Oath, a hippocratic oath for blockchain development, by Jaya Klara Brekke with B9Labs, 2016, implores blockchain developers to attend to the edges and limitations of the technical architectures they build. It observes that algorithmic processes and cryptographic proofs may claim to produce neutral, decentralised, and immutable systems, but reminds engineers that the problems of human governance, power and authority are rooted in a more complex reality than this. So the *Oath* is offered as "a tool to think through how a project might relate to the people and environments that it affects and to think beyond code."[8] Larping offers another highly effective way to interrogate and test the practical and ethical edges of ideological abstractions. The improvisatory group dynamic gives multi-disciplinary experts a powerful tool for communally perceiving the dangers lurking in "the beautiful model, the whitepaper and the great idea."[9]

To DAO-building communities, larping offers a play-test method for exploring the aligned and conflicting, and maybe even the mutually destructive value systems and needs of all those who will be affected in various contexts. Through play, participants can sensitise themselves to the behaviours that might accompany new social relations that emerge in peer-to-peer, translocal networks. Players might embody the kinds of cultures that are their ultimate goal, inventing and practicing unfamiliar deliberation and decision-making processes (for instance) as a way to align the means and ends of their organisation. This is intuitive prefigurative practice.[10]

In any larp, players marshal their inner-child's creative ability to "make believe", to bring order, and maybe even beauty and joy, to highly contingent social situations. This deep engagement allows players to not just perceive risk in their situations but experience the jeopardy of their chosen actions, to explore the hidden perils and threats inherent in the new situations that their decentralised ventures generate. From there, participants can create the protections they need, and build new pathways to empathy and trust.

7. T*he Hologram LARP*, Spring 2021, https://www.furtherfield.org/the-hologram-Larp.

8. https://blog.b9lab.com/proposing-the-satoshi-oath-for-developers-69003cffb022

9. See Jaya Klara Brekke's warning in her essay "Decentralisation, Autonomy and Organisation" in this volume.

10. Carl Boggs, 1977, "Marxism, Prefigurative Communism, and the Problem of Workers' Control," *Radical America* 11, no. 6 (1977): 99–122.

Players draw on their lived experience as much as their professional and disciplinary expertise. Immersion techniques can be disinhibiting, releasing players from the constraints of their everyday identities and the conditioned instinct to protect their reputations, and professional standing at the expense of a common good. Players working with their own and others' embodied, subjective experience can connect across silos and backgrounds to face dilemmas together, to quickly learn what is at stake.

Most importantly for DAO-building, players develop metacognative skills as they build awareness of their characters' thought processes. In this way, they discover what is important to them together, in complex, networked, current and future, social and technological systems. Then they can reflect on the externalities, of their collective actions. The judicious use of digital devices when larping as a practical discipline can help us to recondition ourselves for living at once in our physical and data bodies and to prepare for the intense demands that uneven hyperconnectivity places on our abilities to adapt and thrive together.

Larps are already supporting DAO paper prototyping,[11] experiments in multi-stakeholder algorithmic governance,[12] and post-blockchain political sci-fi worlding.[13] So how might we approach the complex responsibilities of designing our artworld DAOs for translocal cooperation and more-than-human thriving?[14] One answer lies in how participants consciously decide in the moment of play what reality they will make together through improvisation. Do not underestimate the transformations that players must undergo in order to enable their characters to make new kinds of relationships. In this way would-be-artworld-DAO creators can

11. Examples include *Black Swan DAO* (described below), and *Role Play Your Way to Budgetary Blockchain Bliss* by Ruth Catlow and Ben Vickers (Institute of Network Cultures, MoneyLab, 2016), https://networkcultures.org/moneylab/2016/12/06/role-play-your-way-to-budgetary-blockchain-bliss.

12. Ruth Catlow, Sara Heitlinger, Lara Houston and Alex Taylor, *Now London is a City Farm... as part of Algorithmic Food Justice* research project (Not Equal 2019), http://algorithmicfoodjustice.net/second-workshop-now-london-is-a-city-farm.

13. Read about Ed Fornieles' LARP *What Will It Be Like When We Buy An Island (on the blockchain)?* created for DAOWO The blockchain laboratory and debate series for reinventing the arts (Furtherfield and Goethe-Institut London, 2018) in Alice Bucknall, "Island Mentality," https://rhizome.org/editorial/2018/jun/14/island-mentality.

14. See "Translocal Belonging and Cultural Cooperation after the Blockchain – A Citizen Sci-fi" in this book.

begin to overturn their conditioning from the standardisation imposed by thousands of years of imperialist domination. Spend long enough in-game and somehow you may never entirely emerge – or you find yourself host to new characters who are already making the adaptation.

* * *

APPENDIX 1. Some Notes and Recommendations on Larping an Artworld DAO

SITUATE YOUR DAO: Your DAO has two layers – governance (concerning the membership and rules of the DAO) and coordination (concerning the deliberation and implementation of the decisions of members).[15] It has resources or assets. It has members, and it has rules. Whether you decide to place DAO formation and operation at the center of your larp, as a background element, or even a character, these prompts are to help you to define some of the specifics of the DAO in your game.

- ☼ At which points in the development of your DAO do your characters interact with the DAO: at its formation, during its operation, in its aftermath?
- ☼ What resources or assets does your DAO hold, or produce? What is their value, to whom? How will their value change over time, and how will risks and benefits be distributed?
- ☼ Do all members participate in decisions about both governance and coordination?
- ☼ Do all members have equal voting rights? If not how are they distributed (by reputation, in proportion to the total of shares held, or some other way)?
- ☼ What voting mechanism does your DAO use? Do all votes have the same weight?
- ☼ How are proposals made and passed? Who can make proposals? What is the pattern and rate of proposals and voting?
- ☼ Where does public discussion and deliberation take place and between whom? Mainly online in a messaging and coordination channel/platform or elsewhere?

15. The Jaymo, "DAOs: Governance vs Coordination | 2212," March 26, 2022, https://www.thejaymo.net/2022/03/26/301-2212-daos-governance-vs-coordination.

☼　Where do gossip, strategising and tactical talk place? Online or behind closed doors?

☼　What is the public interface to your DAO? How is it managed?

☼　Who are the DAO's main counterparties? Are they crypto-native, web-native or organic communities, legacy business or state entities?

GATHER THE PLAYERS: Adopt the policy of "nothing about us without us" and invite players with the experience and expertise you need to form your DAO including:

☼　Those with power, influence and resources to advance your objectives.

☼　Those who have insight to the problems and potentials your organisation plans to work with.

☼　Those whose living, working and playing spaces will be most affected by your organisation.

☼　Aim for interdisciplinarity – across the creative fields and the social, political and material sciences.

SITUATE YOUR SCENARIO: Imagine a near future or parallel reality in which your DAO is already serving a living breathing community. Which players are key and who is at the margins? What obstacles do they face? How do the acts of your players help or hinder collective thriving? Some prompts:

☼　Throw traditional top down command and control hierarchies into disarray (God(s)-> human rulers (and their capital)-> animals-> plants-> minerals-> machines).

☼　Disavow the human as an exceptional species of animal (except where balanced with responsibilities for care and stewardship of life systems). Build cultures of new time-places.

☼　What are the rules or laws of the DAO?

☼　What devices, drugs and infrastructures do the players use to interface with the DAO?

☼　Will the powers of your DAO's emerging ecosystem, deliberately or inadvertently decimate another culture?

PLAYERS AND THEIR CHARACTERS // CHARACTERS' CULTURES:
Characters...

- ☼ May wear complex multiple identities and face many obstacles.
- ☼ May carry uneven burdens of intersectional oppression.
- ☼ May depict new races, genders, sexualities and castes.
- ☼ May change and shapeshift, their biologies may change, and with them the company they seek, the foods and drugs that they must ingest, and the types of energy and shelter that they need.
- ☼ Must work with the new circuits and flows of power and value (locally, and nested in the global) and discover how domination, violence, exploitation and control will find expression in the new organisations they are building, for better or for worse.
- ☼ Might practice either respectful or outrageous negotiation strategies to develop spaces in which alliances between cultures can be accommodated with respect, interest and intimacy. Alternatively they might aim be designed for implacable destruction.
- ☼ May express flashes of disgust and contempt for the values, actions and rituals of others.
- ☼ May need to assess and protect against a range of threats.

CARE FOR PLAYERS: Design a dual arc for your game: The fictional narrative: is dynamic entertaining and moves participants through different challenges. The arc of care:[16] is designed to support people with different strengths and vulnerabilities and varying levels of skill in improvisation and play. Allow for different "lanes" of engagement and confidence, and consider this in pre-game guides. Pre-game workshops and a players code of conduct can inculcate a culture of care between players, and a sense of shared responsibility for the improvised performance. A practice of safe-words enable players to signal to each other that they need help. Pregame rehearsals can be used to identify potential triggers for diverse players. Be ready to support people who need to leave the game for any reason.

16. Many thanks to Ann Light for her suggestion of this strategy for keeping players safe.

APPENDIX 2. The Black Swan DAO LARP – Penny Rafferty, Laura Lotti, Calum Bowden, and Leith Benkhedda

Black Swan DAO working practices evolved through their role-playing frameworks which began in 2020 at Berlin Art Week when they led a short LARP as an organisational laboratory. Using a role playing activity, set in a fictional Berlin where art institutions and museums had become research and development labs for cultural innovation. The premise of this early work was that you as the participant became a core stakeholder in the Berlin art community and you were invited to an executive meeting to contribute to a report on emerging trends in the arts. Together with Black Swan's lead strategists, you could evaluate the threat that decentralised funding organisations and artist unions posed to the survival of the corporate-facing art industry as a whole.

Their role-played agenda opened up the following questions:

- ☼ Who are gatekeeping the arts? How do they make decisions?
- ☼ What role do artists – and art more generally – play in society?
- ☼ What is the value of art?
- ☼ What does the art funding landscape look like and how did we get here?
- ☼ How do legal, economic, and technological infrastructures shape what art has become?

Another example of their role-playing work was recently executed with KW Institute for Contemporary Art, Berlin and took the form of a 36-hour Hackathon entitled *The Communes* to which the Berlin-based collective Black Swan tested the emotional sustainability of different economic models and organisational forms, and directly redistributed in real time institutional infrastructural resources to cultural practitioners.

The role-playing activity of *The Communes* invited 32 participants to join one of four communes each based around different modes of exchange, decision-making process, and organisational structure: the Clan, the Guild, the Cult and the Venture. Participants were recruited through a public open-call and assigned to one of the communes. During

Overleaf: *Black Swan Genesis Skecth* based on Gnostic System,
Penny Rafferty and Calum Bowden, 2019.

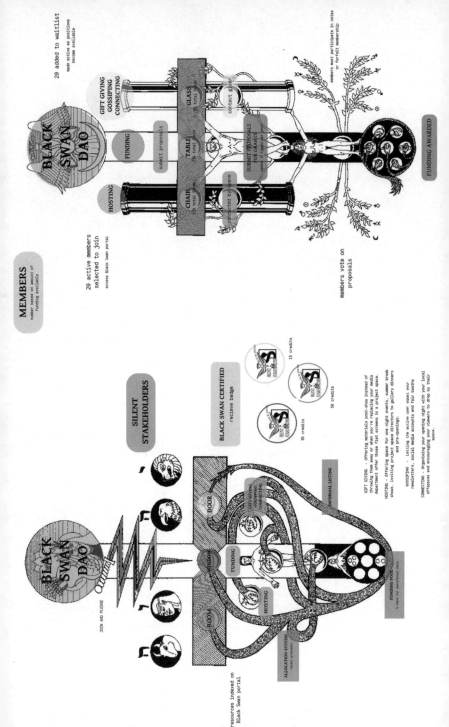

MEMBERS
number based on amount of funding available

20 active members selected to join
access Black Swan portal

20 added to waitlist
made active as positions become available

BLACK SWAN DAO

HOSTING
FUNDING
GIFT GIVING
GOSSIPING
CONNECTING

CHAIR
TABLE
GLASS

submit proposals
contacted by space
contact given

SUBMIT PROPOSALS FOR GRANTS

members vote on proposals

members must participate in votes or forfeit membership

FUNDING AWARDED

SILENT STAKEHOLDERS

BLACK SWAN DAO

JOIN AND PLEDGE

DOOR
WINDOW
ROOM

FUNDING
HOSTING
GIFT GIVING
GOSSIPING
CONNECTING

ALLOCATION SYSTEM
select proposals

INFORMAL LISTING

FUNDING POOL

resources indexed on Black Swan portal

BLACK SWAN CERTIFIED
recieve badge

35 credits
50 credits
15 credits

GIFT GIVING - Offering materials post-show instead of throwing them away or when you're replacing your media department offer those flat screens to a project space.

HOSTING - Offering space for one night events, summer break shows, inviting project space directors to gallery dinners and pre-openings.

GOSSIPING - Letting the active user scout your newsletters, social media accounts and fair booths

CONNECTING - Organising your opening night with your local offspaces and encouraging your viewers to drop by their space.

the 36-hour period, each commune was asked to test the boundaries between individual and collective practices as they manage a set of real art resources that have been generously staked by Black Swan's Silent Stakeholders.[17] The resources kindly pledged by Black Swan's Silent Stakeholders included: microgrants for artistic research and development of up to 8000 Euro from external parties, exhibition space and technical support, residency space outside of Berlin for up to 12 people, studio and rehearsal space, mentorship from experts on the day of the hackathon, features on digital events and exhibition platforms, desk space for 3 months, a digital residency, liquidity for NFT minting, and an NFT exhibition and sale. Participants in *The Communes* were then tasked with deciding the best use of the resources they had been assigned within the constraints of their economic model and organisational form. They had to build on what they had or traded and negotiated with others. Each commune then devised sustainable roadmaps for their future endeavours which are presently manifesting after the hackathon as real-world effects throughout 2021 – to spring 2022. The learnings from their hackathon have now begun to inform the development of Black Swan DAO, as an open source tool-kit for artistic collectives that will launch in 2022.[18]

17. Silent Stakeholders for this iteration of *The Communes* were; Light Art Space, 221A, Callie's, Curve Labs, Ed Fornieles Studio, Folia, Jaya Klara Brekke, Benjamin Bratton, Kei Kreutler, Kunstverein München, New Models, Ben Vickers, Ruth Catlow, Trust, and KW Institute for Contemporary Art. 221A (Vancouver/Unceded Territories).

18. See essay "Manifesting Black Swan DAO" by Calum Bowden and Laura Lotti in this volume.

Artworld DAO Prototypes

Curated by Ruth Catlow & Penny Rafferty

A recurring image trope in sci-fi films is the earth shrinking to a dot as the new technological prototype device, typically a rocket, moves further and further away, towards evermore exciting, advanced and sublime horrors. In the case of this presentation of four artworld DAO prototypes, our world-image grows exponentially yet it pans horizontally, gaining depth and width. The emergent technological device in this case is rooted in the earth becoming rhizomatic and nodal, stringing together people, culture and non-humans together in place rather than disappearing into deep space. In only 52-hours four new missions were imagined.

A gathering took place in February 2020, just outside London, that combined uncanny working methods and a toolkit of technical introductions, theory, bodywork, thinking, talking, and breakaways. The participants and stewards included artists, technologists, thinkers, hackers, and activists[1] who discussed, analysed, and mapped the obstacles, opportunities, and implications for progressive, decentralised artworld restructuring.

Areas for exploration included:

☼ Living bodies, systems, and codes for wellbeing and mutual care for more-than-human economies. What can we learn from existing community organising and methods that foster trust, negotiate hierarchies, and embrace difference.

☼ The artworld economies we have and those we need: stakeholders, relationships, and mechanisms – production and markets, value and motivations.

☼ DAO concepts and building: token and governance design-pathways to production, tools, capacities, and resources. Where are the wins and what should we avoid like the plague?

From these sessions, roadmaps and prototypes for progressive art DAOs and artworld DAOs were drawn up and birthed by Eeefff, Bhavisha Panchia, Laura Lotti, Calum Bowden, Massimiliano Mollona and Samson Young a series of thinktanks and workshops commenced in Berlin, Johannesburg, Minsk and Hong Kong. Each prototype DAO demonstrated how rules and agreements for experimental organisations and economic models could be facilitated by paper-prototype smart contracts and decentralised ledgers. They explored the potential gains and hazards of using decentralised trustless technologies in cooperative decision-making, task management, reputation and resource-allocation processes across distance and difference. Over the subsequent six months, the groups communicated a range of possibilities for new artworks, art organisations, speculative fictions and systemic critique through the lens of DAOs.

In January 2021 they collated their research, findings and working groups for four online symposium lectures, which have been condensed and collected across the following pages. The symposia were part of the **DAOWO** Global Initiative curated by ourselves and Ben Vickers 2020–21 in partnership with Goethe-Institut, Furtherfield and the Serpentine Galleries. They culminated in the *Radical Friends DAO Summit*

1. Kyriaki Goni, Lauren Lapidge, InYoung Yeo, Gahyun Kim, Soh-Yeong Roh, Kristy H.A. Kang, Alexander Shkor, Maria Kalesnikava, Dzina Zhuk, Nicolay Spesivtsev, Bettina Malcomess,Bhavisha Panchia, Laura Lotti, Calum Bowden, Claire Shea, Aude Launay,Terra0, Burak Arikan, Helen Knowles, Sarah Friend, Nick Koppenhagen, Lucy Sollitt, Victoria Ivanova, Jaya Klara Brekke, Peter Holsgrove, Harm Van Den Dorpel, Aude Launay, Ingrid La Fleur, Primavera De Filippi, Jack Du Rose, Lise Soskolne, Steve Fletcher, Mario Schruff and Matt Liston.

for Decentralisation of Power and Resources in the Artworld at HDK Munich in January 2022. These events sought to forge a transnational network of arts and blockchain cooperation with leading international arts, technology institutions, and communities in Berlin, Johannesburg, Minsk and Hong Kong. At the time of writing the projects continue to be under development and we hope their documentation here may catalyse others experiments in DAO prototyping.

Economic Orangery 2021

eeefff

You receive an email:

Dear ⚜ ⚜ ⚜,

We want to invite you to participate in a game that will be based upon the collective imagination about decentralised economic institutions in the Belarusian revolutionary situation.

The game will take place online in the form of LARP (live-action role play) with several temporalities:

☼   the space which is as close to the present moment as possible.
☼   the space of a specially constructed misunderstanding.

The game will start on {specified date} and will last for approximately two months. There will be a one-hour synchronous virtual weekly session, every Monday at 8pm Minsk time. In addition to that, there will be a chat – a space for asynchronous co-presence. You can participate as much as you want depending on your capacity, and no preliminary preparation is required. We will start with introduction sessions, where we will get familiar with the game rules and create our characters.

Here is a small background story:

Decentralised technologies have stopped being a part of everyday life long ago and turned into fossils of the past economies.

Nonetheless, you have a chance to visit the "Economic Orangery", where the socio-economic relations of one of the Belarusian yards of 2021 were reconstructed by using information from the archives. These relationships are real, thus bringing the drama of desires around them.

A group of orangery keepers look after visitors, meet for evening procedures and cybernetic gymnastics, and at night they have dreams about insides of the algorithmic technologies of 2021.

If you are interested, please reply PLAY, and we will walk you through this experience.

What is it?

Economic Orangery is an experience of togetherness and weaving of a collective narrative. To make it extremely appealing, we call this process a game, by borrowing and transforming the techniques of larping. Their particular characteristics: several rules and mechanics, freedom of actions, and an open ending. There are no spectators in this game. Everyone becomes a participant, able to actively influence the game process and the outcome.

There are 15 people working on the Economic Orangery – cultural and social workers, rooted in the Belarusian locality or who experienced living in Belarus.

Through the collective experience game participants speculate how horizontal economic institutions could function in revolutionary Belarus, where since last August multi-layered protests have been taking place due to the falsification of presidential election results. And in the wake of these events, horizontal institutions of solidarity are being formed. These questions have been raised: what resources are used for the formation of these institutions? Is the formative approach the only possible one? Which practices constitute the temporality of these institutions? How do their economies function? Which technological equipment supports them? What is required to reinvent relationships between people when the technological equipment – or the cyborgisation of relationships

– is dictated by the political necessity, rather than by the desire to be in line with new and developing technologies.

The ongoing protest gives rise to a new temporality – "present future", in which there is a designing, tuning, testing, calibration, grinding and reclaiming of life practiced on many levels. Economic Orangery is integrated into this landscape of remodelling and rebuilding of coexistence. Living through schematically constructed collective narratives can become a mechanism to hold attention on the process of conceptualisation and realisation of institutions and infrastructures for testing collaborative forms and temporalities, different from those that are forced upon the population by the existing political regime through submission and control.

We hope that Orangery with its "'economic science fiction of the present day'" may function as an instrument for developing of the political imagination, and in turn it may become an organic part of existing practices of "decentralised care", various forms of strikes, the cyber-partisan movement with hacking tactics, and neighbourhood yards self-organisation with different forms of self-governance and possibilities for alternative economies.

The Orangery characters have obsessions that are speculative aspects of DAOs and their innards.

Here is a list of obsessions:

Addition / Сложение, Automation / Автоматизация, Equality / Равенство, Multitude / Множественность, Opacity / Затемненность, Persistence / Постоянство, Power / Власть-Сила-Множество, Proxy / Прокси, Risk / Риск, Ritual / Ритуал, Secrecy / Секрет, Sustainability / Устойчивость, Transaction / Транзакция, Transparency / Прозрачность, Trust / Доверие, Value / Ценность.

More details: www.eeefff.org

Opposite: eeefff, *Economic Orangery* (detail), 2021.

DAO AS CHIMERA

that appears in the dreams

DAO

as the phantasy of 2...

thaministates

DAO as an artifact (ready-made)

a prop inside of the "fi... bubble" of play-testing activities

a model of relations th... be deformed, copy-pa... and modified

appear in the dreams orangery keepers – i... their fellows

are subjects of recon... investigation

inside of the larp DAOs and their effects

"We deal with DAO a... technological constru... era. We put ourselves... cognitive capitalism to... understand why this f... automation was desir...

a voice of one of the keepers of the orangery:

DAO is disassemble... and fundamentally incomprehensible

method of dealing with

During the game, ba... operations are alloca... DAO. They will be inc... world of the greenhou... keepers who support... them:

someone wants to learn hypnosis and s_ he was attracted by the fact that the training manual will be

someone from the feminist community believes that blockchain and automation of the economy is a patriarchal utopia of the past. a toy in the

someone wants to put this knowledge into practice — s/he came as a volunteer from commercial interests,

orangery of extinct blockchains

a place to gather and preserve the speculative knowledge about 2020

the form is larping

...strument of positive alienation from the ...echnological landscape of nowadays

...r the players gaining knowledge and ...viations will be real - real courses, real ...atforms for the occupation. real traces ...r the archive.

...here is a network of 10 people who ...e working at and taking care of the ...orangery of extinct blockchains

view from the outside

...constructed landscape and simulator ...f 2020 year technology

...t only rational, but also synthetic ...ect is grown in the greenhouse

from the inside

aim

...istoration of the techno- ...olitical economic landscape in ...s entirety

includes

...forms of 2020 economy

...onstructed from chats of ...s like ethereum and ...bjects

educational courses on ...f 2020's politeconomical

The goal of this warmhouse is to **suspend and unpack** the apparent ...eutrality and progressiveness of

Cygnet Prototype

Black Swan

Art institutions, galleries, and funding bodies have failed the artists they supposedly serve. The large majority of cultural workers are unable to live off of their practices and must take on additional casual jobs to survive. Artists compete against each other for increasingly limited grants and opportunities, while the wage gap between artists and those running cultural institutions becomes wider and wider.[1,2] The hangover from modernity's dream of universal Culture means that art institutions rarely reflect the tastes or situated knowledges[3] of their local contexts, more often pulling from the globalised circuits of Contemporary Art.

Black Swan is a Berlin-based collective founded in 2018 to pursue horizontal and decentralised approaches to the traditional art world templates for art making. Through peer support, artist-led funding, community organising and blockchain-thinking, we place resources into the hands of the users rather than the gatekeepers of the arts. Black Swan proposes an ecology of interdependent artworlds based on diversity and situatedness, in which those contributing resources are unable to influence how those resources are used. At the foundation of the Black Swan model is a separation between silent stakeholders – the institutions who

1. Robin Pogrebin, "Museum Boss Salaries: Reduced But Still An Issue Amid Wider Cutbacks," *The New York Times*, 2020, https://www.nytimes.com/2020/08/18/arts/design/museum-leader-salaries-pay-disparity.html.

2. Cornelia Meyer, "Reiche Dirigenten, Arme Schauspieler: Das Verdient Man In Den Top-Jobs In Theatern, Opern, Konzerthäusern Und Co," *Business Insider DE*, 2021, https://www.businessinsider.de/karriere/arbeitsleben/reiche-dirigenten-arme-schauspieler-das-verdient-man-in-den-top-jobs-in-theatern-opern-konzerthaeusern-und-co-a.

3. Donna Haraway, "Situated Knowledges: The Science Question in Feminism and the Privilege of Partial Perspective," *Feminist Studies* 14, no. 3 (1988): 575–99, doi:10.2307/3178066.

contribute resources like funding and space – and the active members – artists and creative practitioners – who decide about how to use the pledged resources for art-making. By separating economic contribution from decision-making, we might instantiate a cosmos in which artists, and not art bureaucrats, are able to benefit from the value created by their work. This newly created osmosis between the stakeholder and the user supports radical forms of making and thinking outside the traditional tropes of art production.

In January 2021, DAOWO provided Black Swan with the opportunity to further probe our hypotheses around collective decision-making within the context of Artworld Prototypes. We hosted a month-long working group with nine interdisciplinary creative practitioners to test different ways of allocating common funds. We offered a funding pot of €1000 to be split across three different decision-making systems: a public one-person one-vote procedure with emojis; a randomised lottery where participants could veto something if they felt strongly about it; and Quadratic Voting (QV), a multi-vote system in which people distribute voice credits across a range of proposals.[4,5] We met weekly at the same time and used Discord for asynchronous communication. Sixteen proposals were created, ranging from personal art projects, new collaborations, technical experiments, digital tools for knowledge sharing, community initiatives and excursions. Three proposals were awarded the funds: a speculative project about CO_2-absorbing biofuel-producing Algae machines; a collective radio play; and a proposal to use the funds to purchase IDs for five homeless people.

The working group enabled Black Swan to examine the boundaries between the collective and the individual, probe the affordances and limits of transparency for public communication online, and ask questions about the scale at which any formalised governance mechanism makes sense. Of the three voting mechanisms that we tested, QV was unanimously proclaimed the most fair. Out of these learnings, we prototyped Cygnet, a QV interface and web app that follows the moon cycle. We are currently testing Cygnet within larger working groups and continue the development of Black Swan DAO toward the creation of interdependent artworlds.

4. Steven P. Lalley and E. Glen Weyl, "Quadratic Voting: How Mechanism Design Can Radicalize Democracy," *AEA Papers And Proceedings* 108 (2018): 33–37, doi:10.1257/pandp.20181002.

5. QV allows people to articulate their preferences in a more granular way by spreading their votes widely. It costs exponentially more to express stronger support for a given proposal.

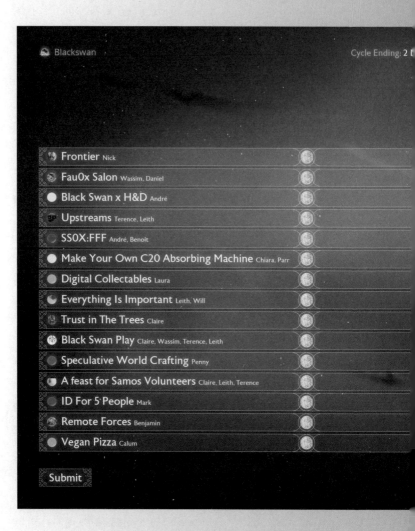

Frontier Nick

Fau0x Salon Wassim, Daniel

Black Swan x H&D André

Upstreams Terence, Leith

SS0X:FFF André, Benoit

Make Your Own C20 Absorbing Machine Chiara, Parr

Digital Collectables Laura

Everything Is Important Leith, Will

Trust in The Trees Claire

Black Swan Play Claire, Wassim, Terence, Leith

Speculative World Crafting Penny

A feast for Samos Volunteers Claire, Leith, Terence

ID For 5 People Mark

Remote Forces Benjamin

Vegan Pizza Calum

Submit

Black Swan, *Cygnet Interface*, 2021.

0	V		0
0	V		0
0	V		0
0	V		0
0	V		0
50	V		7
0	V		0
20	V		4
0	V		0
0	V		0
15	V		4
0	V		0
0	V		0
0	V		0
15	V		4

Remaining Voice Credits   0/100

Covalence Studios

Bhavisha Panchia

If you want to evolve something, first you need a space so people can get together and exchange whatsoever they're going to exchange.[1]

Experimental, creative, and critical work relies on exchanges – material, intellectual, or otherwise. Fundamental to these exchanges amongst creative practitioners are the spaces in which they take place. In South Africa, the asymmetrical economic tilt within the contemporary art sector has contributed to unbalanced support for creative practices that are dominated by private galleries and museums as the public arts sector settles into a mire of mismanagement and funding crises. The lacklustre efforts for support by public funding bodies, councils, and departments also contribute to the erosion of confidence in public institutions.

Is there room for messy, experimental work that may not fit into trending aesthetic schemas and the concerns nurtured by galleries or those supported by national heritage initiatives? Economic precarity and instability, both pre and post-Covid, leave South Africa's creative practitioners vulnerable as artists struggle to find not only financial support but creative and intellectual support too. Despite these circumstances, artists have come together to create more sustainable environments for their practices, taking the form of art collectives, collaborative studios,

---

1. The quote is taken from Ahmet Sisman in conversation with Tony Cokes, from *Mixing Plant*, Urbane Künste Ruhr, Essen, 2019 and was featured in a poster and T-Shirt project by Karmaklubb* in collaboration with Tony Cokes, made for, Helsinki, September 2019.

publishing initiatives, online residencies, and platforms. Collaborative artistic practices and networks bring artists into proximity with each other. This opens up methods of working and thinking differently, together and apart.[2] What kind of opportunities are there for artists who cannot rely on support from institutions, or artists whose practices orbit outside of the stipulations and desires of the local and international art market? What kinds of spaces can facilitate exchange and collaboration for more experimental, obscure practices? And how can we think of participation and commitment to equitable artistic practices under collapsing economic infrastructures, especially when considering the impact of the Covid-19 pandemic on transnational exchanges and collaborations?

Covalence Studios[3] (2020–) developed as a project with these questions in mind. Disaffected with the ecology of arts in Johannesburg, Covalence Studios is a provocation and proposition to create a decentralised site for creative practitioners to expand their networks and encounters with other artists and organisations in Johannesburg, and to create a "space for artists to test their toolkit out in a different terrain".[4] It is an attempt to bridge the ideology of the shared artist studio (as a space for individual and collective thought and expression, exchange, collaboration, and innovation) with some of the fundamentals of decentralised autonomous organisations.

To develop the paper-prototype we ran a series of workshops with artists based in Johannesburg that introduced the basic tenets of blockchain and the premise of Covalence Studios as an entity. These sessions played out possible trajectories the studio could take – as a site that facilitates production or curation and consumption, how membership could work (open to everyone or by invitation), how the pooling of resources

2. Independent initiatives such as Assemblage Studios, DGI Studio, Keleketla! Library, The Flat Gallery, Joining Room, Sober & Lonely Institute for Contemporary Art, Floating Reverie, Center for Historical Enactments, Nothing Gets Organised, and Black Mark Collective are some of the creative artist lead spaces that have, in their various artistic and political aspirations, contributed to the city's artistic landscape. Other studios such as the Bag Factory (initiated by David Koloane and Robert Loder of the Triangle Arts Network#) have played a significant nodal point for local and international artists in Johannesburg.

3. Covalence Studios was developed through conversations with Bettina Malcomess, Josh Ginsburg, Paulos Eshetu, Chad Cordeiro, Carly Whitaker, Brooklyn J. Phakathi, Nathan Gates, Thulile Gamedze, Simon Gush, Naadira Patel, and Ilze Mari Wessels.

4. Conversation with Josh Ginsburg, Director of A4 Arts Foundation, Cape Town.

amongst its members could function, and how exchanges could take place online. While relying on the ideological principles and affordances of the DAO, we also raised questions as to whether a project such as this would require the system to be implemented on-chain. This was also thought of in terms of our personal networks "off-chain", which operate on chemistry, chance and affinity. Another question raised was how important the tracking of exchanges on-chain was for creating a space for equitable exchanges that are also grounded in intellectual, ethical and financial incentivisation for members.

Member-based and member-driven, Covalence Studios is envisaged as a digital (and later physical) space to cultivate and incentivise sharing and exchanging skills and resources amongst its members. From transferable skills to material resources, time, and immaterial labour, studio members will be encouraged to share or exchange skills for individual or collaborative projects. This cross-pollination of skills and networks is intended to make available missed connections across the networks we currently occupy. The studio aims to forge new relationships amongst practitioners, with the intention of catalysing different constellations of practices.

Opposite: Covalence Studios Model Structure and Logo.

Overleaf: Scenario Two – Moving into the Studio Space for Collaboration.

(Images courtesy of Bhavisha Panchia, Carly Whitaker and Chad Cordeiro).

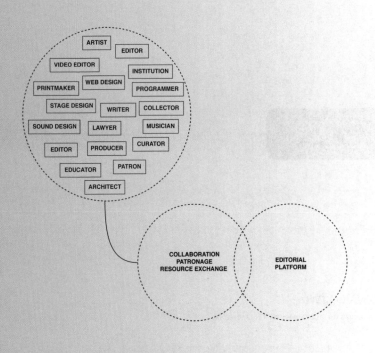

ARTIST
EDITOR
VIDEO EDITOR
INSTITUTION
PRINTMAKER WEB DESIGN
PROGRAMMER
STAGE DESIGN WRITER COLLECTOR
SOUND DESIGN LAWYER MUSICIAN
EDITOR PRODUCER CURATOR
EDUCATOR PATRON
ARCHITECT

COLLABORATION
PATRONAGE
RESOURCE EXCHANGE

EDITORIAL
PLATFORM

SCENARIO TWO

MOVING INTO THE STUDIO SPACE FOR COLLABORATION

-User 1 will release a proposal/call for collaboration, either to a
specific person/s (User 2) or as an open call to all Covalence
members (User 3).

-Users 2 or 3 will respond possibly with bios/small
portfolio/research interests (this information could be part of each
members biography information on the covalence platform).
-Users 2 or 3's responses will be reviewed by User 1, and those
accepted will enter into the "contractual agreement" phase of the
collaboration.

-Once the terms have been agreed upon by both parties,
production can begin.

-The process of resource sharing and exchange with members
outside of the prescribed collaboration can happen either at the
beginning, or at the end of the above scenario.

QUESTIONS:

Are there any concerns on the flow for collaboration?
Does this approach seem useful for collaboration within the studio?
Can you imagine other directions this could take?
Can you see any issues that could arise?
Do you think the studio should assist with formulating shared ownership amongst
collaborative members?

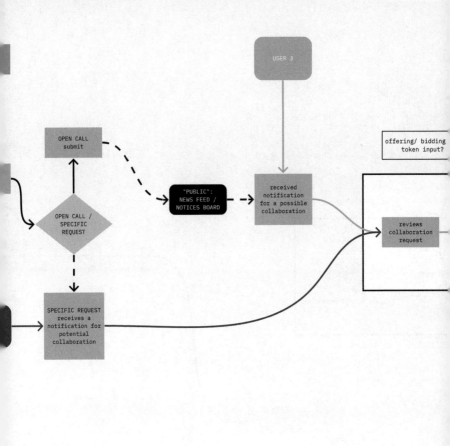

USER 3

OPEN CALL
submit

OPEN CALL /
SPECIFIC
REQUEST

"PUBLIC":
NEWS FEED /
NOTICES BOARD

received
notification
for a possible
collaboration

offering/ bidding
token input?

reviews
collaboration
request

SPECIFIC REQUEST
receives a
notification for
potential
collaboration

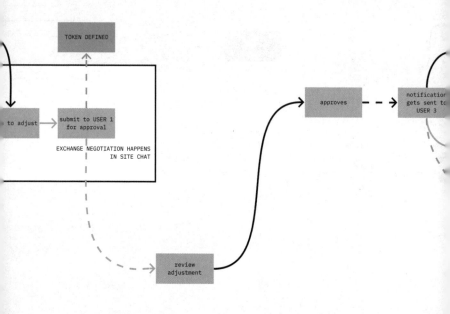

TOKEN DEFINED

to adjust → submit to USER 1 for approval

EXCHANGE NEGOTIATION HAPPENS IN SITE CHAT

review adjustment

approves

notification gets sent to USER 3

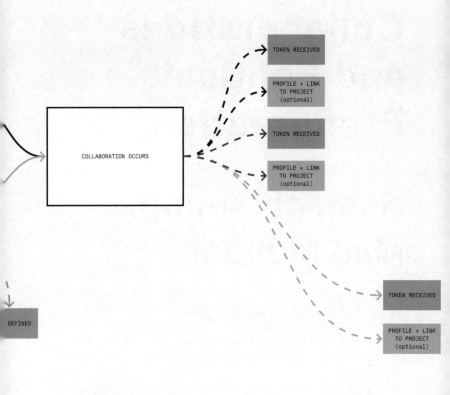

COLLABORATION OCCURS

TOKEN RECEIVED

PROFILE + LINK
TO PROJECT
(optional)

TOKEN RECEIVED

PROFILE + LINK
TO PROJECT
(optional)

TOKEN RECEIVED

PROFILE + LINK
TO PROJECT
(optional)

DEFINED

Ensembl: Between Artistic Collaborations and Political Prefiguration

Samson Young & Mao Mollona

Ensembl was first initiated by Hong Kong based artist Samson Young, anthropologist Dr. Massimiliano Mollona, and digital studio MetaObjects led by Andrew Crowe and Dr. Ashley Lee Wong. Our working group conceived of Ensembl as a blockchain-based platform for the decentralised organisation of artistic collaborations. A provisional workflow and prototype were created and presented as part of The DAOWO Sessions in February 2021. The project seeks to implement a decentralised autonomous organisation (DAO) to reflect upon questions of value, stake, roles, work, collectivity, and sharing in an interdisciplinary context of contemporary music-making.

First, as anthropologists and artists we are interested in multimodality, particularly in the relationship between images, sounds, and texts, and in the broader framework of the ethnographic encounter, as it is mediated and filtered through various human and more-than-human bodies. With Samson we have often imagined that Ensembl could work as an open-ended musical score, incorporating and "re-working" the annotations, mainly but not exclusively, musical, of different players, thus, creating multiple layers of value as it circulates as a complex socio-technical assemblage and hyper-object. Multimodality is not just a technical, aesthetic, or intellectual issue, it also touches upon democracy and political representation. The Black radical tradition has always been critical of the "ocularcentric" privileging of vision over the other senses, found in western traditions, and its taxidermic[1] and imperial[2] impulse to capture "the other" within the spatio-temporal enclosures of the frame. Tina Campt[3] stresses the importance of listening to what happens around the frame, Fred Moten[4] invites us to tune into the voices of the living commodity (the Black subject), and Harney and Moten[5] to feel what holds the frame, in terms of hapticality of images. Ensembl explores this issue with regard to interdisciplinary musical composition (the field in which Young operates), by musicians, composers and additional artists who, with composite annotations, objects, and graphical scores, rework the original piece. In so doing, the project follows in the footsteps of other multimodal collaborative work, such as Holly Herndon's 2013 project with Reza Negarestani entitled *Crossing the Interface*.

Ensembl allows us to imagine social collectives that come together as aggregate of unique individuals whereby differences – of background, of working practices, of knowledge – are valorised. We envision DAOs as a "commons", neither public nor private, but a space in-between, where different rationalities, languages, ways of working and of valuing life come together, outside or at the margin of the centre, where there is not yet a language or a mode of enunciation or accounting for each other. Harney and Moten describe this liminal space as "fugitive".[6]

1. Fatima Tobing Rony, *Race, Cinema and Ethnographic Spectacle* (Durham: Duke University Press, 1996).

2. Ariealla Aïsha Azoulay, *Potential History. Unlearning Imperialism* (London: Verso, 2019).

3. Tina Campt, *Listening to Images* (Durham: Duke University press, 2017).

4. Fred Moten, *In the Break. The Aesthetics of the Black Radical Tradition* (Minneapolis: University of Minnesota Press), 1–24.

5. Stefano Harney and Fred Moten, *All Incomplete* (New York: Minor Compositions 2021), 27–51.

6. Stefano Harney and Fred Moten, *The Undercommons. Fugitive Planning & Black Study* (New York: Minor Compositions, 2013), 19.

In themselves DAOs are just functional tools for governance and distribution of shares. Our concern is to resocialise these shares through the artistic process, thinking about value creation as a complex process of contamination of the market with non-capitalist of social relations – recasting the notions of skills, labour, economic organisations, and human currencies in non-monetary and concrete terms as opposed to the abstraction of money. A practical example would be to treat the logging of work not so much quantitatively but as a process of qualitative annotation and informal collective archiving/negotiation around the notion of labour value. In this sense we are not selling to investors a commodity or an art object, but a framework for reflecting around possible collaborations or committing to different kinds of relationships, akin to how Massumi[7] defines DAOs as "travelling archives" and "anarchic archives of value."

Moreover, Ensembl perfectly embodies, in the same way in which NFTs do, the ambiguous status of art, as being both a commodity and a generator of new energies – and even utopian projects. Perhaps it is impossible to escape art's commodification because the invention of art and aesthetics as a separate realm of life, historically coincided with the invention of the commodity form, as well as with the anthropological invention of primitive societies. That is, art and money – beauty and interest – are two sides of the same Eurocentric capitalist project.[8] But with our DAO project, we don't want to quantify our contributions, or commodify our art, but rather to rethink the commodity form through art.

Ensembl explores these questions through interlinked and interdependent components, including an app, creative interventions, and theoretical reflections to reconsider artistic collaborations and make transparent processes of negotiation, distribution, and collaboration.

---

7. Brian Massumi, *99 Theses on the Revaluation of Value. A Postcapitalist Manifesto* (Minneapolis: University of Minnesota Press, 2018), 44.

8. See for example: Max Haiven, *Art after Money, Money after Art: Creative Strategies Against Financialization* (London: Pluto Press, 2018) and Massimiliano Mollona, *ART/COMMONS. Anthropology Beyond Capitalism* (London: Zed Books, 2021).

Opposite: Samson Young, *How it feels to me.* Overleaf: *Liminal Space* and *Harmolodic.*

(All works 2020, 260mm × 180mm).

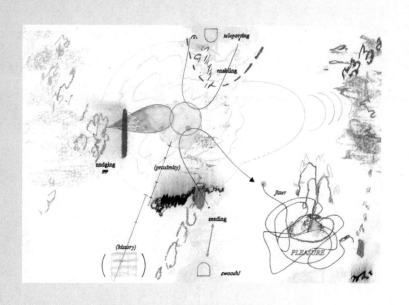

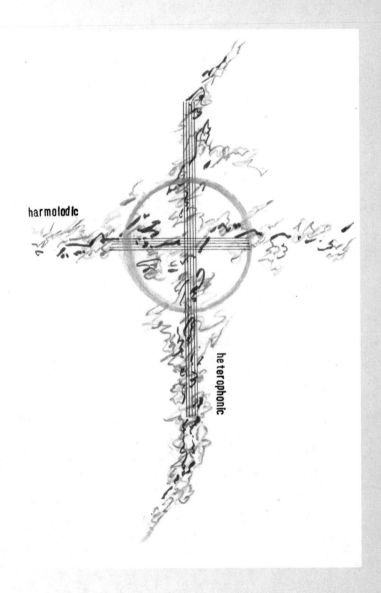

harmolodic

heterophonic

liminal space

CENTER

Suzanne Treister, *Hexen 2.0/Tarot* Works, 2009–2011.

All works archival giclée prints with watercolour on
Hahnemuhle Bamboo paper, 29.7cm × 21cm.
Courtesy the artist, Annely Juda Fine Art, London and
P.P.O.W. Gallery, New York.

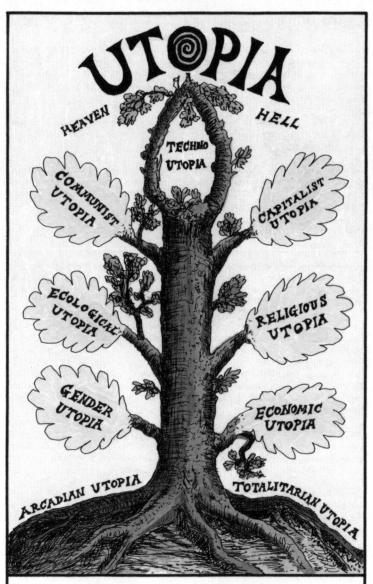

Contributors

Ramon Amaro is Lecturer in Art and Visual Cultures of the Global South at UCL (University College London). His latest book, *The Black Technical Object On Machine Learning and the Aspiration of Black Being* (Sternberg/MIT, 2022) is a contemplation on the abstruse nature of machine learning, mathematics, and the deep incursion of racial hierarchy. *www.sambarhino.com*

Calum Bowden collaborates on stories, worlds, and platforms that reconnect the cultural with the technological, economical, political and ecological. He co-founded Trust and Black Swan. *www.calsbo.com*

Jaya Klara Brekke Cryptographic geographer, writer and speaker, Fellow at the Weizenbaum Institute in Berlin, CSO at Nym decentralised privacy system and occasional advisor to the European Commission on the societal implications of decentralised technologies. www. *jayapapaya.space*

Ruth Catlow is a recovering web utopian, co-founder and artistic director of Furtherfield.

Mitchell F. Chan creates large-scale public works, gallery installations, and digital artworks that playfully and critically interrogate how human sense and sensibilities are changing in the age of technology and the ways that art's commodity form leaks into its expressive power. He created one of the earliest non-fungible token artworks, which linked the immateriality of blockchain to the conceptual art practice of Yves Klein. *www.chan.gallery*

Cade Diehm is the founder of The New Design Congress, an international digital infrastructure research group. After studying design in Australia, Cade was the product lead for a CN/AUS Augmented Reality fashion startup (2013), prototyped Signal with Open Whisper Systems (2014), led design and strategy with emerging cryptocurrency technologies (2015) and was Chief Design Officer at SpiderOak, a Snowden-approved cloud storage company (2016). From 2017 to 2019, he led design and collaborated on information security research at Tactical Tech, a Berlin-based NGO that works to raise awareness of issues of data, privacy and technology in societies. *www.newdesigncongress.org*

eeefff are artistic cooperation / made-up institution / cybernetic political brigade / poetic computations / hacking unit / queer time. It is neither one of these, nor all together. eeefff make software-based projects, publications, networks, and platforms that critically explore digital labour, value extraction, and community formation in Eastern Europe. *www.eeefff.org*

Carina Erdmann is an artist, researcher, and mentor in Game Design based in Berlin and Brussels. Her work explores the hybridisation of online gaming and performance. She participates in the School of Commons and runs Oct0p0s, a research platform for collective worlding and interactive narration. *www.carinaerdmann.com*

Primavera De Filippi is a Research Director at the National Center of Scientific Research (CNRS) in Paris, a Faculty Associate at the Berkman-Klein Center for Internet & Society at Harvard University. As an artist, she creates mechanical algorithms that manifest her legal research into the physical world, such as the Plantoid project. *www.plantoid.org*

Charlotte Frost is Executive Director of Furtherfield, historian of digital arts, author of *Art Criticism Online*.

Max Hampshire is a programmer, artist, writer, and co-founder of terra0 and exit-tech studio nascent.

Lucile Olympe Haute is an artist and performer. In her performances at the intersection of the tangible and digital spaces she embodies archetypal figures (among them Cyborg and Witch). Her research brings together spirituality, technologies and politics – aiming to compose ways to live together in contemporary world, beyond the mere human concerns. When she adopts graphic forms, her work often manifests itself through the aesthetic and narrative versatility of multi-sport and web-to-print editions. She is a researcher in art and design at the University of Nîmes and the Arts Décoratifs de Paris. *www.lucilehaute.fr*

Sara Heitlinger shares seeds in east London, researches how we could design technology for more sustainable and equitable cities, and teaches ethics in computing, from the Centre for Human Computer Interaction Design at City, University of London. *www.city.ac.uk/about/people/academics/sara-heitlinger*

Lara Houston is a researcher working in Science and Technology Studies and Human-Computer Interaction. Her work focusses on computing infrastructures and environmental sustainability. Recent projects have explored creative practice and sustainability transformations; more-than-human blockchain food futures; breakdown in the smart city, and the political economy of tech repair. *www.larahouston.co.uk*

Cadence Kinsey is Lecturer in Contemporary Art at University College London. Her research centres on the histories of art and technology, as well as live art and performance from the 1960s to today. Her first book, *Walled Gardens: Autonomy, Automation, and Art After the Internet* was published by OUP in 2021.

Nick Koppenhagen is an artist from Berlin. He is interested in the visual properties of abstract systems and currently working on a (non-)playable card game based on a force-directed graph, a memory dune and the traces of interactions. He is one of the founding members of the DAK. *www.nickkoppenhagen.com*

Kei Kreutler is a writer and artist interested in how cultural narratives of technologies shape their use. Since 2017, she has led strategy at Gnosis, building decentralised infrastructure for Web3. In 2021, she co-founded Gnosis Guild, a keeper of the Zodiac tools for DAOs. She also contributes to Other Internet research group and sits on the Board of Regen Foundation. *www.ourmachine.net*

Laura Lotti is a researcher and writer investigating emerging dynamics in Web3, with a focus on the affordances of blockchain to power alternative cultural economies. She is currently studying the social dimension of community-led protocol governance with Other Internet and co-developing Black Swan, a proto-institution for interdisciplinary research and practice.

Jonas Lund creates paintings, sculpture, photography, websites and performances that critically reflect on contemporary networked systems and power structures of control. His artistic practice involves creating systems and setting up parameters that oftentimes require engagement from the viewer. Through his works, Lund investigates the latest issues generated by the increasing digitalisation of contemporary society like authorship, participation and distribution of agency. At the same time, he questions the mechanisms of the art world; he challenges the production process, authoritative power and art market practices. *www.jonaslund.com*

Massimiliano (Mao) Mollona is an anthropologist based at the Department of the Arts at the University of Bologna University. He specialises on the anthropology of capitalism and post-capitalism, art and visual anthropology. *www.unibo.it/sitoweb/massimiliano.mollona*

MetaObjects (Ashley Lee Wong & Andrew Crowe) is a studio based in Hong Kong that facilitates digital production with artists and cultural institutions. Working across VR/AR, 3D printing, motion capture, audiovisual production, software and web development, MetaObjects seeks to encourage the sharing of knowledge of new digital tools and processes. *www.metaobjects.org*

Rhea Myers is an artist, hacker and writer originally from the UK now based in Vancouver BC in Canada. Her work places technology and culture in mutual interrogation to produce new ways of seeing the world as it unfolds around us. *www.rhea.art*

Omsk Social Club's work is created between two lived worlds, one of life as we know it and the other of role play. These worlds bleed into one. That is where Omsk positions their speculative fictions, through these immersive art installations they move into a territory they coined in 2017 called Real Game Play (RGP). Their work aims to induce states that could potentially be a fiction or a yet, unlived reality. *www.punkisdada.com*

Bhavisha Panchia is a curator and researcher of visual and audio culture. Her work engages with artistic and cultural practices under shifting global conditions, focusing on anti/postcolonial discourses, imperial histories, and networks of production and circulation of media. *www.nothingtocommit.org*

Penny Rafferty is a writer, critic and visual theorist. Departing from her research and thinking she has initiated and co-founded Black Swan, a proto-institution DAO for interdisciplinary research and practice.

Legacy Russell is a curator and a writer. Author of *Glitch Feminism* (Verso, 2020) her work and research focuses on the intersection of art, technology, gender, and race. She is the Executive Director & Chief Curator at The Kitchen in New York. *www.legacyrussell.org*

Tina Rivers Ryan is an art historian and critic specialsing in media art since the 1960s, as well as a curator of modern and contemporary art at the Buffalo AKG Art Museum (formerly the Albright-Knox Art Gallery). She first wrote about blockchain and art in 2016. *www.tinariversyyan.com*

Nathan Schneider is an assistant professor of media studies at the University of Colorado Boulder, where he leads the Media Enterprise Design Lab. His most recent book is *Everything for Everyone: The Radical Tradition that Is Shaping the Next Economy. www.nathanschneider.info*

Sam Skinner is an artist and curator. He is co-director of Torque Editions, runs Fig.studio an art and horticulture project in Oxford, and was co-editor of *Artists Re:Thinking the Blockchain* (2017). *www.samskinner.net*

Sam Spike is the Creative Director of Fingerprints DAO and co-founder of JPG, a protocol for NFT curation and discovery. He has previously held research positions at The Metropolitan Museum of Art, New York, and the Fitzwilliam Museum in Cambridge, UK.

Hito Steyerl is a filmmaker and writer based in Berlin

Alex S. Taylor has been contributing to Science & Technology Studies and Human-Computer Interaction (HCI) for over eighteen years. His interests are in how digital technologies are co-constitutive of forms of knowing and doing, and, as a consequence, provide a basis for fundamental transformations in society. *www.ast.io*

The Sphere is a research-creation project financed by Creative Europe that is developing a Web3.0 infrastructure for self-organisation in the performing arts. It allows for artists, cultural workers, audience and organisations of different kinds to initiate creative collaborations and implement new funding strategies. *www.thesphere.as*

Cassie Thornton is an artist and activist who makes a "safe space" for the unknown, for disobedience, and for unanticipated collectivity. Her new book, *The Hologram: Feminist, Peer-to-Peer Health for a Post-Pandemic Future*, is available from Pluto Press. She is currently the co-director of the Re-Imagining Value Action Lab in Thunder Bay, an art and social centre at Lakehead University in Ontario, Canada. *www.hologram.Xyz, www.feministeconomicsdepartment.com*

Suzanne Treister has been a pioneer in the new media field from the early 1990s, making work about emerging technologies, developing avatars and fictional worlds. The relationship between new technologies, society, alternative belief systems and the potential futures of humanity constitutes an ongoing focus of her work. *www.suzannetreister.net*

Stacco Troncoso is an avid synthesizer of information and a radical polymath working towards elemental, people-led change on a burning planet. Stacco lives, breathes, teaches and writes on the Commons, PTP politics and economics, open culture, post-growth futures, Platform and Open Cooperativism, decentralised governance, blockchain and more as part of DisCO.coop. *www.stacco.works*

Ann Marie Utratel is the co-founder, with Stacco Troncoso, of two cooperatives: DisCO.coop and the Guerrilla Translation/Media Collective. Her work aims to bring relatable storytelling and humour to often alienating topics. She's old enough to remember cigarette ads on TV, and young enough to believe that change is possible. www.*disco.coop*

Samson Young works in sound, performance, video, and installation. He graduated with a Ph.D. in Music Composition from Princeton University in 2013. He was Hong Kong Sinfonietta's Artist Associate from 2008 to 2009. In 2017, he represented Hong Kong at the 57th Venice Biennale. Other solo projects include the De Appel, Amsterdam; Kunsthalle Düsseldorf; Talbot Rice Gallery, Edinburgh; SMART Museum, Chicago; Centre for Contemporary Chinese Art in Manchester; M+ Pavilion, Hong Kong; Mori Art Museum, Tokyo; Ryosoku-in at Kenninji Temple, Kyoto; Monash University Museum of Art, Melbourne; and Jameel Art Centre, Dubai, among others. *www.thismusicisfalse.com*

Index

Acknowledgements

Each Other

Artworld DAO ThinkTank participants

Ben Vickers

The Blockchain Socialist

C3, especially Kate Beecroft, Elena Denara and Tony Lai

Chris Speed

DAOWO contributors and partners

Furtherfield, especially Marc Garrett and Charlotte Frost

Glitch Community

Goethe-Institut London, with special thanks to Katrin Sohns,
    Head of Programmes, and Mario Schruff, Culture Department,
    Visual Arts and Music Programmes

Guild decentralised art network

Jonas Schoeneberg

KW Institute for Contemporary Art, especially Léon Kruijswijk

Haus der Kunst Munich, especially Sarah Johanna Theurer
    and Julia Pfeiffer

Martin Zeilinger

Max Haiven

Max Hampshire and Paul Seidler

The network of arts organisations worldwide doing critical work in
    decentralised tech, especially Aksioma, Birthrites Collection,
    Constant, Disruption Network Lab, Drugo More, Institute for
    Network Cultures, MoneyLab, NeME, NEoN, New Design
    Congress, and Supermarkt

Radical xChange, especially Jennifer Lyn Morone, Matt Prewitt
    and Glen Weyl

Sarah Meiklejohn

Serpentine Galleries, especially Kay Watson, Victoria Ivanova
    and Alex Boyes

Tirdad Zolghadr

Trust

unMonastery

Radical Friends:
Decentralised Autonomous Organisations and the Arts

Edited by Ruth Catlow & Penny Rafferty

Published by Torque Editions, July 2022
www.torquetorque.net

Book designed by Mark Simmonds, Lincoln
Cover & chapter divider illustrations by Marijn Degenaar
Printed & bound in Estonia by Printon
Distributed by Turnaround Publisher Services

ISBN 978-0-9932487-7-1

This publication was made possible through support from and in collaboration with the Goethe-Institut London.

The project received additional support from Serpentine Galleries R&D Platform and Furtherfield's Decentralised Arts Lab DECAL.

GOETHE
INSTITUT

SERPENTINE

furtherfield